FOR HUMANITY OR FOR THE UMMA?

MARIE JUUL PETERSEN

For Humanity
or for the Umma?

Aid and Islam in Transnational Muslim NGOs

HURST & COMPANY, LONDON

First published in the United Kingdom in 2015 by
C. Hurst & Co. (Publishers) Ltd.,
41 Great Russell Street, London, WC1B 3PL
© Marie Juul Petersen, 2015
All rights reserved.
Printed in India

Distributed in the United States, Canada and Latin America by
Oxford University Press, 198 Madison Avenue, New York, NY 10016,
United States of America.

The right of Marie Juul Petersen to be identified as the author
of this publication is asserted by her in accordance with the
Copyright, Designs and Patents Act, 1988.

A Cataloguing-in-Publication data record for this book
is available from the British Library.

978-1-84904-432-5 *hardback*

This book is printed using paper from registered sustainable
and managed sources.

www.hurstpublishers.com

CONTENTS

CONTENTS

ACKNOWLEDGEMENTS

Jonathan Benthall, a pioneer in the study of Muslim aid and a source of great inspiration, once said that studying Islam can feel like a Jerusalem of the intellect. Post 9/11, researchers studying Islam tread a difficult terrain; they are often positioned (or position themselves) as political actors and their research is presented as ideological statements by people from all sides. Reflecting this, I have often been met with one of two reactions when presenting the topic of my study: some people have warned me not to end up as a mouthpiece for extremist Islamists, while others have praised me for cleansing the name of Muslim NGOs, cautioning me not to write anything that may damage these organisations politically. However, while I am of course aware that there exists no neutral position from which to study such politicised subjects as transnational Muslim NGOs, I wish to emphasise that the aim of this book has not been to condone or condemn transnational Muslim NGOs but, more modestly, to contribute to nuancing the commonly drawn picture of these organisations. With this book, I hope to have contributed to challenging, or at least softening, some of the dichotomies and simplistic categorisations that often surround transnational Muslim NGOs, showing that these organisations—as any other NGO, for that matter—are not inherently 'good' or 'evil', but complex ideological actors, struggling to provide aid in the ways they judge to be most appropriate, and in so doing, being shaped by and in turn shaping the contexts out of which they have grown.

If I have succeeded in this, it is in large part due to the invaluable assistance and support I have received from people along the way. My first and foremost thanks go to staff in the four organisations I have studied—the International Islamic Charitable Organisation, the International Islamic Relief Organisation, Muslim Aid and Islamic Relief. In spite of extremely busy workdays, many people have offered me their time, insights, and knowledge, for which I am deeply grateful. I know that they may not agree with all I have written, but it is my sincere hope that I have managed to convey the respect I have for their work. I would also like to thank the many other people who took the time to talk to me in Britain, Kuwait, Saudi Arabia, Jordan, Lebanon, and Bangladesh, including representatives from the Aga Khan Foundation, CARE, Christian Aid, DFID, Direct Aid, ECHO Bangladesh, the Islamic Center Charity Society, the Islamic Development Bank, the Islamic Welfare Association, Kuwait Zakat House, Muslim Hands, the NGO Affairs Bureau in Bangladesh, the Organisation of Islamic Cooperation (OIC), the Revival of the Islamic Heritage Society, the Society for Social Reform, USAID Bangladesh, the World Assembly of Muslim Youth, and many others.

My field trips were funded by generous grants from the Crown Prince Frederik Foundation, Sasakawa Foundation, Oticon Foundation, and Augustinus Foundation. During my trips, many people have kindly offered their assistance, greatly facilitating my work. I would especially like to thank Yasser al-Khouli for assisting me in the cumbersome process of applying for a Saudi visa and for organising my stay in Jeddah; Niels Bentzen from Save the Children Denmark for assistance with transportation and accommodation during my stay in Dhaka; and Doa'a Awaysheh, Ala'a Awaysheh and Rawaan al-Baseet for keeping me company in Jordan, Kuwait and Saudi Arabia respectively. I also have to thank Rawan, together with Buthaina Shaheen and Hana al-Khamri, for their assistance in translating documents. Finally, I would like to thank my brother, Jens Juul Petersen, for travelling with me to Saudi Arabia. I hope this will not be our last trip together.

Writing up first the PhD thesis, and later the book, I benefited from the expertise and advice of other scholars, for which I am most grateful. My supervisor, Catharina Raudvere, has been a knowledgeable, reassuring and encouraging support. Mamoun Abuarqab, Erica Bornstein, Jonathan Benthall, Atallah Fitzgibbon, Dietrich Jung, Ahmed Ajaz Khan, and Peter Mandaville offered insightful comments and suggestions on parts of the text. Ben Jones was an inspirational sparring partner. Catrine Christiansen has been an invaluable mentor and support. Thanks also to colleagues at the Institute for Cross-Cultural and Regional Studies, the Danish Institute for International Studies and the Danish Institute for Human Rights for encouragement and inspiring discussions over lunch.

Finally, thanks also to friends and family for bearing with my years of absent-mindedness and long hours at the office. Most importantly, I want to thank Thorbjørn and Mona. I cannot wait to come home to you.

I owe the title of the book to Fiona Adamson and Daniel Nilsson deHanas. In 2010, they presented the paper 'For the Ummah or Humanity? Islamic Humanitarianism Between Community and Cosmopolitanism' at the Annual Meeting of the International Studies Association (ISA) in New Orleans. They kindly let me use part of their title for this book, for which I am deeply grateful.

Parts of the book have been published elsewhere. I want to thank Routledge for permission to reprint text from the article 'Trajectories of Transnational Muslim NGOs', *Development in Practice*, vol. 22 (5–6), 2012 in Chapter 3. Furthermore, some of the material in Chapters 4 and 5 has been drawn on for my chapter 'Sacralized or Secularized Aid? Positioning Gulf-Based Charities' in the book *Gulf Charities and Islamic Philanthropy in the 'Age of Terror' and Beyond*, edited by Robert Lacey and Jonathan Benthall, Gerlach Press, 2014.

1

INTRODUCTION

STUDYING TRANSNATIONAL MUSLIM NGOS

Transnational Muslim NGOs: Faith-based organisations
or fronts for terrorism?

'This is how we teach the children about heaven and hell,' Hanin said, opening the door into a colourfully decorated classroom. In the middle of the room were two child-size graves, built from paper, cloth and cardboard boxes. One was covered in dirt and worms; the other was showered with green leaves. It was April 2009 and I was visiting a day-care centre for orphans in Amman, Jordan, run by the Saudi Arabian NGO International Islamic Relief Organisation (IIROSA). Hanin, an elderly teacher with a warm smile, talked enthusiastically about her task of raising the children to become good, Muslim citizens. 'We teach the children to be honest and trustworthy, that is important of course,' she said. 'But the most important thing is to teach them what is right and wrong, especially based on Islam.'

Half a year later, in a small town near Rangpur, Bangladesh, I visited another centre for orphans, run by the British-based Islamic Relief Worldwide as part of its Adolescent Reproductive Healthcare programme. It was international HIV/AIDS day and the teachers had organised an event to celebrate the day. Local politicians, doctors, and other public figures had been invited to tell the adolescent orphans about the disease and a small booklet had been produced, supporting the speeches with facts and figures. 'This is what we do,' a young female teacher named Mona told me. 'We teach them about life skills, reproductive health, HIV/AIDS, sexually transmitted diseases, adolescent life, sexual behaviour, general health, social behaviour, early marriage—if you marry early, your life will be ruined, you know.' I asked her if all this had anything to do with Islam and she looked at me with a puzzled expression. 'It's about awareness-raising.'

Organisations such as Islamic Relief and IIROSA are increasingly visible actors in contemporary aid provision. Around the world, an estimated 400 transnational Muslim NGOs engage not only in orphan care, but in the distribution of food and medicine, construction of schools and mosques, management of refugee camps and coordination of microfinance projects.[1] Since the establishment of the first transnational Muslim NGO at the end of the 1970s, however, most of these organisations have passed unnoticed, receiving public attention only when they were accused of financing or otherwise supporting violent Islamic activism—whether in Afghanistan, Bosnia, Kenya, Tanzania or the USA. In particular after the 9/11 attacks on the Twin Towers and Pentagon in 2001, an understanding of transnational Muslim NGOs as de facto accomplices in Islamic terrorism gained ground. Within a year of the attacks, a number of transnational Muslim NGOs had been designated by the US government, accused of supporting Al-Qaeda,[2] and several other governments followed suit, banning transnational Muslim NGOs from working in their territory (Juul Petersen 2012a). This understanding of Muslim NGOs as inherently political actors has influenced much academic and policy-oriented research, whether focusing narrowly on the role of Muslim NGOs as fronts for militant Islamic movements such as Al-Qaeda,[3] or dealing more broadly with the relationship between Muslim NGOs and political organisations such as the Muslim Brotherhood, Hamas, and Hezbollah.[4]

While such literature sheds light on important aspects of the relation between Islam and politics, it does not necessarily tell us much about the relation between Islam and aid. It does not tell us about the kinds of aid that organisations such as Islamic Relief and IIROSA provide, about their motivations and visions, their underlying rationales and conceptions of aid, or about the role of Islam in all this. Returning to the examples above, what does Hanin from IIROSA mean when she talks about aid as a way to shape 'good Muslim citizens'? What is 'awareness-raising' to Mona and her colleagues in Islamic Relief? And how do we explain the obvious differences in their conceptions of aid and Islam? Without neglecting the importance of unravelling relations between certain transnational Muslim NGOs and militant Islamic activists, this book argues that we need to broaden our analysis of these organisations to include such questions in order to gain a fuller understanding of transnational Muslim NGOs and the role they play in contemporary society. We must, in the words of Alberto Melucci (1989), put aside old habits of viewing social processes only through the lenses of the political, reducing the social to matters of the political. Such an approach may open up for the identification of discourses and practices which may seem invisible, irrelevant or simply uninteresting in terms of formal political power but which may nonetheless play an important role at other levels of society, in particular in relation to the production and reproduction of social norms, values and morality. In line with this, the book directs attention to the transnational Muslim NGOs themselves, exploring how they and their staff members construct and conceptualise the nexus between Islam and aid. More specifically, the book turns on the following questions: how do contemporary transnational Muslim NGOs and the people working in these organisations understand 'aid' and 'Islam'? What are the factors and conditions that have shaped their understanding of these concepts? And where does this place transnational Muslim NGOs in the broader context of aid provision?

In posing these questions, I seek to challenge not only literature on Muslim NGOs as fronts for terrorist networks or political organisations, but also literature casting these organisations as so-called 'faith-based organisations', placing them within the field of international development and humanitarian aid.[5] Reflecting a general increase in attention to religion in the public sphere—in part prompted by 9/11—recent years have seen an almost explosive interest in these organisations among development researchers and practitioners.[6] Much of the literature growing out of this new interest contributes valuably to the study of religion and development, exploring the role of religious organisations in the provision of aid by asking questions such as: are faith-based organisations 'effective development partners' (Harb 2008); do they have the potential 'to help poor people to escape from poverty' (Harper et al. 2008:2); and do 'religious and spiritual resources produce a type of knowledge that is, or could be, relevant to development?' (Haar and Ellis 2006:354).[7] However, while approaching Muslim—and religious—NGOs from an entirely different angle to the literature on Muslim NGOs and politics, much of this new literature ends up sharing some of the same weaknesses. First, the tendency to view Muslim NGOs as either faith-based organisations and as such part of the largely Western 'development system', or as political actors, part of an 'Islamic resurgence', fails to grasp the double identity of transnational Muslim NGOs as organisations which are historically rooted in and constantly move between the development system and the Islamic resurgence. Second, the literature on faith-based organisations shares an instrumentalist understanding of transnational Muslim NGOs. Whereas literature on Muslim NGOs as political actors casts them as tools in struggles for the Islamisation of society, literature on faith-based organisations focuses on the ways in which faith-based organisations may be useful tools in the implementation of development activities. As such, both literatures tend to overlook issues of organisational identity and ideology, rarely asking questions as to how these organisations present and understand themselves, their religion and the aid they provide, exploring how they respond to and are shaped by the different contexts out of which they have grown.

Actors and meanings

This book proposes a different approach to the study of transnational Muslim NGOs.[8] As Deneulin and Rakodi (2011:51) point out, the study of religion and development must, primarily, be a study of the meanings that people give to their social practices. In this perspective, the study of transnational Muslim NGOs should not solely or even primarily be about determining whether or not their religious identity makes them efficient contributors to development or facilitates their connections with terrorist groups, but about exploring their modes of 'self-identification' (Palmer 2011:100) and looking at how they define and give meaning to concepts such as 'Islam', 'development'—and 'terrorism', for that matter. In other words, the analysis of transnational Muslim NGOs should approach these organisations not as instruments, whether in the Islamisation of society or the implementation of effective development projects, but as autonomous actors actively engaged in the production of meaning (Benford and Snow 2000:613), capable of making choices and imposing those choices on the world. Paraphrasing David Lewis et al. (2003:546), this approach is first and foremost an attempt to understand how meanings associated with 'aid' and 'Islam' are produced, expressed, contested and reworked by actors in these organisations, and thus to illuminate not only the multiple significances that these terms hold, but also the processes through which they gain significance and the consequences these processes of signification may have.[9]

This requires micro-sociological studies of concrete organisations and their staff members. Based on empirical case studies, I turn to the organisations themselves, directing attention towards processes and structures of meaning construction in four selected Muslim NGOs—Islamic Relief Worldwide and Muslim Aid from Britain, the International Islamic Charitable Organisation (IICO; in Arabic, *Hayat al-khairiyya al-islamiyya al-'alamiyya*) from Kuwait, and the International Islamic Relief Organisation (in Arabic, *al-Igatha al-islamiyya al-'alamiyya*) from Saudi Arabia. These four organisations were first and foremost selected in the expectation that they would be what Flyvbjerg (2001, 2006) calls 'paradigmatic cases', highlighting general characteristics of contemporary transnational Muslim NGOs. As such, they are not selected because they are 'average' or 'representative' transnational Muslim NGOs, but because they are expected to contain the most information, the richest narratives and the broadest range of characteristics, serving as emblematic examples of transnational Muslim NGOs (Flyvbjerg 2001:78).[10] Established at the end of the 1970s and beginning of the 1980s, these organisations are some of the oldest and most well-established transnational Muslim NGOs. With budgets ranging from US$ 20 million to US$ 100 million, they are also among the largest, working all over the world (see Table 1.1. for a basic overview of the four organisations). At the same time, and as we shall see, they differ with regard to a number of aspects, including historical and geographic origins, constituencies, sources of funding and kinds of activities, thus representing different types of transnational Muslim NGOs and illustrating the heterogeneity of this group of organisations.

Over a period of six years from 2007 to 2013—but most intensively from 2008 to 2010—I have collected organisational material by and about these four organisations (such as website information, annual reports, policies, brochures, and project documents); I have spent time at their headquarters in Saudi Arabia, Kuwait, and Britain, as well as in selected country offices in Bangladesh, Jordan, and Lebanon, interviewing almost 100 staff members, trustees, and volunteers, and visiting more than 30 project sites, including orphanages, vocational training centres, microfinance projects, and dyke construction sites, to mention only a few.[11] Based on this material, the book aims to present detailed, nuanced portraits of the four organisations, exploring the ways in which they give meaning to notions of aid and Islam.

Table 1.1: Overview of the four organisations[12]

Name	Origin	Year	Budget (US$)	Staff	Major countries
Islamic Relief	Britain	1984	101 million	1,650	Palestine Pakistan Somalia Bangladesh Kenya
International Islamic Charitable Organisation	Kuwait	1984	59 million	360	Syria Pakistan Somalia Turkey Sudan
Muslim Aid	Britain	1985	42 million	2,200	Bangladesh Somalia Pakistan Indonesia Sri Lanka
International Islamic Relief Organisation	Saudi Arabia	1979	32 million	2,000	Saudi Arabia Jordan Sudan Pakistan Somalia

Processes of Islamisation

The analysis of aid and Islam in these four transnational Muslim NGOs is not based on a preconceived and essentialised notion of what 'Islam' is. In other words, I do not have any presumptions about the ways in which religion shapes the organisations, their identity and work, but see the exploration of its construction and signification as topics for analysis. Paraphrasing Peter Mandaville (2007:20), '[t]his approach tends to resist making claims about the nature and content of Islam and instead primarily concerns itself with the various ways in which people engage and draw upon religious tradition as they construct and contest social orders.' In this, I am inspired by the historian of religion Bruce Lincoln (2003), who argues that something becomes religion not primarily by virtue of its specific content but by its claims to transcendent authority and truth. Activities, things, phenomena, people, and ideas are not religious per se but become religious when they are given religious meaning through religious discourses, practices, communities and institutions. In other words, something becomes religion by being 'religionised'—or 'sacralised', as Woodhead and Heelas (2000), among others, have termed it. Thus, something is Islamic or Muslim when it is constituted as such through discourses and practices that are concerned with matters of Islam (traditions, figures, concepts, rules, stories, etc.) and claim a transcendent authority by reference to Allah, the Qur'an and the *sunnah*. As such, virtually anything can be recoded as 'religion' or 'religious' (Lincoln 2003:6). This means that one cannot only look for religion in its conventional hiding places, but must be open to finding it elsewhere as well, tracing what Mandaville (2007:327) refers to as 'the migration of religious discourse and symbolic capital into spaces not formally constituted as "religious"'— such as NGOs and aid provision.

At the same time, however, there are limits to what can count as Islam. Religions are not detached from power, history and context, but confined and curtailed by this. As such, the fact that anything can in principle be religionised does not mean that anything does become religionised. In practice, there are very real limitations as to what can be religionised, and consequently what can count as religion. In their constructions of 'Islam', actors build on and are restricted by centuries of Islamic discourses and practices, outlining what is sayable, doable, and thinkable within the limits of Islam. Likewise, certain actors have more power to Islamise than others; Schaebler and Stenberg (2004:xvii) talk about 'Islam' as a discursive field of contesting powers. As a result, interpretations of Islam may vary from setting to setting, but there is also, at any given moment in time, a relatively stable core of Islamic discourses that somehow connect most Muslims (Mandaville 2007:17)—what Benthall refers to as a family resemblance (2011:102)—making the use of terms such as 'Islam' and 'Muslim' meaningful. In line with this, I advance a definition of 'Muslim NGOs' as those NGOs that constitute themselves with reference to

Muslim discourses, that is, NGOs that define themselves as Muslim, either by simply referring to Islam in their name, or by explicitly referring to Islamic authorities, traditions, figures or concepts in their practices, structures and community.[13] At the same time, the meaning conferred on the term 'Muslim NGO' by these organisations themselves is of course precisely the focus of the analysis.

In this perspective, and quoting Deneulin and Rakodi (2011), the task of the present book is to understand how religious discourses are embodied in certain social practices, structures, and communities; how social and historical processes have led to that particular embodiment; and how religious discourses, practices, communities, and structures are redefined in light of changing social, economic, and political contexts. In other words, the analysis of transnational Muslim NGOs cannot simply be about identifying the role of Islam in development aid, based on preconceived notions of what Islam 'is', but should be about exploring the construction of 'Islam', asking questions as to how and when Muslim NGOs 'Islamise' things (as well as how and when they do not 'Islamise' things), and what kinds of 'Islam' they construct in the process, while at the same time paying attention to the structures, actors, and practices delimiting and shaping these processes of Islamisation. This focus on practiced Islam and processes of Islamisation directs our attention to the plurality of meanings associated with contemporary Islam, manifested in the concrete dialogues, debates, and divides along political, theological, geographical or individual lines. As is obvious even from the brief examples given at the beginning of this chapter, Hanin and Mona present widely different conceptions of Islam and its role in aid provision, something which will be elaborated upon in the following.

Ideologies of aid

I employ the concept of 'ideology' as an analytical tool in my analysis of meaning making in transnational Muslim NGOs, conceptualising ideology broadly as the framework through which meanings of Islam and aid are organised and presented.[14] In relation to transnational Muslim NGOs, ideologies of aid can be understood as meaning systems that centre on questions of aid provision (for instance, what is aid, why should it be provided and how should it be provided), are formulated and shared by actors involved in the provision of aid (such as local charities, NGOs, governments, intergovernmental organisations) with the purpose of guiding and motivating them in their provision of aid, as well as justifying and promoting their agenda to the public, garnering support among potential donors and partners and ensuring their legitimacy in doing so. More specifically, I approach aid ideologies as consisting of different elements, or frames—a vision, a rationale, some strategies, and underlying this, a particular kind of authority on which the ideological claims are based. Through these frames, different ideological subjects emerge—the giver and the receiver—outlining conceptions of a basic aid chain.

The relationship between the organisations' ideologies and actions is not characterised by straightforward causality; in fact, there is not necessarily any correspondence between the two. Ideologies are guidelines for what people should do, not what they actually do. As such, a focus on ideologies of aid in transnational Muslim NGOs cannot tell us anything about whether these NGOs are effective providers of development aid, or if they have connections to militant Islamic movements. But that does not mean that it is not important to consider ideological representations. The focus on ideologies of aid is important not so much because it says something about how organisations actually provide aid, but because it says something about how they want to provide aid or think that one ought to provide aid, and as such, it can tell us something about the perceptions, imaginations and interpretations of these organisations.[15] More broadly, a study of organisational ideologies of aid can illuminate aspects of the contemporary politics of aid, analysing struggles over the production of meaning (Benford and Snow 2000:613), and shedding light on issues of legitimacy, alliances and conflicts. Through their ideologies, actors involved in the politics of aid promote certain societal values, norms and principles and reject others, thus contributing to shaping important moral conceptions and categories, and signifying human lives and relations.

Methodologically, to study ideologies of aid in transnational Muslim NGOs is not the same as conducting a full-fledged ethnography of these organisations; it is not even to study organisational meaning making as such. There is much more to these organisations than ideologies (practices of project implementation, staff relations, and budgeting, to mention only a few things). Instead, a study of ideologies is primarily a study of (re)presentations. To be precise, this study is not so much about how these organisations understand themselves and the work they do, as it is about how they (re)present themselves and their work. Overall, this entails a focus on discourses, in the sense of narratives, texts and rhetorical struggles (Williams 1995:126). It is through discourses that ideologies are consciously presented and communicated to an audience and it is through discourses that ideologies are contested, challenged and eventually changed.[16] In concrete, methodological terms, this means that I have based my analysis on material that expresses or illustrates the (re)presentational discourses of the four organisations, including official, negotiated representations as expressed in public documents such as websites, annual reports and newsletters, as well as more unofficial, individualised representations, as expressed by staff members in interviews and during visits to project sites.

Aid cultures

Naturally, aid ideologies are not free-floating meaning systems but anchored in and shaped by particular contexts. Contrary to some existing literature, I propose that transnational Muslim NGOs should not be understood exclusively in the context of either Western development aid or the Islamic resurgence. Instead, I conceptualise transnational Muslim NGOs as growing out of and (increasingly) shaped by both contexts, constructing their organisational identity and ideologies of aid in a dialectic move between the two (Yaylaci 2007). More specifically, I conceptualise the contexts in which transnational Muslim NGOs operate as different 'cultures of aid.' With aid culture, I refer to those larger social structures that outline the overall boundaries for what can be said and done—in other words, what is legitimate—in relation to aid provision. While aid cultures are in no way generic or static, they do possess a certain stability, having over time become institutionalised into relatively sedimented structures, practices, and meanings (Berger and Luckmann 1966), thus producing a climate that is conducive to certain actors and ideologies and not to others. Compared to the concept of ideology, the concept of aid culture denotes a much broader meaning system, incorporating a wide range of tendencies, ideologies, structures, traditions, actors, and ideas. Despite their heterogeneity, however, there are certain aspects that bind them together, making it meaningful to speak of a common culture. A shared language is one such factor, ensuring social integration and functioning as a sort of 'symbolic order'. Paraphrasing Tvedt

(2002:369), this symbolically powerful language may change over time but it always tends to serve as an identity marker for the culture vis-à-vis other cultures. Another, more concrete, factor is the participation in economic exchanges, contributing to the construction of very concrete cultural boundaries.[17]

When it comes to transnational Muslim NGOs, two aid cultures merit attention; namely the, largely Western, culture of development aid and the, largely Middle Eastern, culture of Islamic aid, each of them turning on particular sets of ideas, values, ideologies, and traditions, manifested in concrete actors, structures, practices and discourses, and growing out of particular histories—and as a consequence of this, each promoting a different understanding of aid and religion.[18] This division into a, largely Middle Eastern, Islamic aid culture, and a, largely Western, development culture should in no way be seen as a repetition of Samuel Huntington's (1998) clash of civilisations thesis. As the analysis will show, transnational Muslim NGOs are not easily placed squarely within one or the other of these cultures, but are best conceptualised as growing out of and shaped by both, to different degrees and at different times drawing on different aspects from each, in the process perhaps contributing to building new aid cultures. As such, and contrary to the clash of civilizations approach, this analytical approach seeks to encourage attention to the encounter between cultures, or what Long (1989) has called 'the social interfaces' of meanings. Defined as 'critical points of intersection between different lifeworlds, social fields or levels of social organisation' (Long 2001:243), social interfaces are real or imaginary meeting points of different discourses, ideologies or cultures (Hilhorst 2003:11), and studies of social interfaces can bring out the dynamics of the interactions taking place at such meeting points, showing how the goals, perceptions, interests, and relationships of the involved parties may be reshaped as a result of this interaction (Long 1989:2). In this perspective, the analysis of the ways in which transnational Muslim NGOs navigate in relation to the two aid cultures is in fact an attempt at abandoning 'a binary opposition between Western and non-Western epistemologies and practices, and instead attempt[ing] to deal with the intricate interplay and joint appropriation and transformation of different bodies of knowledge' (Arce and Long 2000:24)

The attacks on Washington and New York on 11 September 2001 and the ensuing 'War on Terror'[19] present us with a particularly interesting window through which to study the interface between different aid cultures as it plays out in transnational Muslim NGOs. While Muslim NGOs have historically been firmly embedded in an Islamic aid culture, relating to the culture of mainstream development aid mainly by way of conflict, competition, and co-existence, the events following 9/11 presented an entirely new situation, blurring the dichotomous relations. As is commonly known, 9/11 and the War on Terror had severe consequences for transnational Muslim NGOs in the form of control, sanctions, and decrease in funding. These 'hard' measures to crack down on 'terrorist' NGOs have been coupled with 'softer' counter-terrorism approaches seeking to encourage cooperation with 'moderate' Muslim NGOs (Howell and Lind 2009:47), coinciding with a general interest in 'faith-based organisations' as the new panacea in development aid. Thus, transnational Muslim NGOs are now navigating in an environment of increasing regulation and control, but with simultaneous openings for cooperation and funding. In this situation, some NGOs have been relegated to the periphery, characterised as 'fundamentalist' or 'traditional', while others have been hailed as 'moderate' faith-based organisations. Seeking to go beyond these simplistic categorisations, this book explores the ways in which some of these transnational Muslim NGOs position themselves in the contemporary aid field, providing detailed descriptions of the different ways in which these organisations construct their identity and ideologies, and attempting to capture what Flyvbjerg (2006:237) has elsewhere referred to as the 'rich ambiguity' of these actors.

Sacralised and secularised aid

Positioning IIROSA, IICO, Islamic Relief, and Muslim Aid in relation to the two aid cultures, the book argues that they relate to them in different ways. IIROSA and IICO are firmly positioned in a Middle Eastern Islamic aid culture, while Islamic Relief and Muslim Aid have become increasingly embedded in a Western development culture. Against this background, the book puts forth the argument that overall, the four organisations present two different kinds of ideologies, resting on different conceptions of aid and Islam, different interpretations of the cultures of Islamic aid and development: the two Gulf-based NGOs present a sacralised form of aid, resting on a very visible, all-encompassing organisational religiosity that influences all aspects of aid provision, centring on notions of Islamic solidarity in the *umma* and echoing core elements in the Islamic aid culture. As the teacher from IIROSA notes in the introductory example, aid is about raising good, Muslim citizens, teaching the orphan children about what is right and wrong in Islam. The two UK-based organisations, on the other hand, provide a largely secularised form of aid, turning on universalist notions of humanity and based on an almost invisible, compartmentalised religiosity relegated to clearly defined spaces of seasonal activities and personal motivation and without significance for other organisational activities, thus resonating with values in the culture of development aid. 'What is the role of Islam in your awareness-raising activities?' I asked Mona from Islamic Relief— and she did not seem to understand my question. Clearly, for her there was no role for Islam to play in these activities.[20]

These notions of sacralised and secularised aid, however, are not static, straightforward or unambiguous, but constantly challenged and changing, testifying to the instability and incoherence of ideologies.[21] For instance, there are signs that the two Gulf-based NGOs are moving towards a more secularised notion of aid, seeking to adjust their ideologies to the culture of development aid, thereby hoping to create resonance with the UN and Western aid organisations. For some of Hanin's colleagues in IIROSA and IICO, then, the quality of aid is no longer measured primarily in terms of its potential contributions to a strengthened *umma*, but also in terms of its professionalism, transparency, and accountability. The UK-based NGOs, on the other hand, seem to be moving towards a re-Islamisation of at least parts of their aid provision, in an attempt to create ideologies that simultaneously appeal to conservative Muslim donors and secular aid agencies. While some staff members in Islamic Relief and Muslim Aid share Mona's understanding of Islam as irrelevant to concrete aid activities, many others insist that Islam can provide an 'added value' to an otherwise secular aid, facilitating access to particular groups of recipients and at the same time ensuring organisational authenticity.

These processes of ideological production in contemporary transnational Muslim NGOs may contribute to the formulation of new conceptions and cultures of aid, questioning, or at least re-articulating, the historical secularism[22] of Western development aid on the one hand, and the religious solidarity of Islamic aid on the other. At the same time, and underlying their ideologies of aid, these organisations present new conceptions of Islam, introducing a this-worldly focus on activism and morality, resembling what Mandaville (2007:3f) has termed post-materialist Muslim politics. The movements of political Islamism as well as conservative Islamic piety, he argues, are increasingly forced to compete with Muslim agendas above and below the state and the religious establishment that seek more broadly to open up spaces for the inclusion of religion in public life and greater recognition of Muslim identity claims (Mandaville 2007:4). Thus, for people in transnational Muslim NGOs, being an 'active' or 'good' Muslim is not necessarily about fighting for political power, nor is it about praying five times a day or wearing the right Islamic dress; it is about engaging in social activism such as the provision of aid, based on Islamic values and ethos. As such, this book is not only about how transnational Muslim organisations conceptualise aid provision, but also about how this in turn contributes to shaping their conceptions of organisational religiosity, and, more broadly, conceptions of contemporary global Islam.

Structure of the book

The book is divided into eight chapters. Following the Introduction, Chapters 2 and 3 take the first steps into the analysis of transnational Muslim NGOs, providing the contextual framework for understanding these NGOs. Chapter 2 presents the two different aid cultures from which these organisations have emerged, namely the culture of development aid and that of Islamic aid. The chapter argues that these two aid cultures are in many ways fundamentally different; that their differences have historically been unnoticed insofar as they have, until the emergence of transnational Muslim NGOs, maintained largely parallel, unconnected existences; and finally, that they have in each of their ways contributed to creating conditions of possibility for the emergence of transnational Muslim NGOs. Against this background, the chapter presents transnational Muslim NGOs as sites of cultural encounters, having grown out of and being shaped by these two cultures. Chapter 3 then zooms in on some of the specific historical events that have contributed to shaping the ways in which Muslim NGOs position themselves in relation to these two cultures of aid, discussing the role of the organisations in relation to the famine in the Horn of Africa, the wars in Afghanistan and Bosnia, and finally 9/11 and the War on Terror. The chapter presents two main arguments: first, that transnational Muslim NGOs have historically emphasised their allegiance to an Islamic aid culture, relating to the culture of development aid primarily by way of parallel co-existence, competition and conflict; and second, that this situation has changed after 9/11 and the War on Terror, at once forcing and encouraging transnational Muslim NGOs to relate more directly with the development culture, and to present new repertoires of relations.

Chapters 4 and 5 move from the macro level of global cultures and historical events, outlining the context in which transnational Muslim NGOs work, to the micro level of four concrete organisations, presenting the first of two case studies. Introducing the two Gulf-based NGOs, IICO and IIROSA, to the analysis, Chapter 4 first gives a description of the two organisations and their members, analysing their organisational identity and claims to authority. Chapter 5 then analyses elements of their organisational ideologies, including their vision, rationale and strategies for aid provision. Discussing the ways in which the two organisations have transmitted, translated, and appropriated elements from different cultures of aid in their formulation of organisational identities and ideologies, the two chapters argue that IIROSA and IICO present a sacralised aid ideology, based on a largely religious organisational authority and resonating with principles of a traditional Islamic aid culture. Following the same structure, Chapters 6 and 7 present a case study of the two British-based NGOs, Islamic Relief, and Muslim Aid. Contrary to IICO and IIROSA, these two organisations present a secularised aid ideology, building on a professional organisational authority and resonating with principles of mainstream development aid. At the same time, however, the two case studies document how this dichotomy between sacralised and secularised aid is never fixed or static, but constantly interrupted and disturbed, whether by IIROSA and IICO's attempts at 'developmentalising' their sacralised aid or by Islamic Relief and Muslim Aid's attempts at Islamising their secular aid. These and other main findings of the book are summarised in Chapter 8, leading to a discussion of their implication for future developments in the field of aid provision.

2

THE CULTURES OF DEVELOPMENT
AND ISLAMIC AID

When the International Islamic Relief Organisation builds a mosque, it often builds a well next to it, at once facilitating the Islamic tradition of ablution and making sure that people in the area have access to clean water. Likewise, in its celebration of the Islamic holiday *Eid al-Adha*, Muslim Aid integrates an element of economic empowerment, making sure that the sheep to be sacrificed are bought from participants in one of its microfinance projects. These examples hint at the fact that transnational Muslim NGOs are not easily conceptualised as either part of an Islamic aid culture or as part of the mainstream development culture, but are better understood as organisations which are simultaneously rooted in and constantly move in between the two, mixing elements from both. Taking its first steps into the actual analysis of transnational Muslim NGOs, the present chapter will outline the historical contexts out of which transnational Muslim NGOs have emerged, sketching the contours of the two aid cultures that have shaped them and providing the background for Chapter 3's analysis of their trajectories in and out of these cultures. By taking a historical approach to the description of the cultures of Islamic aid and development, I seek to emphasise the fact that these two cultures are not permanent or static entities, but fluid and changing processes, and as such, any attempt at characterising them must necessarily be historically specific. In that perspective, the following descriptions of and comparisons between the two cultures are not an attempt at drawing up generic ideal types, but seek merely to outline important traits and differences as they appear at a specific point in time.

A common humanity: A brief history of development aid[1]

Contemporary forms of development aid have their roots in nineteenth-century Europe. Emerging modernisation, manifested in rapid industrialisation, urbanisation and market expansion, prompted parallel sentiments of societal breakdown and optimism. On the one hand, these processes of modernisation led to increased poverty, diseases, and inequality, or at least an increasing awareness of them. On the other hand, technical and scientific inventions encouraged a feeling of optimism that these problems could actually be solved. In the words of Calhoun (2008:76), there was a belief that human action could be mobilised to transform conditions long taken as inevitable. New medicines and vaccinations, for instance, could cure or even prevent formerly deadly diseases such as typhus, yellow fever, and polio (Boli and Thomas 1997:179). Building on a mixture of Christian and Enlightenment ideas, intellectuals, politicians and members of the clergy started employing a language of 'humanitarianism' to push for public interventions to alleviate suffering and restore society's moral basis, emphasising an obligation to take care not only of members of one's own family, tribe or community, but also distant others (Barnett and Weiss 2008:21). Underlying this concern for the stranger were universalist notions of a common humanity, a cosmopolitan rejection of the relevance of national, ethnic or gendered boundaries in determining the limits of rights or responsibilities for the satisfaction of basic human needs (Held 2009:537), coupled with an optimistic faith in the abilities of humans to change the world for the better.

Colonialism and wars: The transnationalisation of aid

While these 'distant others' were initially understood primarily within a national context, a number of events prompted the internationalisation, or transnationalisation, of humanitarian aid. Nineteenth-century colonisation of Africa played an important role in shaping this emerging culture of aid provision. As part of their colonisation efforts, European states established national educational and healthcare systems, introduced vocational training programmes, and founded village banks all over Africa

(Rist 2008:57f), often replicating their own domestic systems and institutions at the expense of those of the local community, and thus introducing the notion of universally valid institutions and systems. In this colonisation of societal structures, states often had the help of non-governmental organisations, many of them Christian. For instance, missionary organisations such as the German Moravian Mission (established in 1732), played an important role, combining missionary efforts with educational activities, establishment of hospitals and aid to victims of natural disasters. Likewise, the many philanthropic foundations set up in this period, often by American industrialists with Christian leanings, spent millions on medical research and the development of vaccines with the purpose of aiding the sick in former and current colonies (Barnett and Weiss 2008:19f). Colonialist efforts to assist the colonies were presented as a moral, philanthropic obligation, while at the same time introducing notions of progress and civilisation as important elements in the provision of aid: As 'highly civilised' societies themselves, the colonising states had a duty to 'civilise' the 'uncivilised' societies. Western colonisation was, in other words, seen as a generous undertaking to help 'backward' societies to progress into civilisation (Rist 2008:43).

Another important factor in shaping contemporary aid was the wars of the nineteenth and twentieth centuries. By the mid-nineteenth century, changes in military technology were making war more brutal. At the same time, war reporting was emerging as a profession, meaning that the public had access to stories and pictures from the increasingly gruesome wars (Barnett 2005:733). This prompted the establishment of several transnational organisations, forerunners of today's NGOs, emphasising the importance of humanitarian relief. In 1862, Henry Dunant, a Swiss businessman, witnessed the Battle of Solferino in which 40,000 soldiers on each side lost their lives. Shocked by brutality of the war and the lack of medical attention for the wounded soldiers, Dunant spent the following years working to establish what was later to become the International Red Cross (Barnett and Weiss 2008:3), concerned with the provision of medical relief to wounded soldiers and victims of war. In a similar vein, the British woman Eglantyne Jebb established Save the Children in 1919 with the purpose of providing food and clothes to German children after the war, declaring that 'there is no such thing as an enemy child' (Chabbott 1999:229ff). In these efforts, the concept of neutrality came to be important, closely related to universalist notions of a common humanity. Taking sides in a conflict, it was argued, would inevitably lead to the exclusion of some people, thus violating the commitment to aid any human being in need. As such, politics came to be seen as a potential moral pollutant of aid (Barnett and Weiss 2008:4). Instead, actors involved in humanitarian and development aid were to remain neutral and impartial, shying away from political involvement.

The institutionalisation of the development system

This idea of a moral duty to provide aid to victims of wars and the 'uncivilised' poor in the colonies, based on notions of neutrality and universality and aimed at promoting progress and civilisation, was further strengthened and institutionalised in the wake of the two world wars. It was formalised in an emerging 'international society' (Held 2009), of which the provision of aid became an integrated part (D. Lewis and Kanji 2009:165). In other words, the new aid culture was not only normatively bound up in notions of universality, but was also structurally and institutionally based on ideas of the world as one place. Calls for international laws and institutions protecting human dignity as a response to the atrocities of the wars led to the establishment first of the largely unsuccessful League of Nations in 1919, and later the United Nations in 1945 (Barnett and Weiss 2008:23), which through different agencies and programmes sought to coordinate humanitarian relief to emergencies arising from war, including hunger, refugee flows and destruction of infrastructure. Parallel to these intergovernmental efforts to attend to the victims of war emerged a growing body of transnational movements and NGOs. In particular the period during and immediately after the Second World War witnessed a remarkable explosion in transnational NGOs, in a few years multiplying their numbers by more than eight (Boli and Thomas 1997:177). Organisations established in this period include Oxfam, Catholic Relief Services, CARE, and Caritas, many of them with Christian leanings.

The wars not only resulted in disasters, requiring immediate attention; they also revealed a tremendous economic inequality that called for more long-term assistance to what would later be called 'the third world' (Barnett and Weiss 2008:23). After the Second World War, not only Europe but most countries in Africa, Latin America, and Asia were in deep financial trouble. A few years after the launch of the Marshall Plan in 1947, President Truman decided to expand US foreign aid to include what he called 'underdeveloped areas' in the South (Degnbol-Martinussen and Engberg-Pedersen 1999:29), often synonymous with the former colonies. Throughout the 1950s and 1960s, European governments followed suit, establishing their own programmes and agencies for the distribution of aid from 'developed' to 'underdeveloped' or 'developing' countries. Likewise, the World Bank—originally established to 'reconstruct' and 'develop' Europe—soon expanded its activities to include what were now known as the 'underdeveloped' countries or 'third world' (Barnett and Weiss 2008:24). In 1956, the Bank founded the International Finance Cooperation, and in 1960, the International Development Association, responsible for lending to the world's poorest countries. And in the UN, a series of agencies for the provision of development aid were established, including the Expanded Programme of Technical Assistance in 1949, followed in 1958 by the United Nations Special Fund, later merging into the United Nations Development Programme (UNDP).

Ideologically, this institutionalisation of aid culture into a system of development assistance in large part relied on the dominant economic and political theories of the time, many of them building on modernisation theory and promoting a unilinear, technical conception of development. Based on notions of poverty as a matter of material deprivation and consequently of aid primarily as facilitation of economic growth, governments and intergovernmental organisations promoted what they considered to be universally valid mechanisms, procedures and practices, assumed to be useful and meaningful everywhere (Boli and Thomas 1997:180). In this, religion came to be seen as a conservative and traditional force, destined to withdraw and eventually disappear from public life as part of societal progress towards an increasingly modern society; a conception which continued to shape development studies and practice until recently. In this perspective, religion was difficult to reconcile with or relate to development's logic of economic progress and bureaucratic rationalisation, and was instead regarded as an irrelevance to development work, to be ignored or even actively fought in the concrete development projects. Donor policies and strategies on development would make little or no mention of religion, just as development workers would rarely pay attention to the topic (ver Beek 2000). This did not mean that the religious, or more correctly Christian, organisations that had until then been heavily involved in the provision of aid were suddenly banned from taking part in the development system, but it did mean that their participation became contingent on their willingness to subscribe to a quasi-secular, largely invisible notion of religion, something which will be discussed further below.

Transnational development NGOs

Since its establishment, the system of development aid has been constantly expanding, strengthening its hegemony in the global aid field. Transnational (often Western) NGOs have played an important role in this, in particular since the 1980s. While NGOs have taken part in the provision of aid since the birth of development culture, they often worked parallel to states and intergovernmental organisations, never fully integrated into their system of aid provision. This started changing in the 1980s, when governmental aid agencies and intergovernmental organisations began channelling aid through NGOs (D. Lewis and Kanji 2009:190; Reimann 2006:49f). By then, the poor performance and corruption of many 'third world' governments had disappointed 'first world' governments, prompting them to turn away from the large-scale, government-organised projects and interventions characteristic of the first decades of aid (D. Lewis and Kanji 2009:173). Coupled with an emerging neo-liberal agenda, this gave way to the so-called structural adjustment programmes, promoting the market rather than the state as the key to economic growth and providing an opening for the inclusion of NGOs. In contrast with governments, NGOs were seen as effective service deliverers, ensuring rapid (and honest) disbursement and utilisation of project funds (Carroll 1992:177). Likewise, a prominent role for NGOs fitted well with the privatisation efforts that were an integrated part of structural adjustment policies. Drastic cuts in governmental social services left room for NGOs to take over the provision of social welfare, education, health services, emergency relief, and other social services, in line with a neoliberal scepticism of the state. Further supporting this turn away from state-led models of aid provision, the end of the Cold War and waves of democratisation in Eastern Europe, the Philippines, Chile, and South Africa prompted a focus on 'civil society'. Among donors, support of democracy became an important element in aid provision and it soon became common sense that in order to be a properly functioning free market and democratic nation, a state would need to have a flourishing civil society (Mercer 2002:7). As Reimann (2006:60) notes, 'NGOs

were viewed as ideal institutions for the new mix of neoliberal economics and democratic theory promoted by the industrialised nations in the
post Cold War world', at once considered to be effective service providers, providers of an alternative to the state, and vehicles of democratisation and good governance.

Ironically, not only the rise but also the fall of structural adjustment
programmes encouraged an increasingly important role for NGOs. In
many countries, privatisation and other neo-liberal initiatives did not
lead to economic growth, or at least only in certain sectors of society,
while others experienced an increasing poverty. Among development
practitioners and academics, this contributed to a reconceptualisation of
development. Inspired by earlier approaches such as basic needs theory,
the narrow conception of development as economic growth was slowly
replaced by a broader and more inclusive understanding, emphasising
the social and cultural (although rarely religious) aspects of development,
under the heading of 'human development'. Introduced in a series of
UNDP Annual Reports the concept of 'human development' broadened
notions of development to include not only economic growth, but also
life expectancy, education and liberty, in the process reducing economic
growth to a means rather than an end in itself (Rist 2008:206). Taking
its starting point in the individual and the community rather than the
state and the market, this new understanding of aid emphasised local-
level and small-scale interventions (Tandon 2000:320). In the implementation of this new kind of aid, NGOs were seen as crucial players—
not, as the neoliberals would have it, as proponents of privatisation and
replacement of the state, but as sources of alternative ideas and approaches
to development (D. Lewis and Kanji 2009:39), and as legitimate spokes-
people of 'the poor', emphasising the importance of principles such as
'participation', 'sustainability' and 'capacity-building' to the success of
'human development'.

In this, governmental and multilateral donors would prefer cooperation with secular NGOs, seen to be proponents of a 'progressive', 'democratic' civil society. Religious organisations, on the other hand, were considered to be 'traditional', 'patriarchal' and perhaps even 'un-democratic'
and as such, they were increasingly marginalised. Those religious organisations that did receive funding and support from donors were typically
mainstream Christian organisations that appeared quasi-secular, avoiding proselytisation and providing aid to Christians and non-Christians

FOR HUMANITY OR FOR THE UMMA?

alike, and as such compatible with the secular development principles of the donors (Clarke 2007:78). In other words, multilateral and governmental donors would engage with religious organisations not because of their religiosity but despite their religiosity, prompting a gradual secularisation of those religious organisations wishing to attract funding from donors. As an employee in a British Christian NGO noted in an interview with Gerard Clarke (2007:84), staff often felt forced to 'leave their faith at the door' when meeting with officials of the UK's Department for International Development (DFID). Similarly, a DFID employee jokingly referred to Christian Aid as 'we're-not-that-Christian' Aid, hinting at their tendency to downplay their religiosity in cooperation with DFID. Thus, while proselytising religious organisations continued to engage in the provision of aid as they had for decades (and even centuries), the culture of mainstream development aid gradually came to prioritise quasi-secular organisations as the only NGOs eligible for donor funding, based on an understanding of aid as inherently secular.

Solidarity with the umma: A brief history of Islamic aid[2]

Almost parallel to the institutionalisation of development aid, another, and in many ways very different, aid culture took form—what we shall, to somewhat simplify, call the Islamic aid culture. Like the culture of development aid, this is an aid culture that has roots that go much further back than the twentieth century. Islamic traditions of charitable giving (*sadaqa*) have existed since the birth of Islam, just as the obligatory alms tax, *zakat*, and the religious endowment, the *waqf* (plural: *awqaf*), have historically been important Islamic institutions of social welfare. This is not the place, however, to enter into a detailed historical account of these theological institutions and traditions.[3] Instead, we shall concentrate on the contemporary history of Islamic aid. Overall, this is a culture that has grown out of 'the Islamic resurgence'.[4] Starting in the early twentieth century, the Islamic resurgence denotes a global movement of renewed interest in Islam as a relevant identity and model for community, manifested in greater religious piety and Islamic solidarity; in the introduction of Islamically defined organisations and institutions; and in a growing adoption of Islamic culture, dress codes, terminology, and values by Muslims worldwide (Lapidus 2002:823). The Islamic resurgence was nurtured by two factors in particular. First, the experience of

European colonialism. In the face of the challenges posed by the West during the nineteenth and early twentieth centuries, Muslim thinkers in a wide variety of socio-cultural and regional settings turned collectively to religion as a form of anti-colonial liberation discourse, calling for Islamic solidarity based on the notion of the *umma* (Mandaville 2001:69; Zubaida 2004). As the Islamic thinker Jamal al-Din al-Afghani claimed, only through unity in a common Muslim identity would people under European colonialism find liberation (Mandaville 2007:279). Second, the emergence of secular Arab regimes after the First World War served as a catalyst for the resurgence. Based on ideologies of modernisation and progress, these regimes, led by secular elites, sought to model their states in the image of Western states. However, rhetoric did not always match reality, and the post-colonial Arab states were largely unsuccessful in their attempts at securing social welfare for their citizens. Coupled with an often oppressive form of government, the ideology of modernisation came to have a radically different meaning to people in the Middle East than in the West. Against this background, Islamic groups and movements started emerging, presenting alternatives not only to the West but to their own secular state and ideologies.

The Muslim Brotherhood: Islam and social welfare activism

By far the most important of these organisations is the Muslim Brotherhood (or *al-ikhwan al-muslimun*), established by the Egyptian school teacher Hassan al-Banna in 1928, a few years after Egypt's independence and the collapse of the Ottoman empire (Soage 2008:54; see also Munson 2001; Mitchell 1969). Under the leadership of al-Banna, the Brotherhood sought to merge Islam and modernity, maintaining the usefulness of modern technology, science and industry (Mandaville 2007:100), but rejecting Western colonial models of modernity and insisting instead on interpreting modernity within an Islamic normative framework, claiming that 'Islam is the solution'. The Brotherhood quickly spread to other Middle Eastern countries, opening up branches in Syria in the beginning of the 1930s, Palestine in 1935, and Jordan in 1942. Later followed Muslim Brotherhood organisations in a number of African countries, including Sudan and Libya at the end of the 1940s, and Somalia in the 1960s. Parallel to this, North American and European branches started emerging, established by Muslim immigrants (more on this below).

As a teacher, Banna had a strong social awareness, and he saw the pro-vision of aid to the poor as an important responsibility of the Brotherhood and of any Muslim. In his pamphlet *The Message of the Teachings* (Banna 1993), he says:

> Be active, energetic, and skilled in public services. You should feel happy when you offer a service to other people. You should feel compelled to visit the sick, assist the needy, support the weak, and give relief to the ill-fated, even if it is with a good and affectionate word. Always rush to do good deeds.

In its first years, rather than formal politics, the Muslim Brotherhood focused primarily on social welfare activities, relief, and the building of schools and hospitals (Yaylaci 2007:12), presenting an alternative to the largely unsuccessful state. Emerging Brotherhoods in other countries copied the approach. In Jordan, for instance, the Brotherhood established an organisation specifically designated to provide aid to the poor, the Islamic Center Charity Society, which is today one of the largest NGOs in the country, running almost 100 community centres, forty health clin-ics, several schools and universities, and two hospitals (Jung and Juul Petersen 2014). Education became a core activity for the Brotherhood, not only in the sense of teaching and transmitting knowledge, but as a way of moulding individual conduct, entrenching faith, stimulating activ-ism, and contributing to the Islamisation of society (Hatina 2006:182; Høigilt 2013). Through education, the Brotherhood hoped to give new generations an Islamic identity, by extension strengthening and reform-ing the Muslim community (Mahmood 2005:58). As such, focus was on the restoration of believers to the fold of righteous Islam; the conversion of non-Muslims became secondary (Hatina 2006:181). In this, moral training played an important part. In the words of Banna (cf. Roald 1994:140):

> A rising nation (*umma*) is in severe need of morality, an exceeding, strong and firm morality together with a high-aspiring, lofty and great soul (*nafs*), because it has to face the demands of the new age which cannot be met except through a distinguished, sincere and strong morality based upon a deep-rooted, firm and profound faith, great sacrifices and deep suffering

For Banna and the Brotherhood, education was closely related to the religiously inflected notion of *tarbiya*, implying a holistic sense of human growth and development that accrues through knowledge of religion (Mandaville 2007:59). This moral training and education emphasises virtues such as patience, sincerity and good intentions, truthfulness, tolerance and hope, discouraging gossip and backbiting, sexual promiscuity and other forms of misconduct (Roald 1994:142). But it does not seek to attain mere individual spirituality, detached from the world. Religious feelings must generate action; in the words of Banna (1993): 'Belief is the basis of action. Sincere intentions are more important than outward actions. However, the Muslim is requested to attain improvement in both spheres: purification of the heart and performance of righteous deeds'.

A number of other organisations directly connected or closely related to the Brotherhood emerged.[5] In 1941, the Jama'at-e Islami (in English literally 'Islamic Party') was established in Lahore by the journalist and theologian Sayeed Abul A'ala Mawdudi as an advocacy organisation and political party seeking Muslim autonomy and rights in India. Later, he embraced Islamic nationalism, and his new cause would be the Islamisation of Pakistan, founded in 1947. Following the partition of India and Pakistan, an independent party was formed in India and today there are also sister organisations in Bangladesh, Sri Lanka and Kashmir. Like the Brotherhood, with which the Jama'at-e Islami enjoys close ideological and organisational relations, members were well-educated people, unwilling to accept the secularist position of the West and what they saw as Westernised regimes (Esposito and Voll 2001:20). But unlike the Muslim Brotherhood, the activities of the Jama'at were always primarily political, aiming at the establishment of an Islamic state, governed by Islamic law. From the 1940s, however, the Brotherhood's activism also took increasingly political forms. Under the ideological leadership of Sayeed Qutb, who had been influenced by Mawdudi, the Brotherhood started to call for the establishment of an Islamic state based on *shari'a* (Mandaville et al. 2009:20), reflecting increasing dissatisfaction with Nasser's secular nationalism. Nonetheless, parallel to their increasing politicisation, both movements continued their engagement in social and cultural activism, which helped to strengthen their popularity.

Transnational pan-Islamism: *Da'wa* and Islamic economics

Apart from the Muslim Brotherhood, the Gulf countries played an important role in shaping the culture of Islamic aid in the 1960s-70s. While the Brotherhood and Jama'at-e Islami's aid was very much shaped by national needs and carried out by local associations, the movement from the Gulf countries was transnational and missionary in its outlook, manifested in organisations such the Muslim World League, the International Islamic Council for Da'wa and Relief (in Arabic, *al-Majlis al-islami al-'alami lil da'wa wa al-ighata*), and the OIC. Many of these transnational initiatives emerged from Saudi Arabia, reflecting the country's increasing importance in the Islamic resurgence. Underlying many of these new Saudi initiatives were elements of a pan-Islamic ideology, articulated largely as a counterweight to Nasser's secular Arab nationalism (Hegghammer 2010:17) as an attempt to compensate for the weak legitimacy of Wahhabi Islam (Schultze 1990, cf. Benthall and Bellion-Jourdan 2003:71).

One crucial factor in shaping the movement of transnational, missionary aid from the Gulf was the emergence of what came to be known as 'Islamic economics'. The sharp rise in the price of oil at the time of the Yom Kippur war in 1973 provoked a spectacular increase in the disposable revenue of producer countries, including Saudi Arabia and Kuwait, seemingly altering the balance of economic power between the oil-producing countries of the Islamic world and the industrialised states in the West. Furthermore, the increased revenues also placed large sums of money in the hands of governments, businesses and individuals of the oil-producing countries, boosting efforts to create distinctively Islamic financial institutions, depending on private capital (Pripp 2006:104).[6] At the same time, there was a widespread disillusionment with the capacities of the (secular) state to act morally and effectively, prompting people to look to the private financial sector for solutions (Pripp 2006:134). Against this background, a number of Islamic financial institutions were established.[7] On the one hand, these institutions were part of attempts at providing Islamically viable alternatives to secular economic systems such as socialism and capitalism, deemed by many Muslims to be morally corrupt. On the other hand, they were also shaped by a desire to develop an effective and workable system that would not only be morally preferable, but would also be capable of generating material development in Muslim countries, eliminating what some Muslim scholars referred to as the 'economic backwardness' of Islamic countries (Pripp 2006:113f). As such, Islamic economics was presented as an alternative to dominant capitalist theories of economic growth, central to the culture of development aid.

A key figure in this new movement (and in the Islamic resurgence as such) was the scholar, activist and soon-to-be TV host Yusuf al-Qaradawi, born in Egypt in 1926. He wrote his doctoral thesis on *The Role of Zakat in the Resolution of Legal Alms* (1972), and became a much-used consultant for financial institutions and businessmen, involved in the establishment of, among others, al-Taqwa Bank (1988), Qatar Islamic International Bank (1991), and Faysal Bank (1994). For Qaradawi and other Islamic economists, the concept of *zakat* is central to Islamic economics—and to Islamic ideology in general. *Zakat* is one of the five pillars of Islam, a religious tax obliging Muslims to pay 2.5 per cent of their wealth as alms, primarily to the poor and needy.[8] Collection of the tax by the state had been widespread in the early centuries of Islam but the duty to pay it had long been left to the individual. However, with the resurgence of Islamic economics, *zakat* was accorded renewed importance by Islamic thinkers as a fiscal mechanism for increasing social justice and public welfare (Singer 2008:201). New governmental and semi-governmental *zakat* systems emerged throughout the Muslim world, starting in Saudi Arabia (1951), followed by Malaysia (1955), Libya (1971), Yemen (1975), Jordan (1978), Pakistan (1980), Kuwait (1982), and Sudan (1984).[9] Some years later, the Qatar Islamic Fund for Zakat and Alms, of which Qaradawi is a co-founder and board member, was established. *Zakat* represents a key component of the moral economy, epitomising a number of ideas which help to define that economy:

> 'the notion that the individual holds property as a trustee for God; therefore that property must be used for a higher end, such as the sustenance and support of those in a less fortunate position than yourself; the idea of mutual social responsibility which ensures the "integration of the individual into a truly Islamic society"' (Pripp 2006:125).

At the same time, and on a more practical note, *zakat* was a convenient tool for the purification of interest money, considered to be prohibited in Islamic economics. Interest was impossible to avoid in a globalised banking sector where cooperation with capitalist banks was inevitable. Instead, the new Islamic finance institutions would convert interest into charitable work (Benthall and Bellion-Jourdan 2003:72), often through the establishment of *zakat* mechanisms for the purification of money. As such, the rise of Islamic economics and Islamic businessmen, or 'religious-minded middle class entrepreneurs' (Roy 2004:96) released large sums of money that had to be distributed to charity, often through NGOs.

Finally, the establishment of transnational organisations also played an important role in shaping this particular, Gulf-based, trajectory of Islamic aid in the 1960s and 1970s. Based on notions of a pan-Islamic solidarity (*al-tadamun al-islami*), King Faisal promoted the idea that all Muslims are one people with a responsibility to support each other in times of crisis. The ultimate expression of this pan-Islamic movement was the Organisation of the Islamic Conference (OIC), an intergovernmental organisation established in 1969 with the purpose of safeguarding and protecting the interests of the Muslim world (Mandaville 2007:159).[10] This also included the provision of aid to fellow Muslim communities and states, primarily through the OIC's Islamic Development Bank and its Islamic Solidarity Fund (1974). Prior to the establishment of the OIC, several non-governmental organisations were established to promote cooperation, mutual solidarity and religious awareness, while at the same time exporting a Saudi-style Islam (Mandaville 2007:159). In 1962 the Muslim World League (in Arabic, *Rabitat al-alam al-islami*) was established. Religious leaders from twenty-two different countries were involved in the launch of the organisation, including Jama'at-e Islami's Mawdudi and a number of high-rank Brotherhood representatives (Schulze 2000:173),[11] as were official religious and political institutions in Saudi Arabia.[12] The purpose of the organisation was to build up a global Islamic public, primarily through mission activities such as publishing, media, education and coordination of preachers and scholars, Arabic language instruction, Qur'an schools, mosques, and Islamic centres, propagating conservative Islamic teachings based on Wahhabi Islam to Muslims as well as non-Muslims (Mandaville 2007:285), but also through relief and charity work. Today, the Muslim World League is one of the largest Muslim non-governmental organisations, with branches all over the world. Other transnational organisations from this period include two of this book's main protagonists: IIROSA, established in Saudi Arabia as part of the Muslim World League in 1979, and IICO, founded by Qaradawi in Kuwait in 1984.[13]

Migration and Islam in the West

Parallel to the aid provided by the Muslim Brotherhood organisations and that of the Gulf states, a third wave of Islamic aid was prompted by the migration of Muslims from Middle Eastern and Asian countries to

Europe and the USA, starting in the 1960s. Among the immigrants were many Muslim Brothers, having fled persecution under secular regimes in countries like Egypt, Syria, Iraq, and Tunisia (Mandaville 2007:159). By the 1980s, some of these immigrants started establishing more permanent Muslim Brotherhood structures in Europe, adjusted to the new surroundings. In 1982, the Islamic Community in Germany (in German, *Islamische Gemeinschaft in Deutschland*) was established, followed the year after by the Union of Islamic Organisations in France (in French, *Union des Organisations Islamiques de France*). In 1989, the Brussels-based umbrella organisation Federation of Islamic Organisations in Europe was established, and in the 1990s, a series of other organisations followed, including the European Institute of Human Sciences (1992) and European Council for Fatwa and Research (1997), both of them established by the Federation (Mandaville et al. 2009:20f). Qaradawi played (and plays) an important role in many of these organisations; he is the founder and chairman of the European Council for Fatwa and Research, and enjoys close relations with the Federation of Islamic Organisations in Europe. A somewhat parallel development took place in Jama'at-e Islami. The economic migration waves of the 1950s and 1960s lead to the establishment of large Pakistani and Bangladeshi communities, in particular in Britain (de Cordier 2009a:611). Among them were some former Jama'at-e Islami activists who soon established a number of European organisations. One of the first was the UK Islamic Mission, established in 1962 by a small group with connections to the East London Mosque. In 1973, the Islamic Foundation in Leicester was established, and in 1979 Da'watul Islam, both of them with close connections to the Jama'at-e Islami environment. More recently, the Muslim Council of Britain was founded in 1997, allegedly associated with older generations of Deobandi and Salafi-influenced leaders (Mandaville 2007:295; see also Eade and Garbin 2006), many of them affiliated with Jama'at-e Islami. Finally, like the Muslim Brotherhood and Jama'at-e Islami, Saudi organisations also spread to Europe and North America following Muslim migration. The Muslim World League, for instance, has established offices in a wide range of European and North American cities since the 1970s.[14]

Together with more independent organisations and community associations, some of them organised around the local mosque, all these organisations engage in a variety of Muslim causes and activities, acting as representatives and places of gathering for the migrant Muslim communities. Some focus primarily on *da'wa*, mosque services and Qur'an lessons, while others engage more broadly in voluntary community services, including youth work, charitable activities and the collection of *zakat* (de Cordier 2009a:612). The majority focus their activities on the local community, but some also engage in activities abroad. Initially, this was primarily in the form of mosque collection of *zakat* and money for *Qurbani* offerings to be channelled to the region from which the contributors originated.[15] Reflecting generational shifts in the Muslim population, this started changing in the 1980s, when the first professional Muslim aid organisations emerged, copying the organisational form and structure of British NGOs such as Oxfam and Christian Aid. Among these are two of the protagonists of this book—Islamic Relief and Muslim Aid. Islamic Relief was established in 1984 by two medical students of Egyptian origin, informally connected to the Muslim Brotherhood; Muslim Aid was established the year after by a group of British Muslim community organisations, many of them dominated by Bangladeshi and Pakistani immigrants with relations to Jama'at e-Islami.

Dichotomies of aid? Comparing the cultures of development and Islamic aid

As the above histories of two contemporary aid cultures show, the cultures of development and Islamic aid are in many ways different. They have both emerged as responses to and are shaped by processes of modernisation, colonialism, and globalisation. But their proponents, or inhabitants, have interpreted these processes in different ways, leading to different cultures of aid provision. Overall, one could argue that this difference, at least in part, grows out of different positions in these processes of modernisation, colonialism, and globalisation: put somewhat simply, the development culture has grown out of an experience of power and hegemony, of colonising, but also out of sentiments of collective guilt and a sense of complicity in the creation of 'the distant sufferer', stemming from the same colonial legacy (Chouraliaki 2010:111). The Middle Eastern Islamic aid culture, on the other hand, is shaped by experiences of marginalisation, of being colonised, and of the poor not as a distant sufferer, but as a fellow member of the community. In concrete terms, and as shall be outlined in more detail below, these differences manifest themselves in the different actors inhabiting the two cultures, the different systems and institutions they have created as well as in the different values that they promote.

Parallel aid cultures

Historically, the cultures of development and Islamic aid have, in terms of actors, structures and geography, had largely parallel existences, with rare overlaps or coincidences. For one, the actors inhabiting the two cultures were different. Development aid, on one side, was dominated by organisational types such as transnational NGOs, governmental aid agencies, and intergovernmental organisations. In concrete terms, the culture was inhabited by intergovernmental organisations such as the UN and the World Bank; governmental aid agencies such as USAID and DFID; and NGOs such as CARE and Oxfam (D. Lewis and Kanji 2009). Islamic aid, on the other hand, was dominated by organisational types such as transnational missionary organisations, networks, national political groups and movements, immigrant community associations, ministries of *awqaf* and *zakat* and prominent individuals. More concretely, powerful actors in the Islamic aid culture were political movements such as the Muslim Brotherhood and Jama'at-e Islami, including their national branches and affiliated associations, missionary organisations such as the Muslim World League and the World Assembly of Muslim Youth, ministries of *awqaf* and *zakat* in Saudi Arabia and other Gulf-based countries, and European Muslim organisations such as the Muslim Council of Britain. Finally, and unlike the highly institutionalised culture of development aid, the culture of Islamic aid has nurtured the authority of charismatic personalities such as Banna, Qutb, and Qaradawi.[16]

Furthermore, these actors worked through parallel economic structures. Development aid came to be based on a formalised, standardised system of economic transactions, while Islamic aid relied on much more informal, personal, systems of transaction. But perhaps most importantly, the two cultures were geographically different. The culture of Islamic aid has grown out of the Middle East, in particular Egypt and the Gulf countries, as well as Pakistan. The Muslim Brotherhood emerged from Egypt, and has traditionally been strongest in the Middle East, while Jama'at-e Islami emerged from Pakistan and spread to other South Asian countries. The majority of the transnational organisations were established in Saudi Arabia, including the Muslim World League, the OIC, and World

Assembly of Muslim Youth. Likewise, most of the funding for Islamic aid provision has traditionally come from Saudi Arabia and other Gulf countries. In contrast, the field of development aid has grown out of a Western context and was dominated by Western actors (Donini and Minear 2006; see also Escobar 1995; Rist 2008). Western states controlled most money flows, the vast majority of transnational NGOs were from the West and even intergovernmental organisations such as the UN agencies, the World Bank, and others were arguably dominated by Western actors, with most contributions coming from Western countries. This is not to imply that there were no non-Western actors in the field of development aid, only that Western actors were dominant, numerically as well as economically. Kuwait and Saudi Arabia, for instance, have had governmental aid agencies since respectively 1961 and 1974, but both preferred to channel their official aid through OIC and the Islamic Development Bank rather than through the UN, the Development Assistance Committee and the Organisation for Economic Cooperation and Development (OEDC) (Kroessin 2007). As other Arab Gulf states, they have always treated the latter as 'Western' channels, providing only symbolic support (Hyder 2007:6).[17]

Different languages, different values

The actors inhabiting the two cultures of aid have historically come to rely on different sets of values, some of which can be conceptualised in the form of dichotomies, shaping the symbolic languages of development aid and Islamic aid.[18] One such dichotomy of values is that between solidarity and universalism. In the culture of development aid, universalism came to be a central value. Universalism is understood first and foremost in terms of an inclusive, non-discriminatory approach to recipients, based on a cosmopolitan understanding of humanity as one, and constituted in sharp opposition to particularistic, often religious, approaches, perceived to be discriminatory and excluding. Islamic aid, on the other hand, centres on notions of solidarity and brotherhood, binding Muslims together in a global *umma*. In this perspective, all Muslims are part of the same religious brotherhood, and as such, closely connected, mutually interdependent, and obliged to help one another. Echoing classical Islamic ideas about the two ontological spheres of *dar al Islam* and *dar al-gharb* (in English, the house of Islam and the house of war), the limits of solidarity were often understood in terms of the West. Qaradawi, for instance, often identifies a specific Western threat to Islamic civilisation and way of life—initially the post-colonial Arab regimes, perceived to be protégés of Western imperialism (Hatina 2006:182), and later the threat of secularism, in the form of a morally decadent and individualised West (Gräf and Skovgaard-Petersen 2009:5).

Closely related to this is the dichotomy between neutrality and justice. In the culture of development aid, neutrality came to be a core value, shaped by the efforts of Western humanitarian organisations and states to aid victims of the world wars and epitomised as one of the seven principles of the Red Cross. The victors of the wars emphasised the neutrality of aid, first and foremost in the sense of being apolitical, thus ensuring a universalist approach to recipients, but also increasingly in the sense of being technical, professional and objective rather than emotional, personal, and normative. On the other hand, in the Islamic aid culture, which had in part grown out of political movements such as the Muslim Brotherhood and Jama'at-e Islami, there was no inbuilt dichotomy between aid and the political, and neutrality did not seem to be an essential value. Instead, actors emphasised the importance of aid as a tool for justice, a way of realising and extending sentiments of solidarity in order to protect fellow Muslims from external threats, whether in the form of dominant colonial powers or oppressive, secular regimes.

Finally, and to some degree underlying the other two dichotomies, is the dichotomy between the secular and the religious. The culture of Islamic aid was based on a notion of religion as all-encompassing and relevant to all spheres of life, including the provision of aid. Religious activities such as *zakat* collection, *da'wa*, religious education and construction of mosques played a central role in the provision of aid, just as Islamic scholars, Qur'an schools, and mosques were important for the implementation of aid. The culture of development aid, on the other hand, had gradually come to rest on a principally secular understanding of aid. This does not mean that there were no religious actors involved in development aid: as we have seen, missionary organisations were historically involved in the provision of aid to the colonies, just as Christian NGOs played a part in the establishment of the United Nations, and some of the largest NGOs of the 1980s were religious, including World Vision and Catholic Relief Services. But it means that the culture was, to a large degree, based on a secular understanding of 'religion' in terms of a dichotomy between the public and the private. In this perspective, the public sphere remains, or should remain, largely non-religious, with 'religion' confined to personal beliefs, religious institutions and other clearly defined 'religious' spaces, leading to a preference for secular or at least quasi-secular NGOs such as Christian Aid.

Creating conditions of possibility for transnational Muslim NGOs

Albeit in different ways, both of these parallel cultures facilitated the emergence of transnational Muslim NGOs in the 1970s and 1980s, creating conditions of possibility for their existence. The culture of development aid has institutionalised a transnational system for the provision of aid that has become a hegemonic transnational system, dominant in terms of economic transfers as well as language. Equally important, this culture has introduced the NGO, carving out a space for such organisations as relevant organisational forms and providers of aid in this system. Facilitated by broader processes of globalisation, transnational NGOs have, especially since the 1980s, gained increasing visibility and influence, coming to be seen as the most appropriate and effective actors in the provision of aid (whether from the perspective of neoliberal anti-state ideologies or visions of alternative development and a strengthened civil society).

More specifically, the culture of Islamic aid has forged a connection between Islamisation and social welfare, promoted by organisations such as the Muslim Brotherhood, Jama'at-e Islami and countless local charities. Likewise, the Gulf-countries' pan-Islamic efforts have presented new transnational relations and organisational types, (re)introducing concepts of Islamic finance and mission. Financially, the explosion of oil prices in 1979 meant that huge funds were suddenly available to donors at governmental level, among businesses, and individuals, many of whom channelled large amounts to aid activities, thus contributing to the strengthening in particular of Gulf-based aid organisations (Ghandour 2004:329), such as the IIROSA and IICO, which were both established at this time. And finally, the emergence of a Muslim diaspora in the West has contributed to the establishment of new donors and transnational structures of *zakat* distribution (de Cordier 2009a:610). While first generation immigrants preferred giving their *zakat* personally or to the mosque, often to be distributed to the villages where people originally came from, during the 1980s, the changing configuration of immigrant Muslim society led to shifts in the patterns and forms of charity. New generations of immigrants also wanted to pay their *zakat*, but they wanted to do so to established organisations, encouraging the establishment of Western Muslim NGOs such as Islamic Relief and Muslim Aid.

Against this background, I argue that transnational Muslim NGOs can be conceptualised as sites of cultural encounters—this is where the cultures of development and Islamic aid meet. To paraphrase Long (2001:243), they can be seen as an interface between different aid cultures, as sites for the intricate interplay and joint appropriation of different bodies of knowledge. What that means is precisely what this book is about. The following chapter will take a first step into the exploration of transnational Muslim NGOs as interfaces for the cultures of Islamic aid and development. Sketching their historical trajectories, Chapter 3 seeks to explore the emergence of transnational Muslim NGOs, analysing the ways in which they have traditionally positioned themselves in relation to the two aid cultures.

Table 2.1: The cultures of development and Islamic aid

	Development aid	*Islamic aid*
Language	Universalism	Solidarity
	Neutrality	Justice
	Secularism	Religion
Geography	The West	The Middle East
Organisational types	Transnational NGOs	Transnational missionary
	Governmental aid	organisations
	agencies	National political groups
	Intergovernmental	Immigrant community
	organisations	associations
		Ministries of *awqaf* and
		zakat
		Prominent individuals
Examples of important	UN	Muslim Brotherhood
actors	World Bank	Jama'at-e Islami
	USAID	Muslim World League
	DFID	Saudi Arabian government
	Oxfam	Yusuf al-Qaradawi
	CARE	

3

TRAJECTORIES OF TRANSNATIONAL MUSLIM NGOs

When I visited Muslim Aid's country office in Bangladesh, I talked to a young man who had worked in the organisation for several years. He told me that he had gone to an international NGO coordination meeting some years before, and staff from other Western NGOs would not sit next to him.

> I sat down in a corner, and then, when the people from Islamic Relief came, they sat down next to me. The space next to me on the other side was empty and this lady from ActionAid came, and she didn't want to sit next to me. I think she thought that it was like the Islamic corner or something like that. I felt very bad. We never thought like that. And now, when I go to the coordination meetings, everyone wants to sit next to me.

This little story gives an example of how relations between (some) transnational Muslim NGOs and mainstream development actors have changed, shifting from avoidance and even hostility to dialogue and cooperation. Chapter 3 looks at these changing relationships in a broader context, exploring the different ways in which transnational Muslim NGOs have historically navigated between the cultures of development and Islamic aid. Tracing the trajectories of transnational Muslim NGOs, the chapter also seeks to provide suggestions as to the concrete political, economic and social factors influencing the emergence and development of transnational Muslim NGOs. The chapter traces the history of transnational Muslim NGOs through an analysis of four events, serving as the windows through which to explore the ways in which the organisations have historically been positioned in the aid field. These events are: the famine in the Horn of Africa in the mid-1980s; the war in Afghanistan in the 1980s; the war in Bosnia in the 1990s; and finally the 9/11 attacks on New York and Washington in 2001, all judged to be defining moments in the history of transnational Muslim NGOs insofar as they have contributed in important ways to shaping the perceptions and room for manoeuvre of these NGOs.[1] At the same time, the analysis of these events also directs attention to the heterogeneity of the group of transnational Muslim NGOs, illustrating how different organisations have emphasised different understandings of aid at different times.

Table 3.1: Important events in the history of transnational Muslim NGOs

Event	Examples of transnational Muslim NGOs established in relation to these events
Famine in the Horn of Africa	International Islamic Relief Organisation (Saudi Arabia, 1979)
	Munazzamat al Da'wa Islamiya (Sudan, 1980)
	Islamic African Relief Agency (Sudan, 1981)
	Malawi Muslim Agency (Kuwait, 1981)[2]
	Islamic Relief (UK, 1984)
	International Islamic Charitable Organisation (Kuwait, 1984)
	Muslim Aid (UK, 1985)
War in Afghanistan	Human Concern International (Canada, 1980)
	Human Relief Agency (Egypt, 1985)
	Islamic Call Committee (Kuwait, 1986)
	Mercy Relief International (USA, 1986)
	Al Haramain (Saudi Arabia, 1988)
	Benevolence International Foundation (Saudi Arabia, 1988)
	International Islamic Council for Da'wa and Relief (Egypt, 1988)
	Office for Services to the Mujahedeen (Saudi Arabia, nd.)
	Committee for Support of Afghanistan (Saudi Arabia, nd.)

War in Bosnia	Humanity First (UK, 1991)
	Foundation for Human Rights and Freedoms and
	Humanitarian Relief (Turkey, 1992)
	Global Relief Foundation (USA, 1992)
	Helping Hand for Relief and Development
	(USA, 1993)
	Muslim Hands (UK, 1993)
	Istanbul International Brotherhood and Solidarity
	Association (Turkey, 1994)
	Deniz Feneri (Turkey, 1996)
	Islamic Center for Help to the People of Bosnia-
	Herzegovina (Iran, n.d.)
	Small Kindness (UK, 1999)
9/11 attacks	Humanitarian Forum (UK, 2004)
	Friends of Charities Association (Saudi Arabia, 2004)
	National Council of American Muslim Non-profits
	(USA, 2005)
	Charity and Security Network (USA, 2008)

Competition: Transnational Muslim NGOs in the Horn of Africa

The first transnational Muslim NGOs emerged at the end of the 1970s and the beginning of the 1980s, prompted by a wish to support fellow Muslims who had fallen victim to wars and natural disasters (Yaylaci 2007:14). One of the first such disasters to attract the attention of Muslim organisations was the famine in the Horn of Africa, encouraging the establishment of several NGOs with the purpose of providing food aid, medicine, and other kinds of emergency relief to people in affected countries. A pioneer transnational Muslim NGO was IIROSA, established in Jeddah in 1979 by a group of wealthy Saudi men. 'We said to each other, listen, people are suffering in Sudan and Ethiopia, we are only 150 km away, we need to help,' one of the founders tells me, noting how he collected shoes and clothes and stored them all in his own house. 'I remember my children protested, but I explained to them what the purpose was, this is for the good work of Allah, and they understood.' A few hundred kilometres away, during a conference of Islamic banks in Kuwait City in 1984, Yusuf al-Qaradawi called for the need to fight poverty, illiteracy, and disease among poor Muslims. Under the motto 'Pay a dollar, save a Muslim' he challenged the audience to raise a billion dollars for this purpose; a campaign which lead to the foundation of IICO, established by 160 Islamic scholars, thinkers, businessmen and other prominent people (Benthall and Bellion-Jourdan 2003:41). That same year, Islamic Relief was founded in Britain by two medical students of Egyptian origin. As Hani al-Banna, one of the founders, recalled in an interview: 'It started with the famines and food shortages that affected Ethiopia and Sudan in the mid-1980s. The images of starving people shocked me, like people around the globe, profoundly' (Marshall 2007). Likewise, Muslim Aid, established in Britain in 1985 by representatives from twenty-three primarily Pakistani and Bangladeshi Muslim community organisations, was prompted by the famine in Somalia: 'Everyone was there [in Africa] but the Muslims. We saw it on TV and we were ashamed,' a board member noted in an interview.

This period saw the establishment of several other transnational Muslim NGOs (see Table 3.1 for some examples). There are a number reasons for this wave of transnational Muslim NGOs at precisely this moment in history. Overall, and as has been described in the foregoing chapter, factors such as the general increase in transnational NGOs at this time, the popularity of pan-Islamic ideals of solidarity, the explosion of oil prices, and the emergence of a Muslim migrant community in the West all contributed to the birth of transnational Muslim NGOs. More specifically, the spread of communication technology also played an important role. Through real-time coverage of emergencies, new media would bring remote events virtually to the door of a Muslim audience, stirring emotions of solidarity and empathy (de Cordier 2009a:612)—a development that was only further strengthened by the emergence of MBC, Al Jazeera, and other Arabic satellite channels in the early and mid-1990s (Meyer et al. 2007:297).[3] As a Muslim Aid employee noted in an interview with de Cordier: 'Of course, the Ethiopian famine was not the first large-scale disaster to shock international audiences [...] But the way it was covered, and the global nature of the charity events around it, were new' (cf. de Cordier 2009a:612).

For the Muslim NGOs the media also crudely displayed the fact that Western NGOs were far more active than Muslim ones, despite the fact that many of the victims of the famine were Muslims. 'I was watching the catastrophe on TV,' one of the founders of IIROSA told me, 'and I realised that the only organisations helping the starving people were the

Western ones. There were no Muslims.' There was for many people a wish to translate the theoretical and much talked-about Islamic solidarity into a practical Islamic aid (Yaylaci 2007:13; Ghandour 2004:328), demonstrating compassion with the starving Muslims and showing the world that not only Western NGOs were capable of providing effective aid. As such, there was also an element of competition and defiance of Western hegemony inherent in the first generations of Muslim NGOs (Bellion-Jourdan 2000:15). For some, this was not only a competition in terms of compassion and efficiency. Among certain Muslim NGOs at the time, there was a widespread conception that the majority of Western organisations in Africa worked either covertly or overtly as missionaries, attempting to attract converts to Christianity through relief and social welfare activism (which some of them undoubtedly did). This understanding of Western NGOs as missionaries included explicitly secular NGOs such as the Médecins sans Frontiers, seen to be promoting Western values that many deemed to be culturally and religiously inappropriate in a Muslim context. Refusing to leave the field of humanitarian action to these NGOs, specifically in situations where recipients were identified as Muslims (Benthall and Bellion-Jourdan 2003:70), some Muslim NGOs took up the challenge by introducing their own missionary projects in Africa. From this perspective, an important objective of Muslim NGOs was not only to provide aid, but to counter the influence of Western, Christian NGOs and protect Muslim faith and identity. This was the case with many Gulf-based NGOs, reflecting the pan-Islamic missionary efforts of these countries. A former staff member in IIROSA, for instance, noted that the expansion of Christian organisations in Africa was what prompted his organisation to engage in aid provision. Likewise, Yusuf al-Qaradawi, the founder of IICO, launched his 'Pay a dollar' campaign as a direct reaction to a conference of missionary organisations in Colorado in 1978 at which Christian missionaries had allegedly announced their intention of investing a billion dollars in an effort to convert as many Muslims as possible (Benthall and Bellion-Jourdan 2003:41).

This understanding of Western organisations as missionary and the need for Muslim organisations to step up in the battle of souls was not restricted to an African context, but was also common in Afghanistan and later in Bosnia.[4] However, taking into consideration the colonial history of Africa, there is reason to believe that the conflict was more pronounced here, building on centuries of Christian missionary activism.

Furthermore, unlike Afghanistan and Bosnia, the Muslim population in many African countries is often a minority, strengthening the perception of vulnerability to missionary activities and the need for protection. As Ahmed (2009:426) writes, Western aid organisations are often depicted as deploying aid as a means to convert Muslims to Christianity and to exercise political control over them. Thus, historically, especially East Africa has been considered an important Islamic frontier, the border of the *umma* (Brenner 1993:15).[5]

Sudan seems to have been a particular battleground for struggles between Muslim and Western organisations, often intertwined with and aggravated by the national political struggles between the (largely Muslim) north and the (non-Muslim) south. Ghandour (2003) has described this situation as a 'humanitarian cold war'. On the Muslim side, organisations such as the Sudanese Organisation of Islamic Call (in Arabic, *Munazzamat da'wa islamiya*, often shortened to MDI) and the World Islamic Call Society have been especially critical of the Western NGOs working in the country, accusing them of being conduits for financial and technical support for Christian rebels in the south (de Cordier 2009b:668) as well as forced conversion, secularist propaganda and neo-colonisation. In 1995, Muslim NGOs such as the Islamic African Relief Agency had worked alongside Western organisations like Médecins sans Frontiers and the Irish GOAL, together with national Christian organisations such as the Sudanese Council of Churches, in the Wadi al-Bashir camp at Omdurman. However, the population, heavily incited by the MDI, drove out the non-Muslim NGOs, accusing them of mission and conversion (Ghandour 2004:335). As noted in a 1995 report, written by MDI staff: 'The missionaries in Africa have brandished the motto that says "Give up the religion of Islam, and we will free you from the hunger, poverty, fear and sickness." Armies of missionaries have crossed Africa with food in their left hands and crosses in their right hands' (cf. Benthall and Bellion-Jourdan 2003:111). In 1997, the World Islamic Call Society launched an initiative called 'Countering the Christianization Efforts', including a seminar on 'Christianization and Colonialist Penetration', which was held in cooperation with Africa International University (Salih 2002).[6] Other organisations, such as the IIROSA and IICO, may not have expressed their scepticism as publicly as the World Islamic Call Society but shared their basic assumptions about Christian and Western NGOs and agreed on the need to counter their missionary activities with Islamic information and education in the provision of aid to the Sudanese people, for instance through building mosques and Qur'an schools. Christian and Western NGOs, on the other hand, were highly critical of Muslim NGOs in Sudan, suspecting them of close relations to the government and the militant *janjaweed* (Kirmani and Khan 2008:48; Benthall and Bellion-Jourdan 2003:123). They were sceptical of cooperation and rarely invited them to participate in coordination meetings (Ghandour 2004:336)—and if they did, meetings would often be conducted in a heavily jargoned English without the benefit of translation, thereby excluding all but the most competent English speakers (see also Ratcliffe 2007:59). Thus, in its first years, Operation Lifeline Sudan, a consortium of UN agencies and NGOs established in 1989 to provide humanitarian aid to Sudan, included no Muslim organisations among its member NGOs (Minear 1991:61). Likewise, the NGO Forum created in the early 1990s to coordinate activities of international and local NGOs in Southern Sudan did not include any transnational Muslim NGOs, mirroring patterns of similar NGO networks in other African countries.[7]

Conflicts: Transnational Muslim NGOs in Afghanistan

Parallel to their involvement in the Horn of Africa, transnational Muslim NGOs became increasingly involved in other areas of the world. Here, Afghanistan came to play an especially important role. Many people saw the 1979 Soviet occupation as an atheist attempt to intimidate a pious Muslim population. This triggered surges of solidarity among Muslims all over the world, and Muslim groups and organisations started collecting funds and in-kind support to send to Afghanistan. Some of the providers of aid to Afghanistan were well-known transnational Muslim organisations, including IIROSA, IICO and Muslim Aid. But the war was also a catalyst for the creation of new organisations. Many of these came from Saudi Arabia, Kuwait, and other Gulf countries, but Muslim NGOs from other Middle Eastern countries also played an important role in Afghanistan, just as Muslim migrants in Europe and North America also established a number of Muslim NGOs (see Table 3.1 for examples).

As in Africa, in Afghanistan, relations between Muslim NGOs and Western ones were marked by defiance. While appreciating the support of the US government for the mujahedeen, many Muslim NGOs saw

Western NGOs as exponents of atheism and what they considered to be generally inappropriate norms and practices that were potentially harmful to Afghan society, while some were suspected of supporting particular political parties (Benthall and Bellion-Jourdan 2003:74f). As such, many Muslim NGOs preferred to cooperate with other Muslim NGOs rather than enter into partnerships with Western NGOs, and in 1986, the Saudi and Kuwaiti Red Crescent societies, the Islamic African Relief Agency and the Muslim World League established an Islamic Coordination Council (Benthall and Bellion-Jourdan 2003:74). When the Agency Coordinating Body for Afghan Relief (ACBAR) was established two years later with the purpose of strengthening broad coordination among all NGOs working in Afghanistan, most Muslim NGOs abstained from joining, seeing ACBAR as dominated by Western organisations (Christensen 1995:144). Only a few Muslim organisations became members of ACBAR, including the Islamic African Relief Agency and the Aga Khan Foundation (which many other Muslim NGOs did not consider a 'real' Muslim NGO).[8]

For some Muslim NGOs, aid became not just a question of providing relief to suffering Muslims, but of supporting them more directly in their fight against the enemy. In other words, whereas the provision of aid in Africa was sometimes simultaneously relief and *da'wa*, here it was sometimes relief and jihad. Speaking about Afghanistan, Qaradawi proclaimed in an interview in the journal *Al-Jihad* (cf. Benthall and Bellion-Jourdan 2003:71) that all Muslims were obliged to commit themselves to support the resistance:

> Jihad is *fard 'ain* an obligation for individuals, as opposed to *fard kefaya*, a communal obligation, for military and medical experts or anyone with a special skill that the *mujahidin* need. They should help the *mujahidin* in the field of their competence and capacity. In general, it is incumbent on all Muslims to provide material and intellectual help in order to live with them in the heart even if they cannot live with them in the body.

While most Muslim NGOs, together with Qaradawi himself, took this to mean non-violent and indirect support through *da'wa* and relief, others, in particular some Saudi NGOs, interpreted it as a call to directly support the armed struggle of the mujahedeen. Making no distinction between peaceful and warlike purposes, they provided the mujahedeen with weapons and equipment, facilitated contacts to volunteers who wanted to join the mujahedeen and supported the mujahedeen financially (Bokhari,

Chowdhury and Lacey 2014:203). A case in point is the Saudi Office for Services to the Mujahedeen (*Maktab khidamat li-l-mujahidin*), founded by a militant member of the Muslim Brotherhood (Ghandour 2002:13) and allegedly particularly active in supporting the mujahedeen. According to a now declassified 1996 CIA report, the organisation's Peshawar office funded at least nine training camps (CIA 1996:6), parallel to its involvement in the provision of relief aid, healthcare, food, and education to Afghan refugees (Hegghammer 2010:43). The same CIA report also claims that the IIROSA helped fund six training camps in Afghanistan (1996:5). Former members of the World Assembly of Muslim Youth support this accusation, claiming that this organisation provided logistical support for young Saudis wanting to fight in Afghanistan. While denying formal involvement, a former IIROSA staff member also hinted at involvement, at least at the level of individual staff members:

> I don't know if the IIROSA supported the mujahedeen, but in Afghanistan everything was mixed up. It is not my impression that they sent funds directly to other activities, but some of their staff may have been involved in other activities. They recruited people in the hundreds, so surely some of them …

In order to comprehend this involvement in military support by Saudi NGOs, it is necessary to understand the international environment and the atmosphere surrounding the war in Afghanistan. The involvement of the NGOs was to a large degree sanctioned by the USA and the Saudi state, which were also heavily involved in supporting the Afghans (Benthall and Bellion-Jourdan 2003:72). Eager to build alliances in their fight against the Soviet Union, the US government would, indirectly or directly, encourage this support to the mujahedeen, or the 'freedom fighters', as they were called (Hegghammer 2010)—including financing of the magazine *Afghan Jehad*, treatment of injured mujahedeen in the US, and publication of leaflets for religious scholars (Benthall 2011:116f). In the early 1980s, the USA requested the Saudi state to match US congressional funding for Afghan resistance, and funding increased in the mid-1980s (Hegghammer 2010:26). The Saudi state for its part provided direct military and logistical support to the mujahedeen. Furthermore, it sent money through the Saudi Red Crescent and the Popular Committee for Fundraising, later the Saudi Relief Committee (Hegghammer 2010:25), knowing that Saudi Red Crescent was part of the weapons pipeline—on at least one occasion, ambulances were used to transport healthy fighters to and from the battlefront. Likewise, the first Saudi mujahedeen were in fact aid workers from the Saudi Red Crescent and the Relief Committee, contributing to further blurring the lines between humanitarian and military assistance (Hegghammer 2010:27).[9] There is no record of the US government expressing concern over this at the time (Bokhari, Chowdhury and Lacey 2014:203). But with the victory of the mujahedeen at the beginning of the 1990s, the international political climate started to change, resulting, among other things, in the increasing control and repression of Muslim NGOs. Yielding to the injunctions of the USA and certain Middle Eastern states, in 1993 the Pakistani authorities arrested more than a hundred people working in NGOs on the border of Pakistan and Afghanistan (Benthall and Bellion-Jourdan 2003:77). Likewise, after pressure from Egypt and the USA, around the same time Saudi Arabia fired the head of the Pakistani branch of the Muslim World League, who was accused of supplying documentation and arms to militants in Afghanistan (CIA 1996:2). As we shall see below, scepticism about transnational Muslim NGOs was only to grow over the years.

Co-existence: Transnational Muslim NGOs in Bosnia

Erupting at a time when the conflict in Afghanistan was drifting into civil war, the 1992–5 war in Bosnia came to be the new focus of attention for many transnational Muslim NGOs, replacing their Afghan involvement (Benthall and Bellion-Jourdan 2003:129). The beginning of the 1990s thus saw a new wave of Muslim NGOs, many of them of a Western origin, established by immigrant communities, but already established organisations also experienced great increases in donations in these years, facilitating their expansion. In 1993 Islamic Relief opened up offices in Tuzla and Zenica; in 1994 Mercy Relief International followed. The war in Bosnia also saw the emergence of the first transnational Turkish NGOs, including the Foundation for Human Rights and Freedoms and Humanitarian Relief (IHH), established by Milli Görüs representatives in 1995 (Solberg 2007). Likewise, Iranian organisations, such as the Foundation for the Oppressed and the Iranian Islamic Centre for Help to the People of Bosnia-Herzegovina were important actors in the provision of aid to the Bosnian people (Benthall and Bellion-Jourdan 2003:139). As in Afghanistan, the main part of aid, however, came from Gulf-based organisations. According to Burr and Collins (2006), the King Fahd of Saudi Arabia gave US$ 103 million to Bosnia in the period

1992–6, some distributed through governmental committees (Benthall and Bellion-Jourdan 2003:72), but much channelled through Muslim NGOs such as IIROSA and Al Haramain. Under the local name of IGASA, IIROSA embarked on sizeable aid programmes aimed at Bosnian Muslims who had taken refuge in Croatia and Slovenia (Benthall and Bellion-Jourdan 2003:130).

As in Afghanistan, the war in Bosnia also saw the more or less direct involvement of certain Muslim NGOs in the armed struggle. As Hegghammer (2010:33) notes, the 'Bosnian jihad' became the first major pan-Islamic battleground after the Afghan jihad and the new destination of choice for large numbers of Arab volunteer fighters. According to the above-mentioned 1996 CIA report, as many as thirteen Muslim organisations operating in Bosnia were somehow involved in the conflict, including the Human Relief Agency and Al-Haramain. Others mention the Islamic Benevolence Foundation and the Office for Services to the Mujahedeen, both allegedly involved in sponsoring volunteer fighters as well as shipping weapons and military equipment into Bosnia, and IIROSA, allegedly involved in the extension of services such as visas and fake ID cards to Arab combatants (Hegghammer 2010:49; Benthall and Bellion-Jourdan 2003:135). But Bosnia, for many reasons, came to be a different experience to Afghanistan: there was more international control of the area, Bosnian Muslims were more secular and not as attached to the Arab world, and the national and international authorities were no longer as welcoming of Islamic fighters as they had been in Afghanistan. For one, the 1990–1 Gulf War had put severe constraints on the relationship between the United States, Saudi Arabia and Islamist movements, with the last denouncing the participation of Muslim countries in the US-led coalition against Saddam Hussein (Benthall and Bellion-Jourdan 2003:76). Secondly, the atrocities in Algeria and Egypt as well as the February 1993 attack on the World Trade Center in New York illustrated with all clarity the threat posed to authorities by the Arab mujahedeen (Hegghammer 2010:33ff). A few years later, the bombings in Riyadh (1995) and Khobar (1996) prompted the Saudi government to crack down on veterans of the Afghan and Bosnian jihads, and mass arrests and interrogations marked the beginning of a more confrontational phase between the Saudi state and the Islamic movement (Hegghammer 2010:76f), as well as more generally, between Arab regimes and the Islamic movement. The involvement of some transna-

tional Muslim NGOs in the 1993 and 1998 attacks on American territories—first the World Trade Center and then the bombings of the US
embassies in Kenya and Tanzania—led to increased control of these
organisations, manifested in a decrease in public funding, arrest of individuals, and bans of certain organisations. Most famously, five transnational Muslim NGOs suspected of involvement in the embassy attacks
were banned by the Kenyan government in 1998—Mercy International,
Help African People, Al-Haramain, IIROSA, and the Ibrahim bin Abdul
Aziz Ibrahim Foundation, the two former with headquarters in the USA
and the three latter based in Saudi Arabia (Salih 2002:24).

This situation of increased control and restrictions meant that many
transnational Muslim NGOs, whether by design or under constraint,
came to adopt a sharp demarcation between aid and jihad (Benthall and
Bellion-Jourdan 2003:70). Instead, they avoided involvement in the conflict, adopting a strategy of neutrality as a way of ensuring legitimacy.
Islamic Relief, for instance, took part in a fundraising campaign organised by the British newspaper *The Independent*, stressing that aid was distributed not only to Muslims but also to Serbs and Croats (Yaylaci
2007:31). Similarly, this period also witnessed the establishment of partnerships between Muslim and non-Muslim NGOs. In the *Independent*
campaign, for instance, Islamic Relief worked together with Oxfam and
Save the Children, just as the Islamic African Relief Agency worked
closely together with the Methodist Church's Fund for Relief and
Development (Benthall and Bellion-Jourdan 2003). And the partnership between the Muslim organisation Merhamet (supported by Islamic
Relief), the Catholic Caritas, the Orthodox Dobrotvor, and the Jewish
La Benevolencija won all four agencies the John XXIII international
peace prize, awarded by Pope John Paul II during a visit to Sarajevo in
1997 (von Hippel 2007:38).

While emphasising neutrality and interfaith dialogue over jihad and
da'wa, however, most transnational Muslim NGOs were still driven by
a religiously defined solidarity, maintaining a particularist focus on fellow Muslim recipients rather than a universalist humanity, like most
mainstream aid agencies. Muslim Aid's Annual Reports and PR material from the 1990s, for instance, frequently referred to 'the Muslim
umma', and 'Muslim brotherhood.'[10] Similarly, most—if not all—funds
were channelled to Muslim countries or Muslim minorities in non-Muslim countries. An important reason for this is that the majority of these

organisations still depended mainly on funding from individual Muslim donors, serving as vehicles for the distribution of *zakat* from wealthy, pious Muslims who expect their contributions to go to the support of their poor brothers and sisters. Although some organisations had started cooperating with non-Muslim, Western NGOs, this had not been translated into the receipt of formal funding from donor agencies: by the end of the 1990s, transnational Muslim NGOs had yet to receive any financial support from agencies such as the UK Department for International Development (DFID) or the European Commission's Humanitarian Office (ECHO). In general, then, Muslim NGOs—whether Western or Gulf-based—remained relatively isolated from the culture of development aid, despite the occasional cooperation with mainstream development NGOs.

A new situation: 9/11 and the 'War on Terror'

This all changed with the 9/11 attacks on New York and Washington and the ensuing War on Terror[11]—perhaps the most defining events in the history of transnational Muslim NGOs, for good and bad setting the boundaries within which these NGOs navigate in the aid field today (and, not least, the framework through which we as researchers understand what they do). After it became clear that the attacks on the Twin Towers and Pentagon on September 11, 2001, killing almost 3,000 people, had been carried out by radical Islamic groups, suspicions quickly arose as to the involvement of certain transnational Muslim NGOs in planning and financing the attacks. Within a year of the attacks, a number of transnational Muslim NGOs, including Al Haramain, the Revival of the Islamic Heritage Society, the Global Relief Foundation, and Benevolence International Foundation, had been designated by the US government, accused of supporting or being otherwise related to Al-Qaeda. Several other governments followed suit, banning a number of transnational Muslim NGOs working in their territory. In 2003, for instance, the Saudi Arabian government, after pressure from the US, closed down Al Haramain's office in Somalia on the grounds that the organisation was supporting Al-Qaeda. In January 2004, a joint US-Saudi action designated four offices of Al Haramain inside Saudi Arabia (Cotterrell and Harmer 2005:19).[12]

In the following years, governments and intergovernmental organisations introduced a wide range of new policies, instruments and regulations, attempting to prevent and obstruct NGO involvement in terrorist activities. Under UN auspices, for instance, the Security Council Committee overseeing Resolution 1267 required member states to 'freeze the assets of, prevent the entry into or transit through their territories by, and prevent the direct or indirect supply, sale and transfer of arms and military equipment to any individual or entity associated with Al-Qaeda, Osama bin Laden and/or the Taliban'. As of 2015, the Committee had designated twelve Muslim NGOs, suspected of association with Al-Qaeda (see Table 3.2). The Philippines and Indonesia branches of IIROSA were designated in 2006 but were removed from the list in January 2014 following several petitions from the organisation. The European Union maintains a similar list of persons, groups, and entities related to terrorist activity. As of 2013, however, only one NGO had been included on this list (see Table 3.2).

Table 3.2: Designated transnational Muslim NGOs[13]

Name	UN	EU	US	Suspected of relations to
Office for Services to the Mujahedeen	x		x	Al-Qaeda
Al Rashid Trust	x		x	Al-Qaeda
WAFA Humanitarian Organisation	x		x	Al-Qaeda
Rabita Trust	x		x	Al-Qaeda
Umma Tameer E-Nau			x	Al-Qaeda
Revival of Islamic Heritage Society	x		x	Al-Qaeda
Afghan Support Committee	x		x	Al-Qaeda
Al Haramain Islamic Foundation	x		x	Al-Qaeda
Aid Organisation of the Ulema			x	Al-Qaeda
Global Relief Foundation	x		x	Al-Qaeda
Benevolence International Foundation	x		x	Al-Qaeda
Islamic Call Committee			x	Al-Qaeda
Al Akhtar Trust	x		x	Al-Qaeda
Taibah International	x		x	Al-Qaeda
Al Masjed Al Aqsa Charity Foundation			x	Al-Qaeda
Al Furqan	x		x	Al-Qaeda
Islamic African Relief Agency			x	Al-Qaeda
International Islamic Relief Organisation[14]			x	Al-Qaeda

Al Rehmat Trust		x	Al-Qaeda
Hilal Ahmar Society		x	Al-Qaeda
Holy Land Foundation for Relief and Development	x	x	Hamas
Al Aqsa Foundation		x	Hamas
Comité de Bienfaisance et de Secours aux Pal.		x	Hamas
Association de Secours Palestinien		x	Hamas
Interpal		x	Hamas
Palestinian Association in Austria		x	Hamas
Sanibil Relief Agency		x	Hamas, Al-Qaeda
Al Salah Society		x	Hamas
Union of Good		x	Hamas
Al Waqfiya		x	Hamas
Al Quds International Foundation		x	Hamas
Islamic Resistance Support Organisation		x	Hezbollah
Martyrs Foundation		x	Hezbollah
Goodwill Charitable Organisation		x	Hezbollah
Iranian Committee for Reconstruction of Lebanon		x	Hezbollah
Imam Khomeini Relief Committee		x	Hezbollah
El Ehsan Society		x	Pal. Islamic Jihad

In the USA, the Treasury Department maintains a list of *Designated Charities and Potential Fundraising Front Organizations.* The Treasury Department oversees and investigates financial transactions of US-based NGOs, and if an NGO transfers material support or resources[15] to designated persons or organisations, the Department has the authority to freeze all assets of the NGO, effectively closing it down. Today, thirty-seven Muslim NGOs are designated by the US State Department for their relations to Al-Qaeda, Hamas, Hezbollah or other supposedly radical Islamic groups (see Table 3.2). This includes the Indonesia and Philippines branches of IIROSA. IIROSA has addressed the Treasury Department several times, petitioning acquittal and removal from the list, so far to no avail. In Great Britain, the Asset Freezing Unit under HM Treasury maintains a consolidated list of individuals and entities designated by the UK, the UN and the EU. The Charity Commission is responsible for registration and control of all major NGOs. Since 2003, 100 organisations and over 200 individuals have had their assets frozen, totalling over US$ 100 million (Danckaers 2008:3). Unlike the Treasury Department in the USA, the Commission has a range of different tools at its disposal in case of misuse of funds, including the removal of certain trustees, handing over of NGO management, transfer of assets to other NGOs, and if nothing else works, closing-down of the NGO. Shaw-Hamilton (2007:24) has likened the difference between UK and US approaches to that between a scalpel and a sledgehammer, pointing out that the US approach 'causes suffering to beneficiaries and alienates donors'.

Governments in other parts of the world, in particular the Middle Eastern countries, accused by many of involvement in terrorism or laxity in acting against terrorists on their territories, have also sought to exert tighter control over the flow of funds in or through their country, resulting in a number of measures to tighten up regulation and oversight of NGO activities (Harmer and Cotterrell 2005:28). This has been particularly acute in Saudi Arabia. In July 2003, for instance, the Saudi Arabian Monetary Agency announced a set of new regulations governing Saudi aid organisations, including requirements for consolidation of funds in a single bank account, licensed by government. Later that year, Saudi charities were banned from transferring funds abroad (Cotterrell and Harmer 2005:19). This was followed in 2004 by the announcement that a National Commission for Relief and Charity Work Abroad would be established, overseeing all NGO activities and public donations, and facilitating greater governmental control over the use of charitable funds (Cotterrell and Harmer 2005:19).[16] All this was due to heavy US pressure but also to the increase in the level of jihad activity within Saudi Arabia, witnessed for instance in the East Riyadh bombings in May 2003, and the Muhayya bombing later that year, which killed more than 50 people (Hegghammer 2010:217).

This increased suspicion and control of Muslim NGOs has had a wide range of consequences for the organisations. First of all, and perhaps most tangibly, a number of organisations had to close down following designations from the US or other authorities, even though they had not been convicted in court.[17] Furthermore, the increased governmental control of international transfers meant that relations with institutional and individual donors from abroad were encumbered, leaving many Muslim organisations in financial straits. In concrete terms, it has become very difficult for the Kuwaiti businessman living in Detroit to send his annual *zakat* contributions to a Muslim NGO in his home country, just as the NGO based in Saudi Arabia might no longer be able to transfer funds to a local partner organisation in Palestine. As a representative from the World Assembly of Muslim Youth put it in a newspaper interview: 'After 9/11, everything shrank when it comes to Islamic work, humanitarian work [...] People are frightened. They stopped giving any money, almost all of the business people [...] We have to go and collect riyal by riyal' (cf. Alterman 2007:74).[18]

But the War on Terror not only led to a focus on supposedly 'extremist' Muslim NGOs, involved in financing terrorist activities; it also encouraged an increasing interest in cooperation with so-called 'moderate' Muslim NGOs, seen as potential bridge builders between Islam and the West (Howell and Lind 2009). In this, the mainstream development system came to be an important site for dialogue. Just as NGOs were enlisted in the fight against Communism in the 1960s and 1970s, they increasingly became implicated in the War on Terror (Holenstein 2005). Through so-called 'soft measures', governmental aid agencies, in particular in Europe, started encouraging cooperation with (certain) Muslim NGOs. One example is the so-called Montreux Initiative, initiated by the Swiss Federal Department of Foreign Affairs in 2005 under the title *Towards cooperation with Islamic charities in removing unjustified obstacles*.[19] These soft measures have coincided with a general interest in religious NGOs among governmental and intergovernmental development agencies. Failures in mainstream aid provision, together with a disappointment in 'regular' NGOs, among other things, forced development agencies to look for alternative ways of doing aid—and in this, many turned to religious NGOs, or faith-based organisations as they are often called, seeing them as the new panacea. Based on factors such as their cultural proximity, historical rootedness, popular legitimacy, infrastructure, networks, and motivation, religious NGOs are seen to have a great potential as promoters of development aid, giving them an 'added value' over secular NGOs.[20] As part of this trend towards increased cooperation, a number of aid agencies opened up to fund Muslim NGOs. The UK's DFID is one of the donor agencies that has been most active in this regard. Despite initial scepticism, since 9/11 the agency has been involved in several initiatives with the purpose of strengthening cooperation with Muslim NGOs. Islamic Relief has a framework agreement with DFID and several other Muslim NGOs have received grants from the agency. Likewise, DFID's Civil Society team holds workshops, one of them in cooperation with the Muslim Council of Britain, targeted specifically at Muslim organisations with the purpose of encouraging them to apply for funding and supporting them in the process.[21]

This trend towards increased cooperation with Muslim NGOs, however, only includes certain organisations. As noted in Chapter 2, DFID and other aid agencies have historically relied on a strongly secularist understanding of aid, avoiding or ignoring issues of religion and spirituality. They would prefer cooperation with secular NGOs, and when cooperating with religious organisations, these would often be quasi-secular NGOs whose religiosity was by and large relegated to the private sphere, invisible to the donor agencies. The 'religious turn' among development donors did not fundamentally alter this preference. For donors, the new focus on religion and religious organisations was not driven by an interest in discussing alternative, religiously inspired, conceptions of aid, but an interest in making the provision of existing aid more effective. It was, in other words, an interest in religion and religious organisations as tools in the provision of secular aid, prompting a focus on institutional and organisational rather than spiritual aspects (James 2009:5). In this perspective, religious organisations can galvanise moral commitment, translate principles of aid into the idioms of faith, mobilise popular support and provide useful networks (Clarke 2007:8), but '[they] should not, however, interfere substantively with what is effectively a secular development agenda with its own understanding of what constitutes rationality, social justice, and modern economic development' (Thomas 2004:22; see also Tomalin 2012).[22] As such, the secular distinction between 'religion' and 'aid' as fundamentally separate categories is maintained: religion can be a tool in the provision of aid, but it cannot be part of aid. Paraphrasing Zaman (2004:151), we may say that religious organisations are acceptable in the aid field only when they unequivocally recognise the functional differentiation of social spheres, that is, when they agree to operate within the framework of secularisation.[23] Combining the discourses on faith-based organisations as tools in the effective implementation of secular development with War on Terror discourses on politically moderate and extremist Muslim NGOs, the mainstream development culture, led by governmental aid agencies such as DFID, came to perceive a quasi-secular, invisible religiosity as a sign of 'good aid' and 'moderation', while a visible, orthodox religiosity is a sign of 'bad aid', 'fundamentalism' and perhaps even 'extremism'.

Table 3.3: Largest transnational Muslim NGOs (2010/2011 figures)[24]

Organisation	Origin	Spending (US$)
Aga Khan Development Network	Switzerland	625 million
Islamic Relief	UK	101 million
Social Reform Society	Kuwait	81 million
Direct Aid/Africa Muslims Agency	Kuwait	66 million
Foundation for Human Rights and Freedoms and Hum. Relief (IHH)	Turkey	63 million
International Islamic Charitable Organisation	Kuwait	59 million
LIFE for Relief and Development	USA	57 million
Muslim Aid	UK	42 million
International Islamic Relief Organisation	Saudi Arabia	32 million
Dubai Charity Association	UAE	29 million
Sheikh Al Nouri Charity Society	Kuwait	17 million
Muslim Hands	UK	15.7 million
Helping Hand for Relief and Development	USA	13.3 million
Comité de Bienfaisance et de Secours aux Palestiniens	France	10.5 million
Human Concern International	Canada	8 million
Interpal	UK	6.4 million
Munazzamat al Da'wa al Islamiya (MDI)	Sudan	6 million
Muslim Charity	UK	4.7 million
Mercy USA for Relief and Development	USA	3.9 million
Human Appeal International	UK	3.8 million
Hidaya Foundation	USA	3.8 million
Kinder USA	USA	0.8 million

*Although they presumably also have million dollar budgets, a number of other large NGOs, such as Deniz Feneri Association (Turkey), Zayed bin Sultan al Nahayan Charitable & Humanitarian Foundation (United Arab Emirates), Qatar Charity (Qatar) and EMDAD (Iran) have not been included in the list, as it has been impossible to obtain information about their budgets.

Navigating between cultures

This brief history of transnational Muslim NGOs, focusing on four defining moments, illustrates how these NGOs have navigated in relation to the two aid cultures out of which they have grown.[25] The analysis has shown how transnational Muslim NGOs are far from isolated entities, predicated on static notions of religion and aid, but part of specific contexts, shaped by and reacting to political, economic and social processes. Against this background, two overall points can be raised: First, albeit to differing degrees, transnational Muslim NGOs have historically emphasised their allegiance to the Islamic aid culture, relating to the culture of development aid primarily by way of competition, conflict, and parallel co-existence; and second, 9/11 and the War on Terror have introduced a dramatically new situation, at once forcing and encouraging transnational Muslim NGOs to relate more directly with the development culture and open up to new repertoires of relations.

In their early years, transnational Muslim NGOs were thoroughly embedded in an Islamic aid culture, relating to the culture of development aid by way of competition, conflict or, at best, parallel co-existence. There are several reasons for this position. As outlined above, during the 1980s and 1990s, relations between Muslim NGOs and Western NGOs and donors were marked by defiance and sometimes outright hostility (Benthall and Bellion-Jourdan 2003:74), blighted by simplistic and stereotypical representations on both sides. In concrete terms, this means that Muslim NGOs have tended to operate in parallel networks away from mainstream development efforts (Ratcliffe 2007:57), rarely coordinating with the Western NGOs, and hardly ever receiving funding from Western donors (von Hippel 2007:32). In particular in the Horn of Africa, many Muslim NGOs perceived Western NGOs as crude embodiments of Christian missions and secularist decadence (Ghandour 2004:333), threatening the faith and identity of the Muslim community by their proselytising attempts at converting the poor, whether to Christianity or secularism. At least in part as a way of challenging this alleged dominance of Western organisations, some Muslim NGOs would start engaging in missionary activities themselves, entering into a sort of competition with Christian NGOs. Replicating their missionary techniques in attempts to bolster the faith of Muslims and convert non-Muslims, Muslim NGOs promoted activities such as the construction of mosques, distribution of religious texts, and establishment of Qur'an schools. This, in turn, strengthened scepticism among secularist Western NGOs, who—while overlooking their own ideological stance—came to view Muslim NGOs as aggressively proselytising organisations and auxiliaries of Islamic states (Ghandour 2004:333).

Involvement in Afghanistan further contributed to worsening the relationship between Muslim NGOs and the Western development culture. As described above, this conflict was interpreted by many (Muslims as well as non-Muslims) in a religious light, pitching a Muslim population against a non-Muslim enemy. This prompted transnational Muslim NGOs to avoid cooperation with Western NGOs, which were seen to be exponents of atheism and what the Muslim NGOs considered to be inappropriate norms and practices, potentially harmful to Afghan society and culture (Benthall and Bellion-Jourdan 2003:74f). Furthermore, some Muslim NGOs started to indirectly or directly support the mujahedeen, seeing aid as meaningless if not including the actual fighters as well.

While the use of aid as a tool to support the mujahedeen was initially supported by Western governments, in particular the USA, this support quickly waned with the changing political climate at the beginning of the 1990s. Further strengthened by a string of attacks by militant Islamic groups, including the 1993 attack on the US World Trade Center and the 1998 attacks on US embassies in Tanzania and Kenya, the involvement of some transnational Muslim NGOs with the mujahedeen was increasingly frowned upon by Western actors, often generalising their criticism to include all Muslim NGOs. In Bosnia, these competitive and conflict-ridden relations were slowly being replaced by attempts at peaceful co-existence. The political situation of increased control and restrictions meant that transnational Muslim NGOs, whether by design or under constraint, came to adopt a sharp demarcation between aid and jihad (Benthall and Bellion-Jourdan 2003:70), shifting from a focus on justice and solidarity to neutrality and universalism as a way of ensuring legitimacy. In this, Western Muslim NGOs such as Islamic Relief had an obvious advantage, and this organisation experienced rapid growth in this period. Some organisations also started cooperating with development NGOs; however, for the main part transnational Muslim NGOs remained at the margins of the development culture, seldom invited to participate in NGO networks or offered funding from governmental aid agencies.

Against this background, I have argued that 9/11 and the ensuing War on Terror has presented a dramatically new situation, blurring the dichotomous relations between transnational Muslim NGOs and the mainstream development culture. Under the leadership of the US government (and supported by many Middle Eastern governments), the War on Terror has introduced harsh restrictions against transnational Muslim NGOs, leading to the marginalisation and ultimately designation of certain NGOs, doomed to be 'extremist' or 'fundamentalist'. At the same time, soft measures of bridge-building and dialogue, coupled with an increasing focus on faith-based organisations, especially among European aid agencies, opened up cooperation with certain Muslim NGOs. Combining War on Terror discourses with discourses on faith-based organisations, and echoing broader dichotomies between 'good' and 'bad' Muslims (Mamdani 2002), these actors promoted the ideal of the 'moderate' Muslim NGO, creating a link between a certain kind of religiosity and 'good' aid provision. Transnational Muslim NGOs are now navigating in an environment of increasing regulation and control, but with simultaneous openings for cooperation and funding. In the post-9/11 aid field it is no longer possible—or desirable—for these NGOs to remain entrenched in the Islamic aid culture, relating to the culture of mainstream development through conflict, competition or parallel co-existence. Instead, the situation calls for new repertoires of action: cooperation, integration, or perhaps assimilation? A central aim of the following chapters is to explore this situation further, and take a closer look at some of the organisations that have been positioned as either 'moderate' (that is, adhering to the norms of Western development aid) or 'fundamentalist' and 'traditionalist' (that is, embedded in a Middle Eastern Islamic aid culture). Analysing the ways in which four concrete Muslim NGOs position themselves in the contemporary aid field, and exploring the ways in which they draw on different cultures of aid in their formulation of aid ideologies, I hope to go beyond these simplistic categorisations of transnational Muslim NGOs, challenging or at least softening such dichotomies.

4

PIETY AND PROFESSIONALISM

CLAIMS TO AUTHORITY IN IIROSA AND IICO

Chapter 3 left transnational Muslim NGOs in a new situation, following 9/11. For some, the War on Terror presented a window of opportunity, leading to new possibilities for funding and cooperation, but for others it led to increasing governmental and intergovernmental control, restrictions, and in some cases sanctions, based on suspicions of involvement with militant Muslim movements and groups. Against this background, the following chapters ask how transnational Muslim NGOs present themselves and the work they do in the contemporary field of aid provision. While broader structures, cultures, trends, and events such as those outlined in the previous chapters play an important role in shaping identities and ideologies of transnational Muslim NGOs, these factors all work through the organisations, not upon them (Hilhorst 2003:214). In their construction of aid ideologies, NGOs do not simply duplicate elements from the aid cultures out of which they have grown; they appropriate, interpret, challenge, and sometimes reject these elements, in the process constructing new ideologies and contributing to changing existing cultures, albeit slowly. In this perspective, it becomes particularly important to pay attention to the micro-sociological level of individual actors and actions. Chapters 4 to 7 therefore present detailed case studies of four transnational Muslim NGOs, asking how these organisations understand themselves and their work, and exploring how they position themselves in relation to the cultures of development and Islamic aid after 9/11 and the War on Terror.

In Chapters 4 and 5 we meet the International Islamic Relief Organisation (IIROSA) and the International Islamic Charitable Organisation (IICO), two of the oldest, biggest, and most famous organisations in the Gulf, based respectively in Saudi Arabia and Kuwait. While Chapter 5 centres on the two organisations' aid ideologies, Chapter 4 analyses their organisational identity—the voice with which they formulate these ideologies, so to say. How do they present themselves? How do they seek to establish authority? Such claims to authority are essential elements in organisational ideologies, insofar as authority is what establishes the legitimacy of the ideologies that organisations present, in turn ensuring acceptance by and resonance with potential audiences. This focus on organisational identities also serves to further emphasise the fact that ideologies are formulated by specific actors wishing not only to promote a particular world view but also to position themselves in a particular way. As noted by Hilhorst (2003), the study of NGOs is always a study of NGO-ing: of the ways in which organisations define what it means to be a good, genuine, and legitimate NGO.

Organisations do not present themselves to an undefined or abstract other, but address particular audiences—donors, partners, and other stakeholders—with the purpose of motivating and encouraging them to support their cause (Benford and Snow 2000:624). In their attempts to present themselves as legitimate authorities, organisations seek to make their identity resonate or align with these audiences (Wagemakers 2010:21): what do audiences consider to be a legitimate organisation? The more an organisation resonates with its audiences, the more legitimate it seems and the more support it will get (Benford and Snow 2000:621). Thus, as Thaut et al. (2012:139) note, legitimacy is audience dependent. In this, organisations draw on existing cultural repertoires and their symbols, stories, rituals, traditions, and ideologies (Benford and Snow 2000; Johnston and Klandermans 1995; Swidler 1986); their choices being shaped and constrained by the particular cultural context in which they—and their audiences—are situated (Williams 1995:126). As such, audiences play an important role in shaping ideologies, insofar as organisations seek to adapt their ideologies to the audiences they target in order to ensure resonance. At the same time, audiences are not simply audiences, indirectly influencing ideologies through the NGOs' attempts at adjusting to their (perceived) expectations, but actors that can actively influence the organisations in more direct ways. For instance, as we shall see, individual donors may prefer supporting concrete, tangible causes such as orphans or schools, to more intangible activities such as 'capacity-building' or 'empowerment'. Likewise, institutional donors may condition their funding on requirements as to accountability, inclusion or gender equality. Partner organisations may introduce NGOs to new conceptions of and approaches to aid. And governments may formulate laws and policies, restricting the ways in which NGOs carry out their work. Audiences thus influence the construction of aid ideologies in very real ways, interchangeably forcing, encouraging, pushing or inspiring organisations to change their conceptions of aid.[1] In the following analysis of IIROSA and IICO's organisational identities and aid ideologies, then, we shall also pay particular attention to the audiences to which the organisations present themselves and their work. Before I embark on the actual analysis, however, let me briefly present the situation in which the two organisations found themselves after 9/11, recounting and elaborating on what was described in the previous chapter.

Designations and financial decline. IICO and IIROSA after 9/11

In August 2002, IIROSA was, together with seven other NGOs, seven international banks, the Sudanese government, and a number of individuals, sued by a group of families of the 9/11 victims, accusing them of financing the attacks on the Pentagon and World Trade Center in 2001.[2] This was not the first time the organisation was accused of ties to militant Islamic networks and groups; in fact allegations had surrounded the organisation since its early years.[3] In Afghanistan, the organisation was, as mentioned above, suspected of involvement with the mujahedeen in the 1980s, funding training camps and supporting the fighters in other ways. In Bangladesh, the IIROSA was allegedly closely related to the political party Jama'at-e Islami and the militant movement Lashkar-e Taiba. In the Philippines, several employees of IIROSA were allegedly involved in the militant Moro Islamic Liberation Front during the 1990s, just like the organisation was suspected of funding Abu Sayyaf, a group of Moro separatists with a heavy record of bombings, kidnappings and assassinations. In Indonesia, the head of the country office was allegedly also a member of the Jemaah Islamiyah. And in Kenya, the organisation was suspected of supporting the militant Somali group al-Itehad, involved in the bombings of the US embassies in 1998, to mention only a few examples (Observatoire de l'Action Humanitaire 2008). After 2001, allegations intensified, and in 2006, the Philippines and Indonesia branches of IIROSA were closed by national authorities and designated by the US—and later UN—on the grounds that they were 'facilitating fundraising for al Qaida and affiliated terrorist groups' (Observatoire de l'Action Humanitaire 2008; Ferguson 2006).[4]

At home, governmental support was also waning, and control of IIROSA and other NGOs would increase. IIROSA had enjoyed strong support from the Saudi government since its establishment—in fact, the Minister of Defence, Prince Sultan bin Abdul Aziz, together with Mufti Abdel Aziz bin Baz, the highest religious authority in the kingdom, were among its first donors. Similarly, several government representatives have served on the board and as members of the General Assembly, just as state authorities have exercised great influence on the nomination of the secretary general and other top management positions in the organisation.[5] But in 2003 the Saudi government introduced a range of restrictions on IIROSA and other transnational NGOs, including requirements for consolidation of funds in a single bank account, licensed by government, and a ban from transferring funds abroad without prior permission (Cotterrell and Harmer 2005:19). Likewise, when IIROSA branches were designated and sued in the US, the government did not offer any assistance. 'The government took a neutral position—it didn't help anybody, it didn't even offer counselling,' says a former trustee.[6]

The Kuwaiti NGO IICO was never under quite the same pressure. In 2002, a trustee of the IICO's Geneva branch was accused of sympathising with militant Islamists (Levitt 2006:168), but apart from that, the Kuwaiti organisation has not been directly accused of connections with any militant Muslim groups and movements. Still, the IICO also suffered from the War on Terror and its 'hard measures'. In 2007 the Kuwaiti government introduced a range of initiatives similar to those of Saudi Arabia, forbidding cash collections in the street or in mosques and restricting international transfers (Benthall 2007:9), making it difficult for people to donate to organisations such as IICO.[7] Furthermore, in a general climate of suspicion and allegations, funding would decline and popular support wane. While many people in the Gulf countries would sympathise with IICO and even IIROSA, interpreting the anti-terror measures as covert and illegitimate attempts of 'the West' to fight (and eventually exterminate) Islam, they would still refrain from publicly supporting them.[8] Afraid of being associated with 'terrorist' organisations, many people instead preferred to channel their *zakat* payments through government, other NGOs or privately, leading to substantial budget cuts, closing of offices and cancelling of projects in many organisations. Thus, in the mid-2000s, the budgets of both IICO and IIROSA had allegedly been halved, compared to the 1990s. The budget of IICO has since then been restored, while IIROSA still suffers from budget decline.

Islamic dignitaries and pious Muslims

Against this background, what kind of aid ideology do IIROSA and IICO present today? And with what authority do they present it? To answer such questions, we will have to first answer a much more basic one, namely: who are the people that claim authority and formulate ideologies? Who are the founders, trustees and staff members that make up these organisations?

IIROSA was established by a group of wealthy Saudis in 1978, organising shipments of food and clothes to people in the Horn of Africa.[9] One of them was Farid al-Qurashi, a university professor with an American PhD, who had close connections in the Muslim World League. He soon managed to establish IIROSA as a formal organisation under the umbrella of the Muslim World League, with the secretary general of the Muslim World League as de facto chairman of the organisation. Today, IIROSA presents itself as 'the long charitable arm of the Muslim World League.'[10]

A few years later, IICO was established in Kuwait. At an Islamic finance conference in 1984, Yusuf al-Qaradawi challenged the audience to 'Pay a dollar, and save a Muslim.' A number of people backed Qaradawi's campaign, including the late Abdullah al-Mutawa, then president of the Brotherhood-related Society for Social Reform (*Al Islah*), who donated a million US dollars to the campaign.[11] The idea was presented to the late Emir Sheikh Jaber al-Ahmad al-Jaber al-Sabah, who issued an Emiri Decree in 1986, formalising the organisation.

Many of the original founders have continued their involvement in the two organisations as either trustees, General Assembly members or high-level managers.[12] They are all prominent personalities with 'Islamic' credentials who enjoy strong popularity, authority and legitimacy among Muslims in Kuwait, Saudi Arabia and throughout the Middle East; they are the Islamic aristocracy, so to speak. Some are former ministers, others are businessmen and bank owners, and yet others are university professors (Ghafour and Shamsuddin 2008). 'We always say that the least of the General Assembly members is a former minister, they are all very prominent and well-known, one is a former president,' the then IICO director says with pride.[13] Several of these people have been awarded prestigious Islamic awards, such as the Islamic Personality of the Year Award and the King Faisal International Award for Serving Islam, known by many people in the Gulf as 'Islam's Nobel Prize'.[14] They have close personal and professional relations to other major Muslim NGOs (national as well as transnational)—as trustees, directors, presidents, chairmen and founders of organisations such as the Kuwaiti Society for Social Reform, the Saudi World Assembly of Muslim Youth, the International Islamic Council for Da'wa and Relief and the Muslim World League. Many of these people and organisations are, indirectly or directly, linked to the Muslim Brotherhood, but represent a much broader Islamic movement, finding their supporters in an audience that includes Muslim Brothers as well as independent Muslim activists and 'regular' individuals. The Society for Social Reform and Yusuf al-Qaradawi are obvious examples of this connection, but the Muslim World League, albeit closely connected to Saudi Wahhabism, is also strongly influenced by the Brotherhood, with several prominent Brotherhood members serving in the organisation (Mandaville et al. 2009:29).

The biographies of the organisations' secretaries general serve to illustrate this strong embedding in an Islamic aid culture: Yusuf al-Hajji, the first secretary general of the IICO, has been Director General of the Islamic Educational, Scientific and Cultural Organisation (ISESCO), is member of the board of trustees of several Islamic universities, founder of the College of Shariah at Kuwait University, founding president of the Kuwaiti Red Crescent Society, as well as founder, co-founder, and chairman of several other NGOs. Furthermore, he has served as Minister of Awqaf in Kuwait, and worked as Secretary of Education prior to that. In 2003, he was awarded the King Faisal Prize. Yusuf al-Hajji resigned in 2010, leaving the position to Abdullah Maatouq, a man who resembles him in many ways. Maatouq has a Master's Degree from Imam Muhammad Ibn Saud Islamic University, and a doctorate from a Scottish university. He is a former Minister of Awqaf and Islamic Affairs, former Minister of Justice, as well as advisor to the Emiri Diwan. In IIROSA, Farid al-Qurashi, who was also one of the organisation's founders, served as its first secretary general until the mid-1990s. Qurashi was a professor in economics at King Abdul Aziz University. Like Hajji, Qurashi was well known all over the Gulf, and was well connected with the Muslim World League and other key Muslim organisations. In an interview, a former colleague and trustee describes him like this: 'Farid was very open-minded, he had a PhD from America. He was a wizard in collecting funds, he could communicate with very high-rank officers and government level and got both money and protection.' In 1996, Qurashi was replaced by Adnan Khalil Basha, a university professor and public figure who also had good relations to government, the religious authorities, and Muslim organisations.

Like the two secretaries general, the majority of senior staff members in the two organisations are well-educated people, many of them with a PhD from a North American or European university. Very few people, if any, have work experience with the UN or any Western aid organisations, but in particular among IIROSA staff, several top managers and assembly members have worked in the Islamic Development Bank for many years, and now work as volunteers, having retired from a well-paid job. The assistant secretary general is a case in point, having worked in the Islamic Development Bank for fourteen years and now working as a volunteer in IIROSA. Many are prominent businessmen, often with work experience and education from North America and Europe. The assistant secretary general of IIROSA, for instance, is a professor in economics. He has a PhD from Bloomington, Indianapolis, and runs an insurance company in Jeddah. Likewise, IICO's current director has an MBA in Business Administration, and has previously worked as director of several different investment and industrial corporations in the USA. At the same time, they are both well-educated in Islamic Studies; IIROSA's assistant secretary general recently finished a BA in Sharia Studies from a Saudi Arabian university, and IICO's director has a diploma in Islamic Studies.

Among regular staff, many people have a degree in computer science, administration, or Islamic Studies. Of the (few) women working in the organisations, most have a degree in accounting or teaching. Many staff members have worked in the private sector or in government prior to working in IIROSA and IICO. Very few people have worked in NGOs; however, there does seem to be an exchange of staff between IIROSA and the World Assembly of Muslim Youth—for instance, the latter's current secretary general, Mohammad Badah-Dah, is a former supervisor of IIROSA's Health Department and worked in IIROSA for fifteen years. Like him, many people have worked in the organisations for several years, and there does not seem to be a high turnover. This also goes for the director of IIROSA Jordan, a typical staff member. He has a degree in computer science, and worked as a volunteer in a Muslim organisation for orphans in a Jordanian refugee camp, where he heard about IIROSA's work. Now he has worked in IIROSA for eighteen years and he has no plans of leaving:

> I started working in the Bakra Camp many years ago as a volunteer in a local orphan organisation. I worked there for three years, then I came here and I have been here for eighteen years [...] First, I just wanted a new experience, I wanted to try something new. But then, when I started doing the job, I came to love it. I feel comfortable here, I feel like I am working with honest people. I like when the mothers say nice things to me, I like that people are happy with the work we do, I like to make the orphans smile.

Everybody working in IIROSA and IICO is a practising Muslim, often a conservative one—at headquarter as well as country office levels. People pray together, dress according to religious precepts, and the language used among staff is full of Islamic terms and phrases. Relations between men and women are defined by conservative Islamic ideals, meaning that each gender attends to different functions. Women primarily work in fund-raising, teaching, nursing, and other activities deemed suitable for a Muslim woman, while men work in management, project implementation, and the like. Some offices also practice gender segregation. In IIROSA's headquarters in Jeddah, for instance, the women's department is in a different part of town, and female staff members rarely enter the main building but mostly communicate with male staff through e-mail, phone or Yahoo Messenger. In IICO, women also work in a separate department, but in 2008, the first woman was hired to work in the main (male) department, as manager of the then newly established Center for Charitable Studies. This was 'a shock to me and to the men here', she says, and continues: 'But I will fight to hire more women [...] Every organisation has a ladies' committee, but I want women to be a part of everything, not just in one room, dealing with other women. But sure, they need their time.' To sum up, members of both IICO and IIROSA can be characterised as Islamic dignitaries and pious Muslims, reflecting a strong organisational embedding in the Islamic aid culture. What do these people say? How do they present their organisation? How do they claim authority as providers of aid? These are some of the questions that the next sections seek to answer, exploring the ways in which IICO and IIROSA present their organisational identity.

Islamic authority: 'Because of believing in God...'

'[I]t is because of believing in God and in the limitless bestowal of the IICO that its charitable work has gone up to a high place.'[15] These are the introductory lines to one of IICO's publications, illustrating with all clarity that the main source of IICO's organisational authority is religion. The same can be said for IIROSA. As their names also indicate, the two organisations frame themselves as religious authorities, claiming to be legitimate providers of aid because they follow prescriptions of religious authorities, doctrines, and traditions. They seek to legitimise themselves as religious authorities by building on—or aligning with—religious beliefs, values, and ideas common to Kuwaiti and Saudi societies, thus hoping to create resonance with, and by extension gain support from, their potential audiences (Benford and Snow 2000:624).

One strategy for generating legitimacy and authority is to emphasise knowledge (Slim 2002:9). IICO and IIROSA have different ways of displaying their religious knowledge; one is the use of religious symbols. Comprehensible only to the initiated, religious symbols serve as a powerful way of demonstrating knowledge. For instance, the website of IICO is designed in shades of green—the colour of Islam—while its logo—also green—contains several references to symbols in Islam. The logo has the shape of a house, perhaps a mosque, with a window the shape of a globe. Together, the globe and the building can also look like a woman with a hijab. On the right side of the logo, at the bottom of the building, there is an outstretched hand, reaching for the globe. The hand is a common symbol in different charity traditions, including Islam, referring at once to the physical acts of begging for and giving alms. But the hand also resembles an angel's wing (in Arabic, *al Janah*), another common symbol in Islam. Hovering over the building is a crescent, perhaps the strongest contemporary symbol of Islam and the Muslim community.[16] Another, more explicit, way of displaying religious knowledge is the frequent reference to religious texts. Hadiths, Qur'an verses, and pictures of the Kaba adorn office walls as well as websites, annual reports, and PR material, serving to underline the organisations' status as legitimate religious actors. On its website, IICO even offers lengthy theological explanations of *zakat* practices and rulings, coupled with practical information on how to calculate *zakat*.[17] Furthermore, the website offers people the possibility to 'ask al-Mufti' or 'chat with the Mufti' about religious issues,[18] all of which serves to demonstrate that the organisation is knowledgeable of and adhering to Islamic doctrines and principles. References to religious texts also came up quite frequently in interviews where staff would recite from the Qur'an as a way of emphasising a point or illustrating an example, subtly demonstrating their religious literacy.

Another strategy serving for IIROSA and IICO to generate legitimacy as religious authorities is the promotion of religious practices and traditions inside and outside the organisations. What they do is 'real Islamic philanthropy'.[19] On a general level, at least in IICO, the so-called Fatwa and Sharia Supervisory Board, consisting of four religious scholars, reviews the organisation's activities and determines whether they are in accordance with Islamic laws. A recent topic for discussion was the question of administrative charges in relief programmes, and the Board concluded that these could not exceed 10 per cent of the total budget.[20] Members of the board are well-known religious scholars in Kuwait, and they are often members of other sharia boards, in particular in financial institutions.[21] More specifically, Islamic holidays such as Ramadan and Eid al-Adha are enthusiastically celebrated, and traditional Islamic aid activities such as orphan sponsorship, mosque building and Qur'an lessons are central to the organisations' programmes (something which we will discuss much more below). Furthermore, the two organisations promote and rely on Islamic sources of finance. Presenting themselves as legitimate channels for *zakat* payments, they both have mechanisms for calculating *zakat* on their websites, just as their flyers and brochures promise religious rewards to those that pay their *zakat*. Both organisations get a large part of their funds from individual *zakat* payments. In 1990, Abdulhadi (1990:7) estimated that as much as 80 per cent of IICO funds were *zakat* contributions. There is nothing that indicates that this should be any different today—or that it should be different in IIROSA, for that matter.[22] The recent re-introduction of the *waqf* may also be interpreted as a way for the two organisations to boost religious legitimacy.[23] In part prompted by the decline in funding after 9/11, the two organisations have re-launched the system of *waqf* as an alternative, and potentially more sustainable, source of income, investing in buildings and channelling the revenue back into charitable activities.[24] Finally, staff members are encouraged to pray together in the organisations' many prayer rooms, dress according to religious precepts, and comply with conservative gender practices, adhering to conservative Saudi and Kuwaiti ideals of what it is to be a believing and practising Muslim (see, for example, Meyer et al. 2007).

A third strategy for generating religious legitimacy is to emphasise association with existing and recognised religious authorities. Who an organisation knows is a major source of its legitimacy (Slim 2002:9). In this perspective, legitimacy is a precondition for support but it can also be a result of support (from the right people). The frequent references to renowned religious authorities serve to heighten organisational credibility, insofar as the credentials of these personalities reflect back on the organisations. For instance, both IIROSA and IICO often underline the religiosity of the organisations' founders, all of them pious Muslims, or, as noted in an IICO publication, 'sincere and leading thinkers of the Muslim nation.'[25] Both organisations also frequently underline their external relations and cooperation with respected Muslim individuals, organisations and institutions. IICO, for instance, has a section on its website entitled 'Testimonials' with quotes from prominent people praising the work of IICO.[26] Of the seventeen people quoted, fifteen are Islamic sheikhs, all of them praising not only the work of the IICO but also its status as a 'solid bastion of Islam,' as noted by Sheikh Issa Ben Mohamed Al Khalifa, former Minister and President of the Social Reform Association in Bahrain.[27] Similarly, the organisations' partnerships with major Muslim organisations such as the Muslim World League, the OIC and the International Islamic Council for Da'wa and Relief are often mentioned on websites and in interviews. IIROSA promotes itself as the 'charitable wing' of the Muslim World League, while IICO claims to cooperate in 'spreading Islamic awareness and virtues all over the world'.[28] National Muslim authorities also play an important role. Letters of appreciation posted on IIROSA's magazines and reports testify to good relations with provincial governments, ministries of *awqaf*, and local religious authorities in Indonesia, Afghanistan, Ethiopia,

Pakistan and elsewhere.[29] Likewise, both organisations cooperate with national and local Muslim NGOs. For instance, in Jordan both IICO and IIROSA have for many years cooperated with the Islamic Center Charity Society, the country's biggest NGO and the charitable wing of the Jordanian Muslim Brotherhood.

These relations all tell us something about the kind of Islam that the organisations wish to be associated with. At least three things are worth noting here: First, most of the religious authorities mentioned are formal religious authorities rather than self-taught preachers such as Amr Khaled or Tariq Ramadan. Second, many are associated with government. IICO's list of quotes, for instance, includes four ministers and three emirs. Finally, Muslim Brotherhood organisations and representatives play a prominent role, including for instance Yusuf al-Qaradawi, the Islamic Center Charity Society in Jordan, and the Society for Social Reform in Kuwait. As such, IICO and IIROSA position themselves as part of a particular religious community. They do not associate themselves with new trends of 'Islam lite' as expressed by for instance Egypt's popular TV preacher Amr Khaled; instead, they promote a much more conservative and orthodox understanding of Islam. At the same time, they distinguish themselves from the individualistic piety that is found in, for instance, the Salafi movement, building instead on Muslim Brotherhood traditions of a close relation between social activism and Islam, as discussed in Chapter 2. As one IICO staff member puts it: 'We have this saying, "To go and help another human being is better than to stay and pray for years." So helping is much more than worship. Worship is so important, but helping is even more important, it's much better.' With this understanding of Islam as a conservative, but activist, collectively oriented religion, IICO and IIROSA position themselves within a broader, religious culture in the Middle East, perhaps dominated by Muslim Brotherhood interpretations of Islam, but still capable of accommodating governmental voices.

Furthermore, in particular IICO's claims to a religious legitimacy are also based on an understanding of Islam as a religion of moderation. 'We have different thoughts than others,' a high-level staff member tells me. 'We think that the best is in the middle. That's a basic rule in Islam. Some things in Islam are very clear—salah, *zakat*, hajj—but some things need interpretation. And some of these interpretations are extreme and some are not. The best is to be in the middle.' The director of IICO explains the concept as follows:

For instance, to be brave is the middle way between being a coward and being reckless. To be generous is between misery and crazy spending. Islam is the middle way. Its followers should be moderate—but without compromising. To be patient is in between being angry and cold. Islam says the best man is one who can get loved and who can love. A good person, in the eyes of Allah, is someone who is easy to deal with, someone who does not make problems with others.

'Being in the middle', or moderation (in Arabic *wasat*), is an important element in IICO's framing of itself as a religiously legitimate organisation, manifested, among other things, in the organisation's many initiatives to promote 'the culture of a moderate *umma*'. The director explains: 'Very early, we saw the misunderstandings of Islam among some groups, so we wanted to promote the moderate way—it's the real way, the best way. We want to confront this twisted understanding of Islam.'[30] In 2001, the organisation hosted the symposium *The Culture of a Moderate Umma* for Muslim religious scholars and thinkers in Kuwait, followed by the conference *Tolerance and Moderation are Ways for Life* in 2005. Later, it co-hosted a conference in Italy in cooperation with ISESCO 'to introduce the culture of the moderate *Umma* and to train the preachers about this moderate approach in Europe',[31] as well as two conferences in Singapore 'emphasiz[ing] the need to reject violence in all its forms and [explain] the method of the Prophet in pursuing da'wah work through wisdom, good advice and convincing arguments.'[32] In this, the organisation is strongly inspired by Qaradawi. In his own words, Islam is about moderation and balance—about finding the middle way between religious fundamentalism and Western secularism, between socialism and capitalism, between greed and ascetics (Gräf and Skovgaard Petersen 2009). As such, the reference to moderation as an important source of religious legitimacy places IICO as part of a broader Islamic movement, centred around Qaradawi, but including a wide range of actors and initiatives from the Muslim Brotherhood to the Amman Message, launched by Jordan's King Abdullah.

While IICO and IIROSA's claims to authority seem to be directed primarily at individuals, institutions and organisations in Kuwait and Saudi Arabia, this emphasis on 'moderation' can also, at least in part, be seen as an attempt by IICO to broaden its audience and legitimating environment by referring to a new kind of legitimacy, based on notions of politics and security. As was discussed in Chapter 3, following the War on Terror, a new discourse on so-called faith-based organisations has emerged among Western aid agencies, promoting 'moderate' Muslim NGOs as tools for bridge-building and dialogue. In this perspective, moderation is not so much about theology, but about politics, and a 'moderate' Muslim NGO denotes a politically neutral, or ideally liberal, organisation that does not sympathise with Al-Qaeda or other so-called extremist groups and movements. Using the religious concept of moderation, or *wasat*, the IICO attempts to merge these two kinds of legitimacy, at the same time appealing to a Kuwaiti donor base and reaching out to a new constituency, consisting of Western institutional donors interested in cooperating with 'moderate' Muslim NGOs. In other words, the IICO claims to be a legitimate organisation because it seeks to 'convey the truly peaceful picture of the religion of Islam,'[33] at once saving people from ignorance and extremism. On a side note, this emphasis on moderation points to an important difference between Muslim and other religious NGOs. For Muslim organisations to be legitimate in the eyes of Western development agencies, they cannot simply be providers of aid, but must simultaneously engage in activities of bridge-building and dialogue, pledging allegiance to 'moderation', and as such making amends for the damage allegedly done by other Muslim NGOs, whose guilt and shame they somehow share.[34]

Professional authority: 'Our activities are transparent'

Parallel to their emphasis on religious legitimacy, IIROSA and IICO increasingly seem to frame their authority in terms of professionalism, based on claims to professional relations, practices and knowledge. Religiosity is without doubt the main source of authority, but in some domains claims to professional authority are presented alongside these religious claims. In this perspective, the NGOs claim to be legitimate actors not because of their obedience to God or because of their moral values, but because their work is professional, understood in terms of concepts such as 'accountability', 'science', and 'strategic planning'. As such, they seek to demonstrate their fluency in professional aid speak, often conceived in terms of an international, or 'Western', mainstream aid discourse.

As IICO and IIROSA seek to establish religious authority through different strategies, their claims to professional authority also rely on different strategies. One such strategy is to create allegiance with established authorities in the field of mainstream aid provision as a way to demonstrate their authority as professional aid providers. For IICO and IIROSA, professional authorities in the field of aid provision are not fellow Muslim or Middle Eastern NGOs, but 'international' and 'Western' organisations, often explicitly distinguished from 'Islamic', 'Arab' and 'local' organisations,[35] and presented as the standard against which to be measured, the ideal towards which the organisations should be striving. IIROSA, for instance, has included in its new strategy the objectives to 'implement the international quality standards' and to 'uplift its human resources to the international professional levels'.[36] In recent years, both IIROSA and IICO have taken concrete steps to establish relations with such 'international' organisations, including the UN, the World Health Organisation (WHO), and large Western NGOs. In an interview in *Arab News*, the IIROSA secretary general says: 'We would like to have partnership with more UN agencies and international organisations to benefit from their experience. This will give us an opportunity to learn from them. They can also learn from us, and this interaction will help us become more professional in our mission' (Ghafour and Shamsuddin 2010). Overall, both organisations are actively seeking to reach a broader English-speaking audience through English-language annual reports, PR material, websites, and campaigns. For instance, at the time of writing, both organisations had been updating and improving their English websites for a number of years, and they had both recently launched an English language Facebook profile (although IIROSA had little more than 2,000 friends and IICO a mere 54). More specifically, they have both introduced a number of initiatives with the purpose of facilitating cooperation with international organisations. As noted above, IIROSA has launched a new strategy, including specific plans to establish alliances with Western governments, companies, banks and organisations (Ghafour and Shamsuddin 2008). In concrete terms, this has resulted in, among other things, a partnership agreement with the WHO to cooperate on health programmes in Afghanistan, Jordan, Pakistan, Sudan, Egypt, Morocco, Tunisia, and Yemen;[37] a memorandum of understanding with United Nations Children's Fund (UNICEF) to cooperate on projects for children's rights in Saudi Arabia; and a US$ 500,000 Food Aid Project in the Gaza Strip, implemented in coordination with United Nations Relief and Works Agency for Palestinian Refugees (UNRWA) (Saudi Press Agency 2009). In 2012, during the civil war in Syria, IIROSA representatives met with United Nations High Commissioner for Refugees (UNHCR) and United Nations Office for the Coordination of Humanitarian Aid (OCHA) officials, discussing possibilities for cooperation on the provision of relief to refugees (Aziz 2012). Similarly, IICO has made efforts to establish partnerships with international organisations. In 2004, the organisation joined the Humanitarian Forum, a network established by Islamic Relief's founder, Hani al-Banna in cooperation with Oxfam and British Red Cross and including a range of Muslim NGOs, Western NGOs and governmental aid agencies.[38] The Forum has organised several workshops and conferences with the aim of 'creat[ing] dialogue and understanding between Muslim organisations and their Western and multilateral counterparts'.[39] In 2012, IICO, together with OCHA and Direct Aid, cohosted an international conference with the theme *Effective Partnership in Information for Better Humanitarian Work*, inviting representatives from more than 100 aid NGOs, intergovernmental organisations, and companies.[40] Such relations with international organisations are heavily promoted by both IIROSA and IICO and both maintain long lists of all international partners on their websites and in their reports, displaying their logos and presenting photos from meetings and conferences as proof of these relations.[41]

Another strategy for building authority is to make claims to professional knowledge and practices. The IICO's Center for Charitable Studies is an obvious example of the organisation's attempt to position itself as an aid authority, promoting and producing professional knowledge on aid provision.[42] The centre was established in 2008 to 'introduce the newly developed philanthropy theory and practices to workers and organizations in the Middle East and developing countries [and] develop philanthropy systems and practices that suit the cultural needs of different regions and countries in the third world.'[43] It was explicitly modelled after 'Western institutions', because, as the website states, 'in the Middle East region [...] charitable organisations and charitable activities have no or little scientific basis.'[44] As the director of IICO says:

> [T]he theories for helping the poor have changed. There are several different schools of theories regarding orphans. You can help them by improving their living conditions, giving aid such as clean water and education to the whole community instead of just giving to the individual. And you can educate the mother. These are new concepts. And it's all based on research.

But more than scientifically based aid provision, IICO and IIROSA seem to conceive professionalism in terms of management and strategic planning skills. In IIROSA, the secretary general of IIROSA, Adnan Khalil Basha, is quoted for saying that IIROSA aspires to be 'the first NGO to lay down [a] strategic basis and principles for charity work.'[45] Similarly, the IICO considers itself 'one of the advanced charitable and humanitarian organisations which uses developed technical and managerial methods in its different areas of work,'[46] '[w]orking according to well-designed plans, and a management system that is characterized by proper organisation, clarity of responsibilities, and great flexibility.'[47] The Center for Charitable Studies recently organised a management training course for thirty directors of Kuwaiti aid organisations, hiring an international management company to teach the directors 'to become more qualified' and learn about 'how to do meetings, negotiations, dealing with others', as the manager tells me. 'Most people who work here are not specialised in charity. They need training,' she explains. 'They were all very impressed, it's a new science for them.' Since then, the centre has started offering a wide range of courses with titles such as *Strategies for Institutional Development*, *Quality Management and Its Application in Charitable Work*, and *Management and Implementation of Charity Projects*, seeking to disseminate its professional knowledge to other aid actors, in turn confirming its position as a professional authority in the field.[48]

Claims to organisational professionalism also centre on knowledge and practices of financial 'accountability' and 'transparency', witnessed in a number of—not always successful—initiatives of the two organisations. In 2005, IIROSA launches the, now defunct, US-based Friends of Charities Association together with five other Saudi NGOs,[49] with the specific aim of 'clarify[ing] misconceptions about charities through transparency in their funding and operations of their headquarters and branch offices'[50] as part of a strategy to confront the 'unfair allegations' against Muslim organisations by 'refuting them with facts and figures in a way that does not leave any doubt about the good will of Islamic charities.'[51] Although the initiative was not successful, its mere existence and purpose testify to IIROSA's interest in being received as 'accountable' and 'transparent'. Such claims to professionalism are also reflected in the two organisations' strong emphasis on relations with globally recognised auditing and accounting authorities. At its 2008 General Assembly meeting, for instance, IIROSA appointed the internationally renowned company

Ernst & Young as IIROSA's official auditors. 'The appointment of such a reputable international firm as auditors would strengthen IIROSA's credibility and transparency,' said the secretary general (Ghafour and Shamsuddin 2008). Both organisations have, at least to some degree, started making annual reports and budgets publicly available on their websites, sending signals of financial transparency to potential audiences. IIROSA was recently awarded the ISO 9001 certificate, and IICO is also aiming for ISO certification, introducing new procedures for document control, auditing, and evaluation. ISO is a global certificate for organisational and business management systems, controlled by the International Standardisation Organisation. As such, the ISO certificate sends a strong signal of adherence to global standards of financial professionalism. Displayed on the front page of IIROSA's website, marked in red and in type as big as that used for the organisation's name, the certificate serves as a symbol of professional authority, sending subtle signs of adherence to common norms and values of professionalism, much in the same vein as the crescent and the mosque send signals of a common religiosity. Summing up, the claims to professionalism that we find in IICO and IIROCA are claims to a very particular kind of professionalism, centring on knowledge and practices in the domains of management and finance rather than, for instance, staff or actual aid provision. As such, and perhaps more than as an attempt at introducing radically new ways of providing aid, IIROSA and IICO's claims to professional authority can be seen as a way to respond to international accusations of terrorist financing, emphasising the political neutrality of the organisations by way of claims to transparency. As noted by IIROSA's secretary general in an interview in one of the organisation's bulletins: 'We don't support any terrorist group. Our relief activities are transparent. There is no room for suspicion.'[52]

Unlike their claims to religious authority, IIROSA and IICO's claims to professional authority may not always be heard, at least not by Western and international organisations. In Bangladesh, for instance, ECHO and USAID representatives have not heard about the Kuwait Joint Relief Committee (through which IICO works), and other NGOs have not met them at meetings and in networks. Likewise, in Jordan, few UN agencies and Western NGOs have ever heard of either IICO or IIROSA.[53] And so far, neither of the two organisations has succeeded in attracting significant funding from the UN or other major development agencies.

UNESCO has contributed with some funding to the IICO's Center for Charitable Studies, but apart from that the organisation has not, at time of writing, received any funding from mainstream development agencies. For IIROSA cooperation is primarily in the form of IIROSA donations to UN organisations, not the other way around. For instance, IIROSA donated US$ 500,000 to the abovementioned WHO health programmes; in 2007, it allocated US$ 265,000 to support UNICEF's Family Security Program; and in 2008 and 2009, it gave two US$ 1 million contributions to UNRWA's work in Palestine.[54] Following criticism from Fox News, however, Chris de Bono, UNICEF's chief of media, had to specify that 'UNICEF does not and will not engage with' the designated branches of IIROSA, but would only cooperate with the Saudi headquarters, coordinating relief for children living within Saudi Arabia (UNICEF 2008; Abrams 2008).

Running a health clinic or working in an Islamic organisation?

The above analysis has presented a picture of two organisations that are firmly embedded in an Islamic aid culture. Founders, board and assembly members are all 'Islamic dignitaries' with strong personal and professional relations to key Islamic organisations and persons. All staff members in the organisations are practising Muslims; many have experience from other Muslim organisations; and few have experience from Western development organisations. Likewise, the vast majority of donors are Kuwaiti and Saudi Muslims wishing to pay their *zakat*; partners are primarily other Islamic organisations and institutions; and recipients are mainly Muslim majority countries or Muslim minorities in non-Muslim countries. However, recent years have also seen clear signs of approximation towards the culture of development aid. Indicators of this are for instance the IIROSA's recent cooperation with different UN agencies, and the IICO's participation in the Humanitarian Forum, together with major Western development agencies and NGOs. In other words, IICO and IIROSA may have both feet planted solidly in the Islamic aid culture, but they are reaching out to mainstream development actors. From this position, they seek to present their organisational authority as simultaneously religious and professional, combining terms such as 'accountability', 'strategic planning' and 'transparency' with a strongly moral and religious language. In an Annual Report, IIROSA writes that the organisation will continue with the will of God to provide its services and donations for years to come and will strive to develop and maximize its programs and to improve its performance, based on long-term well-studied strategic plans that it has adopted with a view to institutionalizing its work in order to uplift charity work from all aspects. Praise is to God, Lord of the Worlds![55]

Similarly, the IICO lists its five organisational values as being 'development,' 'institutionalization,' 'transparency,' 'networking' and 'pleasing Allah'.[56] According to the director of IICO, this mix of professional and religious values is not problematic. Talking about the professionalisation of Middle Eastern NGOs, he says: 'We have our charity culture in Islam, but contemporary development is huge—we want to mix the two. Goodness is goodness, this idea is universal. So there are no problems in mixing the non-Islamic with the Islamic. There are almost no differences, if any.' In many respects this is true. Naturally, a religious organisation can be professional in terms of financial accountability, strategic planning, and the like. As noted in IICO's *Administrative and Financial Report*, 'seeking to please Allah when carrying out charity work [...] enhances giving, self-motivation for achievement, continuity in giving, and [promotes] the spirit of self-accountability'.[57] That said, however, there are some fundamental differences between the two kinds of authority, making a straightforward merging potentially problematic in the long run. This is particularly the case when it comes to staff. Here, professional authority is predicated on systems and functions, while religious authority tends to emphasise the personal. An illustrative example of this is the prominent position that the chairman occupies in IICO. As a staff member in IICO Jordan says, praising the now former chairman Yusuf al-Hajji:

He is trusted. He is eighty-five years old. There are elections every four years, but people don't want him to resign. They want him to stay. He is very well-known. You know, when people come to donate money, they ask 'where is Mr Hajji?' and we say, 'he's away, he's at a conference or something, just give us the money', and they say, 'no I want to meet him, I want to talk to him'. It's not like in the West, there you have institutions, systems. Here, it is all about persons. The person is important.

Another aspect of this is the question of professional aid expertise versus religious devotion, qualities which are most often assessed and prioritised differently in a professional aid organisation and a religious one. In a professional aid organisation, the ideal staff member is an expert in aid provision, a specialist working to do his or her job as efficiently as possible. In an Islamic organisation, on the other hand, she or (most often) he is a devoted Muslim working to please Allah and advance the religious cause. Theoretically, there is of course nothing to hinder staff members in possessing both qualities, but in practice organisations will at some point have to prioritise one quality over the other. Will the organisation hire the development worker with several years of experience from Oxfam or another large development NGO, but no religious expertise? Or will it go for the religious expert, with a degree in Islamic studies, but with only a few years of experience from a local community organisation? So far, IICO and IIROSA have prioritised religiously devoted staff over professional development staff. As we saw in the above chapter, the vast majority of trustees and staff members are Islamic dignitaries and practising Muslims, displaying religious expertise rather than expertise in aid provision. A manager of an IIROSA health clinic in Bangladesh, one of the organisation's few development professionals, expresses this preference very precisely when he says of his colleagues: 'They work in an Islamic organisation, while I run a health clinic.' His statement is an indication of the conflicts that may lie ahead for IICO and IIROSA should they continue their transformation into professional aid authorities. What happens when professional development staff are introduced to an organisation that has historically relied on religious authority? Is their integration into the organisation always smooth and unproblematic? This is something we shall discuss further in Chapters 6 and 7, exploring organisational developments in Islamic Relief and Muslim Aid after 9/11. For now, suffice it to say that IIROSA and IICO present themselves primarily as religious authorities, albeit with claims to professional authority in particular areas. How these aid authorities conceive aid is the topic of the next chapter, in which we will explore the actual aid ideologies presented by the IICO and IIROSA.

5

'IT'S ALL IN ISLAM!'

AID IDEOLOGIES IN IIROSA AND IICO

'It's all in Islam!' This is what people in IIROSA and IICO often say when asked about the relation between their religion and the aid they provide. Aid is Islam—and Islam is aid. In this chapter, I explore the ways in which IICO and IIROSA conceptualise the provision of aid and Islam, showing how their organisational compositions and historical trajectories have contributed to fostering a particular ideology of aid, positioning the organisations in relation to the surrounding cultures of development and Islamic aid. More specifically, the chapter shows how different ideological elements are formulated and presented, based on an understanding of ideologies as consisting in three main elements. Inspired by Wilson's (1973) decomposition of ideological dimensions, I conceptualise the ideological framework in terms of a vision, strategies, and a rationale. First, the vision outlines the purpose of the ideology and the problems it seeks to solve: is the problem economic poverty, spiritual degeneration, inequality, physical suffering, or something else? And, correspondingly, is the purpose of aid to generate income, strengthen faith, restore justice or relieve suffering? Second, the strategies explicate how these problems should be solved and the vision achieved, outlining directions for the NGO: is aid about provision of food and medicine? Is it about education and technical advice or about building schools and mosques? And third, the rationale provides the underlying reasons for the provision of aid, answering questions as to why aid should be provided: is it a religious obligation, for instance, or a human duty? Underlying all ideologies of aid is a basic chain of aid provision, outlining who are the rightful givers of aid and who are the rightful recipients. Aid ideologies produce different versions of these subjects, often expressed in the basic, somewhat clinical terms of 'donors' and 'beneficiaries', sometimes more emotionally as 'generous donors' and 'grateful beneficiaries', and other times as 'supporters' and 'clients', or simply 'partners'. Likewise, the aid chain explicates the ideal relations between these subjects, based on underlying theories of giving. Is aid a personal gift from an individual donor to an individual recipient, with the NGO serving merely as a facilitator? Is it an institutional gift from an NGO to groups of recipients, facilitated by the individual donor? Or is it an obligation of the NGO and the donors, meeting the rights of the recipients?

The concrete analysis of these ideological elements and subjects takes the form not so much of a word for word analysis focusing on specific narrative structures, metaphors, and discursive devices, but instead presents a focus on substantive themes, patterns, and meta-narratives (Wuthnow 2011:12). In this, I have been inspired by the so-called framing approach. Framing is a handle for examining the interpretive processes through which extant meanings are debated and challenged and new ones are articulated and amplified (Snow 2004). The concept of frames refers to 'interpretative schemata that offer a language and cognitive tools for making sense of experiences and events in the "world out there"' (Wiktorowicz 2004:15). Frames are, in the words of Benford and Snow (2000:614), action-oriented sets of belief and meanings that inspire, organise and legitimate the ideas, activities and identity of an organisation, and framing is the construction of these sets of meaning, denoting 'an active, processual phenomenon that implies agency and contention at the level of reality construction' (Benford and Snow 2000:614). In this perspective, frames can be usefully conceptualised as constituting the different elements of ideology, and framing as the process through which organisations construct and articulate these ideological elements, thus emphasising a dynamic and processual understanding of ideology.

Visions of aid

Speaking as religious and professional authorities in the field of aid provision, IICO and IIROSA formulate particular ideologies of aid. An important part of this is the definition of organisational visions. What is aid? Is it a response to economic poverty, spiritual degeneration, inequality, physical suffering, or something else? And, correspondingly, is the purpose of aid to generate income, strengthen faith, restore justice or relieve suffering? In other words, how do the organisations define the problems they seek to solve, the solutions they present to these problems, and the ideal situations they strive to obtain through their solutions?

Addressing material and spiritual needs

For IICO and IIROSA, the main problem is poverty and suffering. The IICO is 'dedicated to the alleviation of the ramifications of poverty, distress and deprivation of people,'[1] seeking to 'remove the suffering of people wherever they are.'[2] Likewise, the IIROSA 'aims to alleviate the suffering of distressed and needy people worldwide.'[3] Drawing on what Chouliaraki (2010) refers to as 'grand emotions', the organisations present poverty as a situation characterised by individual agony, shame and humiliation. Recipients of aid are characterised by their needs and wants: they are 'the poor', 'the needy', 'the deprived', 'the hungry', 'the sick', 'the homeless', and 'the distressed'. As such, the discourses of IICO and IIROSA echo those of countless other NGOs, whether religious or not. But poverty is not only about hunger, diseases, and lack of education; it is also about religious ignorance, humiliation and backwardness. In other words, it is about 'economic, health, social and religious needs.'[4] Poverty is, in other words, both spiritual and material and as such, markedly different from secular development conceptions of poverty. This understanding of poverty builds on conceptions of the inseparability of the material and the transcendent, underlying the thinking of most contemporary Islamic movements and groups. At the same time, it has parallels among Christian NGOs. Studying World Vision in Zimbabwe, for instance, Bornstein (2003) finds elements of 'a theology of holism', presenting an understanding of development as simultaneously addressing both spiritual and material needs. She quotes a World Vision director as saying: 'Holistic [development] in our sense is that we want to change the situation from the social point of view, economical point of view, and spiritual point of view' (cf. Bornstein 2003:49). Similarly, Samarian Purse describes itself as an evangelical Christian organisation with the mission to offer 'spiritual and physical aid to hurting people around the world', not only providing food, medicine and other assistance, but also 'sharing God's love' (Thaut 2009:342).

A dignified Muslim and a strengthened *umma*

Closely related to and corresponding with this multifaceted conception of poverty is the organisations' vision of a dignified life for the poor. The overall objective of IICO's work is to 'help the needy [to] live in dignity'.[5] Through the provision of aid, the organisations seek to enable the poor and needy to take care of themselves, so that they will no longer be humiliated and ashamed, but will be able to regain their God-given dignity, living 'a decent and useful life.'[6] This entails not only access to health, education, food and housing, but also religious education and facilities for worshipping (as we will see in the following sections). Underlying this explicit vision of a dignified life for the poor is another, more implicit vision. Based on a notion of poverty as simultaneously individual and collective, IIROSA and IICO introduce the vision of a strengthened *umma* as a response to problems of spiritual poverty in the Muslim community. The *umma* is threatened at different levels: from within, by immoral and ignorant Muslims on one side, and religious extremists and fanatics on the other;[7] and from the outside, by 'an organized invasion' of Christian NGOs, trying to take Muslims away from their religion,[8] as well as by 'baseless allegations' of terrorist connections launched against Muslim NGOs as 'part of a concerted effort by some [people] in the West to stop all Islamic relief efforts'.[9] Responding to these problems, the organisations formulate visions of a strengthened Muslim *umma*, based on 'brotherhood ties' and 'social solidarity'.[10] In this society, Muslims are raised in the right faith, nursing a balanced Muslim character and encouraging 'observance of Islamic morals, sharia virtues, [and] activation of da'wa'.[11] As a project manager in IICO explains:

> If the Islamic ideas were being inserted then society would be happier, more secure, there would be an abundance of wealth—both psychologically and materially. When we spend money for the poor, society will be safer, there will be no crime. There will be more happiness and the economy will be strengthened. So we don't only help the poor, we also help society as such.

By assisting individual Muslims, ensuring their right Islamic education, then, IICO and IIROSA not only ensure their self-reliance and a dignified life, they also contribute to strengthening the Muslim *umma* (see also Kaag 2008:5). To be a good Muslim is not only about individual piety and dignity, but about rescuing and maintaining the distinctively Islamic character of society. As such, the moral reform of the individual is closely linked to that of society (Hatina 2006:182), strongly echoing Hassan al-Banna's ideas of Islamic activism, as laid out in Chapter 2. Aid provision, in other words, is not only for the poor individual, but for society. The motto of IICO—'[If we stand] together…the needy will never ask again'—expresses this double function of aid: it is about helping the poor to become self-reliant so they do not have to ask again. But at the same time, it is about standing together, uniting ties of brotherhood, to create a better society, a strengthened *umma*, in which nobody has to ask for help. Like the conception of poverty as simultaneously spiritual and material, this idea of aid as a tool for strengthening the religious community resonates with certain Christian conceptions of aid, exemplified, in for instance, Samaritan Purse. This is what Thaut (2009), in her analysis of Christian NGOs, calls an evangelistic humanitarianism: 'they provide relief and development assistance largely with the goal of helping to extend the church, build up the community of Christians globally, and serve the spiritual needs of humanity' (Thaut 2009:342).

Helping Muslim brothers and sisters

If a strengthened *umma* is the vision, then recipients are primarily Muslims (or potential Muslims).[12] As such, IIROSA's and IICO's missionary aid necessarily breaks with mainstream notions of universalism. Recipients are not distant strangers, but citizens of the same Muslim nation, brothers and sisters of the same Muslim family. We assist poor people, 'regardless of their race or nationality' and 'without any racial or ethnic distinction', the IICO claims, copying common declarations of humanitarian universalism almost to the word. But only almost. While the organisation proclaims a racial, ethnic and geographical universalism, it does not mention religion. In other words, the IICO may help people of any race, nationality or ethnicity, provided they are Muslim. As such, recipients are subjectified within an overall framework of the Muslim *umma* rather than a global humanity.[13] IIROSA presents a slightly more inclusive approach than IICO, claiming to have provided aid to 'all cases of sick people irrespective of religion, caste and creed.'[14] At the same time, however, this organisation also displays a strong religious particularism, working in 'different parts of the Muslim world and Muslim minority communities worldwide'[15] to 'augment to spirit of Islamic solidarity'.[16] A look at the actual areas in which the organisations work further substantiates this, showing that both work primarily in Muslim majority countries, and with Muslim minorities in non-Muslim countries (see Table 5.1.).[17]

Table 5.1: IIROSA, top five countries (2003)[18]

Country	Percentage of budget
Saudi Arabia	16
Jordan	9
Sudan	5
Pakistan	4
Somalia	3

Table 5.2: IICO, top five countries (2010)[19]

Country	Percentage of budget
Syria	31
Pakistan	26
Somalia	13
Turkey	5
Sudan	2

As noted in Chapter 3, it is precisely this particularistic approach that Muslim NGOs (and other religious NGOs, for that matter) have been criticised for by secular, Western NGOs, claiming that they discriminate among recipients, thus violating principles of universalism and neutrality. With the War on Terror, this distinction between universalistic and particularistic approaches has been coupled with a distinction between moderate and extremist or fundamentalist organisations. In other words, a particularistic, missionary religiosity is seen not only as a sign of discrimination, but also as a sign of religious fundamentalism and potentially political extremism. In this perspective, IICO and IIROSA cannot maintain a strictly particularistic approach, if they want to attract an 'international' audience, but have to find a way to align their vision with mainstream principles of development aid. A few people maintain that the organisations do in fact adhere to universalist principles: 'We don't differentiate between Muslims and non-Muslims—relief is relief,' says a top manager in IIROSA's headquarters. A staff member in IICO's Jordan office echoes this: 'Charity is a human idea.' Most, however, admit that the organisations focus primarily on Muslims. As a staff member in IICO puts it: 'In general, to be honest, they help Muslims first, but if there are non-Muslims in the area, they will also help them.' This is a prioritisation of Muslims over non-Muslims with reference to what I, inspired by Bellion-Jourdan (2000:15), will call a pragmatic particularism or a principled universality: in principle the organisations will help everybody, but in practice they work primarily among Muslims and therefore help primarily Muslims. A high-level staff member in IIROSA says: 'In Jordan, we work mostly with Muslims. The Christians don't ask us for help, they have their own organisations.' Likewise, staff in IICO's Jordan office says that because most people in Jordan are Muslim, discrimination is not an issue. Another version of this argument focuses on the fact that the majority of the world's poor are Muslim, justifying special attention to this group of poor people. As an IIROSA representative writes in an article about Islam and social welfare in the organisation's bulletin (on a side note serving as an example of the ways in which the organisation seeks to generate professional authority by using statistics and references to international organisations):

> In fact, the United Nations reports on poverty indicate that more than one quarter of a billion people or 20 per cent of the world population are poor and that 40 per cent of them live in the Muslim world while reports from the UNHCR reveal the presence of 10 million refugees all over the world, 71 per cent of them from the Muslim world and that 6 million children die annually of starvation.[20]

In this perspective, IIROSA and IICO help Muslims, not so much because they are fellow brothers and sisters in an Islamic *umma*, but because they are poor. And as such, the two organisations attempt to maintain a particularistic focus on Muslims without challenging international discourses of universalism and non-discrimination.

The rationale of aid: A religious duty and a moral responsibility

But why should organisations like IIROSA and IICO engage in aid provision at all? Underlying conceptions of poverty, a dignified life and a strengthened *umma* is a rationale that goes beyond the diagnosis of problems and the formulation of visions, answering more fundamental questions as to why the organisations engage in this work: Is it a religious obligation, for instance, or a human duty? There is a strong motivational element in this, outlining why people should support this work.[21] Often, this also entails a certain educational element; when trying to motivate people to support the organisation and donate money to aid provision, the organisations send subtle messages of moral education, instructing people in how to feel and act towards the suffering (Chouliaraki 2010).

Overall, IIROSA and IICO explain their involvement in aid provision as 'a religious duty' and 'a moral obligation', referring to Islamic sayings.[22] 'There are many verses and traditions in the Qur'an that give us instructions to do charity work. When you give to the poor, you don't just give to the poor, you give to Allah as well,' says an IICO staff member in Kuwait. And IIROSA presents its Annual Report 2011–2012 with a quote from the Qur'an: 'Those who have faith and do righteous deeds, they are the best of creatures.'[23] To comply with these obligations is not only to be a good Muslim; it is to follow the example of Islam's 'good men', in particular the Prophet Muhammad, who is regarded as the perfect man (*al-insan al-kamil*). It is about following the 'prophetic guidance'[24] and 'noble examples of charitable work in Islamic history',[25] thus building on, and passing on, religious traditions and practices. The IICO tells us that the organisation 'came to life as a result of an outcry Qaradawi made',[26] prompting 'people with good intentions and will' to respond. Aid, in other words, is the work of good men, practising 'Islamic high virtues of generosity, brotherhood, equality among mankind.'[27] Three different rationales substantiate these claims to a religious duty, each leading to slightly different conceptions of givers and recipients in the aid chain.

Religious rewards: 'A good deed that lasts for you'

First, the provision of aid is a way to gain religious rewards and a place in Paradise. According to Islamic traditions, when doing good deeds for the sake of Allah, be it prayer, *zakat* or other good deeds, a Muslim collects religious rewards, known as *thawab*—the opposite of *ithim*, which refers to the negative marks recorded by Allah whenever one commits a sin. When a person dies, Allah considers that person's account of deeds before deciding whether he or she goes to heaven or hell. Among the good deeds that one can carry out for the sake of Allah, doing charity, helping others, paying *zakat* and *sadaqa* are considered some of the most important, and consequently, some that result in the most rewards. What the donor gives is not important; what is important is the intention (*niyya*) and the act of giving. This is perhaps most clearly expressed in the frequently mentioned saying from the Qur'an: 'If you save one person it is as if you saved all of humankind.' It is not important whether you save one or hundred people, but that you save—in other words, it is not the result of the action, but the action itself (and the underlying intention) that matters.

In this perspective, the aid chain is a relationship of reciprocity (Mauss 1990 [1923]): the donor gives something to the recipient, but gets something in return. Campaign slogans promise donors 'a chance for more rewards from God,' 'a good deed that lasts for you,' and 'a one-time donation but a continuous reward for you.'[28] Likewise, different projects are presented by reference to common religious sayings. In the presentation of a project for distribution of fridges to poor families, for instance, the PR material urges the donor to '[r]emember that whoever makes it easy for people, God will make it easy for him on the Day of Resurrection.'[29] Another obvious example of this is orphan sponsorship, consistently legitimated and motivated by reference to the Prophet Muhammad. 'The Prophet Muhammad himself was an orphan and he said that whoever took care of an orphan would be like this with him in heaven,' people tell me repeatedly, illustrating the closeness between the sponsor and the Prophet by holding together two fingers. 'That's why we have this programme'.

A consequence of this focus on rewards as the underlying rationale for aid is that the donor comes to plays a central and powerful role in the aid chain. 'My intention is to help people get rewards from God,' the former IICO director says. This priority is echoed in one of IICO's publications: '[T]he IICO seeks to achieve two goals: first to provide a long-lasting source of livelihood for the needy; second, to encourage donors to be generous so that they earn, by the will of Allah, a meritorious and long-lasting reward.'[30] Addressed in a language of sentimental gratitude, donors are praised, as in an IIROSA Annual Report: 'Our honourable philanthropists […] the meticulous relievers and rescuers […] May God Almighty bless them, their progeny and property!'[31] Likewise, the organisations hail their donors through the award of special memberships, hierarchising donors into 'Platinum members', 'Golden members' and

'Silver members'. At the IICO's twenty-fifth anniversary in May 2010, a substantial part of the ceremony was dedicated to the celebration of individual donors. And when Abdul Razzaq al-Sani, lawyer, member of National Assembly, business man, and one of IICO's foremost donors, died in December 2009, a lengthy obituary was posted on the website, celebrating him as 'one of the leading philanthropists who have donated a lot of their money in alleviating the suffering of the poor and needy.'[32]

Another consequence is the invisibility of the recipient. If the purpose of aid is to ensure rewards for the donor, the recipient easily becomes irrelevant as anything but an instrument to obtain these rewards.[33] A look through one of IIROSA's bulletins or IICO's magazines testifies to this tendency. The few photos of recipients rarely portray individuals, but show groups of people—desperately reaching out for food, working in the field or standing in front of a newly built school (always in uniforms)—often photographed from a distance, and sometimes even with their backs turned to the camera. Seldom presented by name, profession or even gender, the recipients remain devoid of individualising features (Chouliaraki 2010:110), representing a generalised, impoverished other, or, as Stirrat and Henkel (1997:69) note, 'the undifferentiated poor'. In contrast, pictures show donors at meetings or in ceremonies, always well-dressed, smiling and referred to with name and title, emphasising their importance in the chain of aid.

This tendency is further strengthened by the tradition of conferring almost unconditional power to the donor. According to Islamic traditions, the donor decides how money should be spent; as a high-level staff member in IICO says: 'It is a religious rule that we should follow the orders of the donor.' At times, the willingness to satisfy donor wishes is even stronger than the wish to comply with common religious principles. An IICO staff member in Kuwait says:

> Sometimes the donor says: "I want to build a mosque for my zakat money." There are eight different ways of paying zakat. But it's not normal to build a mosque for the zakat money. So we have to ask the council, and they can say, in this specific situation, yes it is permitted.

Likewise, a top manager of IIROSA states that in order to comply with donors' wishes, the organisation focuses primarily on orphan sponsorship and mosque building, even though health projects may be more needed: 'The orphan programme is the biggest—people feel sympathy with the orphans, they like to help them. The second largest is the building of mosques; the Prophet said that whoever builds a mosque, God will build him a castle. So people like to pay money to that.' This almost unconditional power of the donor is not seen as entirely unproblematic for staff in the two organisations. At least one person expressed slight frustration with donors, telling me about the difficulties he had trying to convince them to start funding other kinds of activities:

> It is hard work to convince the donors. They want to see buildings. We would tell them about our training activities, capacity building, vocational training and so on. And they would say, good, that's great, but I want to sponsor a building. They want somewhere they can place a sign and you can't do that on a capacity building project. This is often important to them, because they want to honour deceased family members with a building.

As we shall see in Chapter 7, this conflict between donors' wishes to live up to religious obligations and the organisation's wish to provide what they consider to be relevant aid is much more pronounced in Islamic Relief and Muslim Aid.

'Solidarity between the sons of the *umma*'

Another motivational frame—slightly different, but not necessarily contradicting—turns on notions of solidarity. Solidarity is about a mutual interdependence among people, stemming from what they have in common. This community obliges its members to stand together and show solidarity, supporting one another. To let another person down, to turn one's back on a needy person in the community, is to pretend there is no community—it is to break the bond of solidarity. According to this rationale, Muslims should engage in the provision of aid to the poor, because they are part of the same religious community, the *umma*, and as such, are obliged to help one another. As IICO formulated it:

> [Charity] is one of the faith's most effective tools for spreading the values of solidarity and support between the sons of the Ummah. It encourages them to remain united like one body, when one part of it suffers a complaint, all other parts join in, sharing in the sleeplessness and fever.[34]

Using terms such as an 'Islamic society', an 'Islamic brotherhood' and a 'Muslim nation', the two NGOs nurse a strong sense of solidarity (Bayat 2005), emphasising 'ties of interdependence, compassion and tender sympathy'[35] between members of this community and pointing out the responsibility of members to take care of one another. As noted in an IIROSA publication, the organisation 'connects the kind donor with his needy brethren around the world and augments the spirit of Islamic solidarity.'[36] The donor gives to a fellow Muslim brother (or sister) in a country far away, because he sees himself and his fellow brother as members of a deep horizontal brotherhood, the *umma* (Kochuyt 2009:106). An IICO headquarter staff member explains his commitment like this: 'A Muslim should help his brothers and sisters. In Islam, it is not allowed to sleep when your neighbour is hungry.' By receiving the gift of solidarity, the recipient likewise aligns him or herself with the *umma* (Kochuyt 2009:110). As an IIROSA publication notes, 'the Islamic society is a closely knitted society where the well-off helps the poor and the elder cares for the younger',[37] and furthermore, helping the poor and needy 'illustrates the principle of solidarity that Islam encourages and calls for'.[38]

Chouliaraki (2010) claims that relations between donors and recipients are often based on what we may call 'a logic of complicity': because the donor witnesses the suffering of the recipient, he or she is complicit and therefore obliged to help. This sense of complicity is further strengthened, she argues, by the legacy of the colonial past of the West, evoking a sense of responsibility on the part of the West for the misfortunes of the developing world, and consequently for contributing to redressing these. As such, the relationship between donor and recipient is 'anchored on the colonial gaze' (2010:110); it is an affective regime of collective 'guilt, shame and indignation' (2010:111). This explanatory model, however, seems to be of somewhat limited use outside a Western donor context. While Muslim donors from Saudi Arabia and Kuwait are obviously not immune to human sentiments of guilt, they have no memory of a colonising past and as such, their relationship to the recipients is not— to the same degree at least—weighed down by a massive collective guilt. Instead of evoking emotions of guilt and shame, photos and narratives of the suffering poor can hope to stir sentiments of solidarity. Building on notions of a 'Muslim nation' and an 'Islamic society' and interpellating recipients as Muslim subjects, using terms such as 'brothers', 'orphans' or simply 'poor and needy Muslims', the organisations appeal to a common Muslim solidarity, encouraging donors to assist—not out of guilt, but out of fraternity. 'I feel responsible for these people, I cannot leave them,' says a staff member in IIROSA's Jordan office, quoted above. 'It's like a big family.' In this, there may be a collective memory of suffering and poverty, building on experiences not many generations away. Many Muslim families, whether in Saudi Arabia, Kuwait or elsewhere in the Middle East, were once poor too, or know people who were.

While the reciprocity rationale may create an invisible recipient, the solidarity rationale creates a personalised recipient. Turning on notions of family and brotherhood, this rationale encourages conceptions of a personal and intimate relationship between recipient and donor (whether understood in terms of the NGO or the individual donor). A former IIROSA staff member tells me about his experiences in Sudan, emphasising this special bond of solidarity and family between Muslims:

> When we went to Sudan, we would wear the same clothes as the Sudanese, we would eat the same food, do the same things—and many people there speak Arabic. So they felt that we were closer to them. We gave aid with no strings attached, we considered ourselves brothers in humanity. I felt that we were much closer to them—because we share the same life habits. Likewise, in Afghanistan, people received us with deep respect and love. They might have received the Christian organisations with respect as well—but not necessarily with love.

According to some staff, their understanding of aid is different from the way many other (non-Muslim/Christian/Western) organisations understand it: 'Compared to other organisations, we have a different way of dealing with people,' an IIROSA staff member says. In other organisations, their employees do not care about the work or the beneficiaries: 'They don't have the same feeling of family as we have, that the orphans are a part of our family, that it's about humanity, family, about making the orphans feel important. For them, it's routine, it's just a job they need to do, it's about finishing work to get home to your own family,' an IROSA staff member says. Emphasising the sincerity, trustworthiness, and persistence of staff members, the organisations display a personalised, emotional rhetoric. 'We care about the feelings of the needy', as staff members often say. Staff have 'taken [it] upon their shoulders'[39] to save the poor; they have 'managed to alleviate many problems related to poverty,'[40] bringing 'hope to the poor.'[41] In this perspective, an aid based on religious solidarity comes to stand in stark contrast to values of professionalism.[42] According to the rationale of religious solidarity, personal care and compassion are more important qualities than efficiency and professionalism; in fact, professionalism may even be counterproductive to the sense of solidarity between recipient and donor. Thus, when IIROSA and IICO frame themselves as professional organisations, it is a professionalism that does not extend to relations with recipients. An illustrative example of this is an incident an IIROSA top manager tells me about. He had been invited to a coordination meeting with other organisations working with orphans to discuss possibilities for coordination and cooperation:

> Some suggested making a control mechanism, to make sure that orphans don't get money from two different organisations. But I didn't like this idea. I was the only one who protested. I don't think we should minimise the income of the orphans. This is their only salary, and 20 or 30 dollars is not a lot. Some of them need more, they might have bigger families or different circumstances. You can't give the same to all. I don't think we should give all the same. So we cancelled this coordination. One sponsor for each orphan is not enough, they need more sponsors, at least two. […] I was the only one who thought this way, but I have worked with orphans for 18 years, and I feel like their father, I feel responsible for them.

While predicated on notions of personalised care and compassion, at the same time this relationship carries inherent risks of hierarchy and inequality. In the personalised relation of solidarity, the reward is gratitude as much as religious rewards. In an IIROSA magazine, letters from orphan children to their donors are reprinted, lifting recipients out of the mass of 'undifferentiated poor' to deliver a personalised message from the recipient to the donor. In a language of sentimental gratitude, one child writes:

> My dear sponsor. May Allah reward your goodness because you sponsor me and support me, together with Allah, so that I can make my hopes and ambitions come true and be of use to my religion and my community and my family, and I pray that Allah will save you on the Day of Judgement and that you will be saved from the torment of Allah, since you helped me.[43]

Gratitude relies on the social logic of the gift between unequal parties. The gift without reciprocation binds the grateful receiver into a nexus of obligations and duties towards the generous donor; the recipient becomes a perpetual object of the donor's generosity (Chouliaraki 2010:113). As such, the rationale of solidarity may end up creating an equally hierarchical relationship as that of religious rewards—not between a visible donor and an invisible recipient, but between a generous donor and a grateful recipient.

Islamic rights of the poor

There is a third frequently referred-to frame that somehow contrasts the two interpretations above, to a much larger degree emphasising the perspective of the poor. In this perspective, social assistance should not be considered a gift or a favour from the wealthy person to the poor; and it should not be seen as the poor person's begging. Instead, *zakat* is a duty imposed by Allah upon the wealthy, and it is a right endowed by Allah to the poor. As noted on IICO's website: 'Zakat is the third pillar of Islam and it is an obligatory payment made to those Muslims who are in financial need.'[44] A hungry person has the right to receive a share of the meal of the well-fed person and is allowed to use force if he or she is denied this right (Benthall 1999:36). Thus, social assistance is framed as a right the poor can claim rather than a gift he or she must accept from a benevolent donor, whether given in solidarity or with the aim of getting religious rewards. Underlying this frame is an understanding of wealth as a gift or a loan from Allah, rather than a reward. Likewise, poverty is not a punishment from Allah, but a visitation or trial that can come upon everybody. Therefore, the poor must be treated with respect and dignity. As the director of IICO explains:

> Is poverty a punishment for something? No, Islam is not like that at all. Islam doesn't have to do with pessimism, unlogic things. There is always a reason. Poverty is something that exists and you have to get rid of it. To leave your children rich is better than to leave them poor is a saying in Islam. You have to worship and you have to work. To give is better than to take, and the upper hand is better than the lower—but both are good. So it's not bad to be poor.

In this perspective, the donor comes to play a much less dominant role. With the donor out of sight, this leaves room for increased focus on recipients and alternative ways of conceptualising the chain of aid as a relationship based on notions of equality and justice. 'We make people feel the importance of their existence,' an IIROSA staff member says. 'People can contribute to building society, they are special. The poor are not just somebody you can treat like you want to. They deserve respect.' This is often explained by reference to Islam: 'We take this from a hadith by al-Hakim. It says that you can't buy people with your money. You have to deal with them in a respectful way, with good manners and a smile,' the IIROSA staff member says. Others mention the Muslim tradition of making sure that the person receiving the money has the upper hand as a symbol of the uniqueness of Muslim organisations: 'The recipient should not have the lower hand. We care about these details, this is important to us,' says a person in IICO. Interestingly, despite obvious similarities, this discourse of Islamic rights is rarely, if ever, combined with a discourse on universal human rights. Historically, many Muslims have been sceptical of the concept of human rights, in particular, seeing these as neo-colonial attempts at promoting particular Western values. In particular women's rights and reproductive rights have been subject to criticism, seen to be counterproductive to religious values (a criticism that is shared by the Catholic Church and many Pentecostal churches). Thus, although alignment with a human rights discourse would facilitate inclusion in the culture of development aid, this might at the same time jeopardise IIROSA and IICO's relations to other, more conservative, Muslim organisations and individual donors.

Strategies of aid: Relief, da'wa, education, and empowerment

'Our strategy is to present an Islamic model of integrated modern charitable work,' IICO declares on its website. But what does this mean? Having outlined the vision and rationale of the organisations, the following section takes a closer look at their strategies, exploring the specific remedies or solutions and the general means and tactics for achieving their vision. In concrete terms, the two organisations seek to obtain their vision through activities such as 'relief', 'community development', 'social welfare', 'orphan care', 'education', and 'drilling of wells', but also 'building of mosques', 'ifthar for fasting people', 'Islamic centres', 'Holy Qur'an and da'wa', and 'aid to Muslim minorities', echoing the language of Islamic aid more than that of mainstream development. For both organisations, the 'social welfare' programme makes up the largest activity, including orphan sponsorships. For IICO, this programme also includes mosque building, ifthar and Qurbani, while in IIROSA these activities are included under 'Engineering' and 'Community development and seasonal projects'. See Tables 5.2 and 5.3 for an overview.

Rather than engaging in a comprehensive description of these activities, the following section argues that they can be described in terms of four overall strategies denoting different repertoires of action. While often overlapping, each of these strategies presents different ways of conceptualising the provision of aid: one frame turns on the provision of immediate relief; another on mission and worship; a third on education; and a fourth on empowerment.

Table 5.2: IICO, activities (2011)[45]

Activity	Per cent
Social projects	48
Health	16
Relief	16
Cultural and da'wa projects	11
Education	8
Production projects	1
Total	100

Table 5.3: IIROSA, activities (2007)[46]

Activity	Per cent
Social welfare	39
Engineering (wells and mosques)	18
Urgent relief program	15
Community development and seasonal projects	15
Healthcare	6
Educational welfare	5
Holy Qur'an and da'wa	3
Total	101*

*Numbers have been rounded up/down which is why the total slightly exceeds 100 per cent

Aid as relief: 'Food for the hungry'

One strategy of IICO and IIROSA is relief or *igatha*—the straightforward and immediate provision of goods and services, attending to the urgent needs of the poor. As is stated in an IIROSA report, '[the organisation] strives to provide food for the hungry, medical care for the sick, clothes for the unclothed, helps wipe the tears of the orphans, provides shelter, social and educational care for those who have lost their homes due to wars or natural disasters.'[47] Similarly, IICO declares that 'IICO emergency relief program offers immediate help for the victims of war, civil conflicts, famines and natural disasters. In case of disasters, IICO provides immediate and sustained relief funding for basic needs, medical aid, and daily living requirements for the victims.'[48]

The strategy of relief is shaped by sentiments of spontaneity, immediacy, and urgency, rather than long-term planning and sustainability. This idealisation of immediacy is particularly explicit in the organisations' origin myths: 'It wasn't planned or structured—no, it was an immediate response to people in need,' says one of the founders of IIROSA, referring to the establishment of the organisation. 'It's just like Bob Geldof—he never thought of establishing an organisation, he just wanted to help, but it mushroomed from there.' The emphasis on immediacy echoes ideologies of traditional humanitarian organisations in the West, pointing to differences between ideologies of development and humanitarianism. As Bornstein and Redfield (2007:4) note, in contrast to the long-term strategies of development, humanitarianism is inherently presentist, focusing on the immediate needs of living humans in distress: 'the lives and welfare of those now living fundamentally matter and cannot be consciously sacrificed in the pursuit of other goals.'[49] In terms of concrete activities the medical caravans epitomise this aspect, characterised by their temporary, flexible and immediate nature. Popular in both IIROSA and IICO, the caravans consist in a team of (often volunteer) doctors and nurses who travel through a country, organising consultations and carrying out simple surgeries on the way (Kaag 2008:10). Speaking on the occasion of the World Health Day on 7 April 2011, IIROSA's secretary general said that IIROSA, with the help of volunteer Saudi specialists, had conducted heart surgeries and catheter operations in 'a number of Arab and Islamic countries', including Yemen, Egypt, Syria, Morocco, Pakistan and Kazakhstan, benefitting almost 1,200 children. He also noted that the organisation had recently organised four campaigns for optical surgeries and eyesight corrections in Indonesia, Sri Lanka, Nigeria and Burkina Faso, operating more than 2,000 people and distributing more than 10,000 eyeglasses.[50]

As was also the case with many of the early humanitarian organisations in the West, religion is consistently framed as an integrated part of relief in IIROSA and IICO. 'It's all in Islam,' people say when I ask about the relation between aid and religion. Echoing the organisations' multifaceted and holistic understanding of poverty, the prognostic frame of relief is inseparable from Islamic frames. 'This project represents Islam!' an article about IIROSA's medical caravans declares. Several examples testify to this fundamental integration of relief and Islam. Staff and organisational material consistently equate activities such as surgeries, food aid and religious care as part of relief. IICO's website, for instance, notes that the most needed services for the poor include not only orphanages and water wells, but also mosques. In fact, the construction of mosques and wells is often combined in many of IIROSA's and IICO's projects. Motivated by a wish to facilitate the Islamic tradition of ablution (ritual purification before praying), the organisations often build a well next to a mosque (Kaag 2008:10). At the same time, the well of course serves common aid purposes, offering poor people access to clean water. IIROSA's *ifthar* meals during Ramadan also illustrate this largely unproblematic integration of relief and Islam, serving at once as humanitarian food distribution to many thousands of poor families, and as celebration of an important Islamic tradition.[51]

Aid as *da'wa*: 'The best thing to do is to get people to Islam'

A second, and more controversial, way of framing strategies for aid provision turns on education about Islam, or *da'wa*. Through a wide range of missionary activities, the IICO and IIROSA seek to educate poor and needy Muslims about Islam, raising 'the consciousness of people about the magnificence of the true Islam'[52] with the purpose of helping them to 'preserve their culture and identity'[53] and 'boost the morale [...] spiritually,'[54] and by extension strengthening the Muslim *umma*. The most concrete and visible examples of this are the numerous mosques that the organisations have built. As noted in an IIROSA publication: '[T]housands of mosques have been built, with an average of one mosque a day.'[55] In Bangladesh alone, IIROSA has built almost 600 mosques, and IICO, under the auspices of the Kuwait Joint Relief Committee, around 1,000. Other activities include construction and running of Qur'an schools, training of religious teachers, establishment of Qur'an study circles, distribution of Qur'ans and other religious material as well as the launching of radio channels with religious contents.

Unlike the strategy of relief, which is promoted openly by staff and in organisational material, narratives about *da'wa* are ambiguous and diverging—some people speak openly about these activities, while others try to downplay them—and it is difficult, at least for a Western non-Muslim, to get a complete picture of their extent. Kaag (2008:6) had the same experience. In her analysis of transnational Muslim NGOs in Chad, she writes that most of the NGOs spoke quite openly about their material assistance, but stayed silent about their *da'wa* activities. This is a sign of the hegemony of mainstream development norms, requiring a sharp distinction between mission and relief. In this perspective, *da'wa* is not a legitimate activity in itself, but must be justified in order to be accepted.

The organisations present a number of reasons for their engagement in *da'wa* activities, seeking to justify this engagement in different ways. A common argument is that the organisations simply respond to the demands of the poor. Poor people contact the IICO or the IIROSA, asking for assistance in building or re-building a mosque in their village. Another argument focuses on the donors: they want to spend their money on mosques, and the organisations have to obey them, complying with religious principles as described above. A third way of justifying *da'wa* as a legitimate aid strategy is to frame it in terms of a competition with Christian organisations. Using a language of cultural sensitivity and identity, many argue that the aggressively proselytising efforts of Christian organisations have forced them to respond with similar measures, protecting the faith of fellow Muslims. 'If we build a mosque, suddenly there will be three or four churches surrounding it,' says one person, a top manager in IIROSA's headquarters, implying that this religious invasion has to be countered in order to protect the identity of Muslims. As noted above, this was in fact a particularly strong motivational factor for the IICO, which was established to 'protect Muslims from those who were striving to change their faith and obliterate their identity'.[56] The concept of the Christian threat continues to play a role in IICO discourses. At the inauguration of the new IICO headquarters in 2000, Qaradawi gave a speech in which he emphasised the necessity for charitable organisations to unite Islamic efforts and gather the Muslims 'especially because the church organisations have allocated more than one billion dollars to take the Muslims away from their religion'.[57] Similarly, at a 2010 workshop for Qur'an recitation, the IICO chairman spoke about 'evil campaigns against the *umma*,' 'organised intellectual and cultural invasion' and 'increasingly fierce campaigns.'[58] Finally, and perhaps most common, is the argument that the activities the organisations carry out are in fact not 'real *da'wa*', based on a distinction between activities aimed at conversion and activities aimed at information and education. This, in turn, is often linked to a distinction between Muslims and non-Muslims— what Roald (1994:54) refers to as 'home missions' or 'domestic missions': 'We only inform and educate fellow Muslims; we do not try to convert non-Muslims,' people often say. In this, IIROSA and IICO distinguish themselves from other Muslim NGOs such as al Makka al Mukarrama, from Saudi Arabia, and Direct Aid, from Kuwait, both of which carry out 'real *da'wa*', i.e. missionary work among non-Muslims (Kaag 2008:11). One person, from the IICO headquarters in Kuwait, explains:

> There are specific organisations that carry out da'wa, there are rules for this. Da'wa should not be aggressive, it should always be peaceful and nice. In our organisation, we don't do da'wa, we just present Islam. It is not about conversion, it's just presentation for those who are interested. We cannot ask the poor who is dying from hunger, 'what is your religion?' But we work mostly in Islamic countries, so most people are Islamic. There are no conditions for our work. In the beginning of the Islamic era, Muslims went to Asia, and many people there converted—not because they were forced to, but by example. People admired the Muslims, they were kind, trustworthy, they never lied. The best way to promote Islam is behaviour, not talk.

Another person, a former IIROSA trustee, says:

> The best thing you can do is to get people to Islam. It's our duty to salvage people of the world. I will not deny that we are influenced by this, but it is not a point of access. We don't use charity as a hook to get people to Islam. We tell them about Islam wherever we can—mostly orally, because many people cannot read. Islam is simple, it's a religion that gives you an immediate relationship with Allah and that's appealing to many people. A lot of people are impressed with this—not just in Africa, but in Europe as well. But da'wa is not a focal point for the IIROSA, it might be for Direct Aid. IIROSA works mostly in Islamic communities, so preaching is not really a problem, it's more about guiding people from their bad habits such as smoking, violence, improving their individual and social habits.

In this perspective, IIROSA and IICO staff do not consider themselves advocates of *da'wa*, but as Islamic educators, informing fellow Muslims about Islamic values, norms and morality and protecting their cultural identity. 'When Qaradawi started the IICO, he said "We don't want others to become Muslim. Our aim is to make people stay in Islam. We want to improve their social and educational status, we want to strengthen their faith,'" an IICO high-level staff member explains. This way of framing missionary activities is closely related to the third strategy, presenting aid as a matter of (Islamic) education, and covering activities such as the establishment and running of schools, universities, orphanages and day-care centres.

Aid as (Islamic) education: Teaching right and wrong

Historically, the provision of education has been a core activity of both IICO and IIROSA, and in both organisations, the education department was one of the first departments to be established. IICO supports hundreds of orphanages, schools, institutes and community centres as well as eight universities in Asia and Africa:[59]

> Through their educational activities, the IICO seeks to 'provide high-standard educational services to a generation who, hopefully, will be the future leaders of the community [...] able to deal with the different aspects of modernity as well as to maintain the fundamental values of Islam and the Muslim nation.[60]

Likewise, one of IIROSA's objectives is '[t]o help young pupils overcome the darkness of ignorance, disease and poverty while ensuring a sound moral education for them.'[61] In a 2008 interview with Arab News, IIROSA's secretary general stressed that the organisation was 'keen to contribute to the spread of education and reduction of illiteracy in Islamic countries and Muslim communities in non-Islamic countries' (Ibrahim 2010b). According to the secretary general, IIROSA has provided education to more than 31,000 students in 23 countries, contributing to financing the establishment and operation of several schools, institutes, colleges, and universities.[62] Apart from schools and universities, both organisations run several orphanages and other orphan's programmes, providing education to more than 100,000 children.

On the one hand, the education strategy is often contrasted with *da'wa*: *da'wa* is about prayer and rituals, which may be important, but Islam is more than prayer and rituals, and this 'more' is what the strategy of education can bring: 'We teach them how to deal with other people,' says the IIROSA country director in Jordan, adding: 'For me, it's about showing the children that Islam is not just about praying and going to the mosque, it is about dealing with people in a good way, whatever their religion is.' On the other hand, this strategy is also different from relief: 'It's not just about relief, not just about giving the poor help,' the director of IICO says. Instead, it is about educating people in a holistic manner, raising them to become good Muslim citizens in modern society: 'We offer them lectures about different things—morals, social life, how to deal with other people, how to build good people. We raise them to be good citizens. If they are good, this will be reflected in society,' says a teacher in one of IIROSA's day-care centres. IICO's curricula in its so-called model schools also reflect this approach. Through courses in topics such as 'Practical fiqh', 'Faith and belief', and 'Social revival',[63] the organisation seeks to 'help produce efficient and trustworthy cadres and leaders who can participate in various activities in the society, and who can also preserve its great values and maintain its identity'.[64] And in IIROSA's orphanages and day-care centres, the children learn about topics such as social skills and good manners, health and hygiene, praying and fasting through lectures, sports and creative activities. Through life-style evangelism (Bornstein 2003), staff seek to 'build good people'. The IIROSA teacher says: 'The most important thing is to teach them what is right and wrong, especially based on Islam. So when they go out into society, they can recognise the right, they know what is good and what is bad. They learn through our example, through role models.'

In this perspective, being a good Muslim is not only or even primarily about learning the Qur'an by heart and going to the mosque; it is about being an active citizen and about treating others well. In this focus on 'the right behaviour', the strategy echoes earlier traditions of Islamic education, aimed at inculcating *adab*, or morals, manners and human conduct, among students (Siddiqui 1997:429). It is about becoming 'a righteous man' as Muhammad Qutb put it in his book *Program for Islamic Education* (in Arabic, *Manhaj at-tarbiya al-islamiyya*) (Roald 1994:80), in turn contributing to the construction of a just and well-functioning society, the *umma*. By building strong leaders and good citizens, the organisations contribute to strengthening the Muslim community—as reflected in one of IICO's mottos: 'Build a school: Revive a nation.'[65] Echoing Hassan al-Banna's ideas of *tarbiya* as an important tool for building up the Muslim *umma*, an IICO magazine states that 'IICO considers education one of the important factors for the development of poor communities through the elimination of illiteracy, the fight against ignorance and backwardness and preservation of the identity of the Islamic Umma.'[66]

This focus on life-style evangelism over Qur'an recitation may sometimes contract with donors' expectations. An IIROSA staff member in

Jordan explains: 'We show the orphans what Islam is like in an indirect manner, through our examples, through the way we do things. In Saudi Arabia, they do da'wa activities, they teach about the Quran, they give lectures, they explain about Islam. Here, we do it more indirectly.' A small anecdote serves to illustrate this. Once a year, staff members in IIROSA's orphanages and day-care centres fill out a file about each child, to be sent to the child's sponsor in Saudi Arabia. Here, staff have to list a wide range of data about the child, including information about their health, educational status, hobbies and religiosity. 'Is the child religious?' is one question, to be answered by one of the following four options: 'Yes, he prays a lot', 'He reads a lot about Islam', 'He is not old enough' and finally 'He does not know a lot about Islam'. Another question refers to the child's abilities to memorise the Qur'an, and if so, which parts of the Qur'an and what Qur'an school he goes to. Visiting a day-care centre in Jordan, I ask the teacher what consequences it has if a child cannot memorise the Qur'an or does not pray. 'Most of the children pray,' she says and sends me a sly smile. 'Some don't memorise a lot, but they always know a short verse or two, so we write that. Of course we encourage them to learn more, but not everyone can memorise the Quran. It's not for everybody.' Instead, the teacher emphasises creativity as an important part of education. 'With the kids, it's all about learning through having fun. We do theatre, we go camping, we do all kinds of things. We look on the internet for new ideas. What's important is to keep them updated, to be creative, to have fun,' she says, telling me that last year, she made a big tent and invited an old woman to come and tell the children about the old days. 'Children love that,' she says. 'We don't keep them in class all day, it's boring for them.'

It is the same teacher who shows me the classroom briefly described in the introduction to this book, giving an insight into the ways in which IIROSA staff teach children to become 'righteous men'. The room is small, perhaps 20 square meters, and the colourful scenario that the teacher has built from paper, clay, plastic and other material takes up almost all the space. This is to explain heaven and hell to the children in a way they can understand, she tells me, pointing to two child-size graves in the middle of the room. One grave symbolises hell; it is grey and broken, and on top of it are worms and soil; the other, symbolising heaven, is showered with green leaves. On the sides of the graves are two small staircases, one painted red, the other green. On the walls next to the staircases are handmade posters with quotes and drawings, outlining the doors to heaven or hell. The posters next to the red staircase, leading to hell, list the sins of lying, adultery, not wearing hijab, gossip, treating people badly, and praying at the wrong time. The green staircase, leading to heaven, lists the virtues of prayer, *sadaqa*, jihad, to regret sins, to live a good and balanced life, to forgive people, to fast (not only during Ramadan but once or twice a week), and to be good with one's parents. Some posters quote different Qur'an verses, or *ayas*, to be discussed in class. One tells the story of a group of people in hell, trying to argue for their innocence. They tell God that they are not to blame for what they did, because they just followed the orders from their leader. But this is wrong, the teacher says, of course you have to think for yourself. Another poster lists all the signs of Doomsday, accompanied by quotes from the Qur'an; yet another illustrates the temptations of drinking and dancing with little drawings. In a corner is an envelope full of little pieces of paper, each with a short handwritten quote: 'Remember to pray,' 'Forgive people for what they do', 'Please your parents' and so on. The teacher tells me that the children have to pick a quote each and explain to the others what it means, thereby practising their presentation and argumentation skills.

When framing education as a relevant strategy, IICO and IIROSA staff often focus on bridging Islam and modernity. In IIROSA and IICO schools, for instance, students are taught mathematics, physics and computer science, along with religious studies. According to the IICO, it is about 'striking a balance between Sharia sciences and modern disciplines to train the graduates to respond to the requirements of society'.[67] Likewise, staff members underline that their educational material is written by experienced and well-educated professors and has been subject to scientific and linguistic reviews, 'in tune with the modern and state-of-the-art-educational services'.[68] In this, the organisations clearly rely on the thinking of Qaradawi. In his perspective, Islamic education and 'rational sciences' (*al-'ulum al-'aqliyya*) are not in opposition to each other; on the contrary, they reinforce and are mutually constitutive of each other. In fact, specialising in the rational sciences benefits the community and is tantamount to fulfilling the imperatives of Islam (Hatina 2006:192). An IICO staff member in Jordan says that Qaradawi is a model for Islamic education: 'He read modern economy and Islamic science, what we call fiqh, and that made him able to compare the old and the new. He tries to make a model that combines the two.' At the same time, 'Western' concepts, techniques and approaches are often included, explicitly recognised for their 'Westernness' and praised for their modern qualities such as professionalism, efficiency, and scientific rigour. Kaag (2008:5) claims that in Chad, Arabic Muslim NGOs seek to provide an antidote to the effects of Western colonialism and contemporary influences through Islamic education. But, at least for the IIROSA and the IICO, the relationship is not that simple—something which the discussion of organisational authority also showed. Breaking with traditional Salafi scepticism of foreign innovations (*bid'a*), but also with Banna's scepticism of Western modernity, they promote a kind of Islamic integrationism (Schulze 2000), advocating the integration of at least certain elements of Western traditions into the provision of Islamic aid.

Aid as empowerment: 'Give a man an axe'

Recent years have witnessed the emergence of a fourth strategy in IICO and IIROSA. This is the strategy of 'empowerment' (in Arabic *tawkeel* or *tafweedh*), underlying and indirectly assumed in IIROSA,[69] but explicitly pronounced in IICO through its 'productive projects':

> The IICO gives priority to productive projects that provide job opportunities for people, such as factories, farms, training institutes and other similar projects. In doing so, it empowers people, by the Grace of Allah, to work and earn their livelihood, away from the shame of begging or the humiliation of asking people for help.[70]

The director of the IICO's office in Jordan tells me that he introduced the 'productive projects' in Jordan a few years ago, inspired by the Zakat House in Kuwait, which offers poor people small loans with no interest, and the Grameen Bank in Bangladesh, one of the pioneers among microfinance institutions. Today, the director says, more than 1,000 people have taken loans with the IICO office in Jordan, and 'productive projects' have spread to other offices in Asia and Africa. In 2005, the IICO headquarters encouraged their country offices to increase their focus on microfinance projects that would help empower people. In 2007, the organisation set up a specialised unit, the Community Development and Productive Projects Unit, with the purpose of promoting these projects, and in 2009, the headquarters decided to launch a programme costing several million dollars, implementing productive projects in countries such as Uganda and Sudan and supported financially by the Islamic Development Bank. The principles of IICO's productive projects are the same as in mainstream microfinance projects, except for the fact that no interest is taken: The organisation provides poor families with small loans between US$ 700 and 1,400, which have to be paid back in small instalments starting after three months. Assisted by the IICO or one of its partner organisations, the family then uses this money to establish a grocery store, a carpentry workshop or another income-generating project. More than 96 per cent have paid back their loan, a success rate that staff ascribe to the close monitoring of and support to families who take loans: 'We follow the families closely, we are active, we make agreements with the families and make them sign a form. After two months, we go and see how they are doing and to make sure they don't just sell their equipment,' says the IICO country office director in Jordan. Adding to this is, according to him, a mechanism of social control and solidarity: if a family does not pay, the whole community will be denied any new loans. But if the money is paid back it is then used to fund new productive projects.

IICO's concept of empowerment is based on core principles of Islam. 'Our gracious religion, Islam, values and promotes hard work and productivity, and it discourages indolence and dependence on others,' an IICO brochure states.[71] Various hadiths are used to define, explain and legitimise the concept in Islamic terms; perhaps most famously the story about the Prophet Muhammad and the poor man who came to ask him for money, but was told to go and cut wood to sell at the market instead, here told to me by a senior staff member in the IICO:

> We have this saying about the Prophet, he is sitting with his companions and a poor man comes to ask for help. The companions want to give him money, but the Prophet says no and asks him, do you have anything at home you can sell? The man says no, all I have is a copper cup. Bring it, the Prophet says, and the man brings the cup and the Prophet asks his companions who wants to buy it. One of them buys it and the prophet asks the poor man to go and buy an axe for the money. When he gets the axe, the Prophet says, now go and cut some wood and sell it at the market. The man does what he says and some time later he comes back with enough money to buy back the copper cup and with savings. We use this as a slogan—'Give a man an axe', it's similar to the slogan with the fish.[72]

At the same time, the language of productivity, sustainability and individual self-reliance strongly echoes core values of post-structural adjustment development, envisioning the poor as latent economic players and microfinance as a 'self-help' mechanism through which they can be allowed into the market, supposedly transforming them into dignified and self-reliant actors (Cons and Paprocki 2010:639). 'Rather than helping the poor or people in need with something which will not be sustainable, it is better to help them by building their capacities, so that they can be productive and independent'[73]—this is a sentence from one of the IICO's publications, but it might just as well have been taken from a UNDP human development report. IICO staff are aware of and emphasise these similarities, noting with pride that empowerment is an 'international' concept.[74] Thus, unlike the discourse of human rights, the discourse of empowerment seems to be easily aligned with Islamic values. As such, this strategy of developmentalising Islamic aid has the potential to facilitate entrance into the mainstream aid field, serving as a common language or a 'bridging frame' (Benford and Snow 2000:624) through which to communicate with mainstream development actors.

A sacralised aid?

Emphasising a vision of a dignified Muslim and a strengthened *umma*, a rationale that turns on notions of a religiously defined solidarity among fellow Muslims, and strategies of *da'wa* and moral education, the ideology of IICO and IIROSA reflects mainstream trends and values in the Islamic aid culture, resonating with a relatively conservative Middle Eastern Muslim audience. Underlying much of their ideology is a conception of aid as fundamentally sacred. In this perspective, aid is both practically and theologically intertwined with religion. It is a kind of aid that is, at least in part, religiously legitimated, building on religious rationales, promoting religious strategies and striving for a religiously defined vision. This does not necessarily mean that religion is part of all aspects of the ideology (as we have seen above, there are many ways in which the organisations' ideologies in fact resemble those of non-religious organisations), but there is no systematic or principled division; Islam is potentially relevant to all aspects of aid. This conception of Islam and aid as closely related is not unique to IICO and IIROSA, but reflects common conceptions in Kuwait and Saudi Arabia. A few examples serve to illustrate this: in Saudi Arabia, for instance, King Faisal's International Award for Serving Islam is frequently awarded to NGOs and charities, reflecting the extent to which 'serving Islam' and 'providing aid' are seen as mutually constitutive. And in Kuwait, it is the Ministry of Awqaf rather than the Ministry of Social Development that is engaged in the provision of aid on behalf of the state, serving as the only governmental member of Kuwait Joint Relief Committee. We also find examples of this particular understanding of the nexus between aid and religion in many Christian organisations. As mentioned above, organisations such as World Vision and Samaritan Purse bear some of the same traits as IICO and IIROSA, relying on notions of 'holistic development' and seeking to provide 'spiritual and physical aid to hurting people around the world' (Thaut 2009:342). As in IICO and IIROSA, in these organisations religion is potentially relevant to all aspects of aid provision, providing an important and explicit motivation for action and in mobilising supporters, playing a significant role in identifying beneficiaries and partners, and providing the dominant basis for engagement (G. Clarke 2007:33)

This understanding of aid as inherently religious is based on a particular understanding of religion. In IICO and IIROSA, Islam is framed as an all-encompassing religion, or, to use Lincoln's (2003:59) terms, a maximalist religion, constituting the central domain of organisational community and influencing all organisational discourses, practices and structures. This means that Islam is a source of social action as much as individual piety, echoing ideas of Hassan al-Banna and the Muslim Brotherhood. As people repeatedly say, 'helping is better than praying'. But it is not social action understood in formal political terms; instead, it is about education, culture, economy, social welfare, and relief. The vision of the strengthened *umma* is not a vision of a concrete political *umma*, a rejection of the nation state in favour of a transnational pan-Islamic political unit. It is a normative, moral vision, positing the *umma* as a transnational community of values. In this, the organisations are in line with Islamic scholars such as Qaradawi, who scorns the Islamic movement for having focused too much on political issues, promoting instead a much broader focus on culture, economy, education, and social welfare as drivers for Islamisation.[75] As such, Qaradawi as well as IICO and IIROSA reflect what we may call a 'cultural turn' of the Islamic movement, representing a shift from formal politics towards a focus on social and cultural practices. In this perspective, the Islamic state is no longer the principal actor in processes of Islamisation, essential to the establishment of a true Islamic society. Instead, individuals, media, and civil society actors (such as the IICO and IIROSA) play an increasingly important role in the Islamisation of society, what some refer to as a shift from Islamisation from above to Islamisation from below (Caeiro and al-Saify 2009:111).

This firm position within an Islamic aid culture, however, does not mean that the organisations entirely reject or ignore the Western culture of development aid. In particular since 9/11, they have both opened up to development audiences, seeking to attract UN and other 'international' aid agencies. To varying degrees, the two organisations seek to construct ideologies that are simultaneously legitimate to audiences from both the Islamic aid culture and the development culture, merging, translating and appropriating elements from the two cultures. Taking into consideration their firm grounding in the Islamic aid culture, we may conceptualise these attempts in terms of a 'developmentalisation' of Islamic aid. At least three distinct approaches to this developmentalisation of aid can be identified: Adoption, pragmatic alignment and integration. First, adoption refers to the uncritical embracing of elements from the culture of development aid without noticeable modifications or alterations. IICO's and IIROSA's incorporation of mainstream Western ideals of professionalism may be seen in this light, demonstrating that since 9/11, discourses of professionalism have become the frame of reference for all aid actors. Both organisations display an explicit focus on issues of professionalism, praising Western actors for their transparency and accountability, and rejecting old Islamic traditions of secrecy and anonymity in an attempt to counter allegations of corruption and suspicious connections. Pragmatic alignment is another approach to the developmentalisation of Islamic aid. This refers to the alignment of opposing ideological elements but without fully adopting one or the other. Instead, one frame is justified by reference to the other's underlying values. A case in point is the introduction of what I have referred to as a principled universality or a pragmatic particularism, aimed at aligning IIROSA and IICO's solidarity-driven focus on fellow Muslims with principles of universalism, central to the culture of development aid. Seeking to avoid accusations of discrimination, the organisations argue that they do in principle support a universalist approach, but they focus primarily on Muslims out of pragmatic reasons (for instance because the majority of people in the countries they work are Muslim, or because the majority of the world's poor are actually Muslims). In a somewhat similar vein, missionary activities, or *da'wa*, are justified with reference to issues of cultural sensitivity.

Attempting to align their ideologies with values of neutrality and non-confessionalism central to the culture of development aid, IIROSA and IICO increasingly coin their *da'wa* activities in terms of 'home missions' that focus on strengthening the faith, and by extension, identity of Muslims rather than converting non-Muslims. Finally, a third approach seeks to integrate the two frames, seen to be ideologically congruent (Westby 2002:288). One frame is not prioritised over the other, as in the approaches of respectively adoption and pragmatic alignment; instead, the two frames are merged into a new frame. The integration of the concept of empowerment into the ideology of in particular IICO testifies to such processes of ideological integration. Emerging as a development buzzword in the 1980s, empowerment has now been translated into an Islamic aid context as *tawkeel*. Originally understood in the sense of delegation of authority, the organisations have re-interpreted *tawkeel*, equating it with the concept of empowerment, often in the form of income-generating activities and vocational training. Justified by reference to Islamic sayings and adjusted to fit Islamic principles of *riba* (usury), these activities remain thoroughly Islamised while at the same time serving as tools for individual self-help, almost indistinguishable from mainstream empowerment projects of the development culture. In a similar vein, the concept of moderation, brought into fashion by the War on Terror, has been adopted by the IICO, attempting to integrate it into Islamic aid traditions it by reference to theological traditions of *wasatiya*.

This portrait of two Gulf-based Muslim NGOs has shown that these organisations are perhaps best understood in broader terms than simply as 'fundamentalist' or 'traditional' Muslim organisations, relegated to the periphery of the mainstream development culture. The ways in which these transnational Muslim NGOs relate to respectively the Islamic aid culture and the culture of development are not conditioned on dichotomies of rejection or accept, but are blurred, ambiguous, and shifting. On one hand, for instance, the organisations build on a rationale of solidarity, often implicitly or explicitly referring to a dichotomy between the warm and personal Muslim organisations and the cold and professional Western organisations. On the other hand, they hail the same organisations for their professionalism, copying their structures and using Western accounting companies to ensure organisational 'accountability' and 'transparency'. As such, the above analyses of IIROSA and IICO's organisational identities and aid ideologies have presented us with numerous examples of how the two organisations navigate between the cultures of development and Islamic aid, drawing on, rejecting, accommodating and merging different cultural repertoires, and in the process perhaps contributing to creating new aid cultures.

6

PROFESSIONALISM AND (A BIT OF) PIETY

CLAIMS TO AUTHORITY IN ISLAMIC RELIEF
AND MUSLIM AID

'Because it's Muslim, Islamic Relief enjoys greater access to funding,' a staff member from Islamic Relief once said to me, talking about the financial situation of the organisation after 9/11 'It's included everywhere, people listen, they have access to the government. In these times, people want to be seen to be involving Islam.' This quotation illustrates very well how 'these times' have provided transnational Muslim NGOs with very different rooms for manoeuvre: while organisations such as IIROSA and IICO are seen as 'traditional' and even 'fundamentalist', subject to sanctions and designations, Islamic Relief and Muslim Aid have gained a reputation as 'moderate', something which has led to increased cooperation and funding from development donors. In an attempt to go beyond these dichotomies, Chapters 6 and 7 discuss how Islamic Relief and Muslim Aid have reacted to this new situation, exploring their claims to organisational authority and their ideologies of aid and comparing them to those of IIROSA and IICO.[1]

Fame and new funding opportunities: Islamic Relief
and Muslim Aid after 9/11

Only two months after 9/11, Islamic Relief was visited by Prince Charles, who priased the organisation for its 'wonderful work' and made a personal donation to its Afghanistan Appeal.[2] Some years later, he gave similar praise to Muslim Aid, stating that Britain was 'incredibly fortunate to be able to count on organisations like Muslim Aid'.[3] These quotes provide evidence, albeit anecdotal, of the privileged position that Islamic Relief and similar organisations have been given after 9/11—not only by the royal family, but by British authorities in general. When attending a meal to mark the breaking of the Ramadan fast organised by Islamic Relief in August 2010, the then Deputy Prime Minister Nick Clegg said that he was 'full of admiration' for Islamic Relief's work, providing 'moral and organisational leadership' in the international community (cf. Khan 2012:111). And to mark Muslim Aid's twenty-fifth anniversary, Gordon Brown, then Prime Minister, praised Muslim Aid for its 'valuable work'.[4] Overall, Muslim Aid and Islamic Relief (like other British Muslim organisations) have historically enjoyed good relations with the British authorities, although in the early years there was not much contact.[5] After 9/11, the relationship between British authorities and Muslim organisations intensified. As was mentioned in Chapter 3, the British authorities took a decidedly different road to, for instance, US and Middle Eastern governments in the treatment of Muslim NGOs in the War on Terror. The UK put in place a much more supportive and cooperative NGO regulation regime while the latter emphasised strict control and sanctions (Benthall 2008a:93). Likewise, the British government, in particular through the Charity Commission and the Department for International Development (DFID), has been active in promoting what were in Chapter 3 referred to as soft measures, encouraging dialogue with Muslim organisations. In this context, in particular Islamic Relief, but also Muslim Aid, have come to be conceived as ideal partners. Unlike, for instance, Interpal and the Green Crescent, two other UK-based NGOs, neither Muslim Aid nor Islamic Relief were subject to allegations of 'terrorist' connections, but were widely considered to be 'moderate faith-based organisations' and as such, useful in dialogue initiatives, aimed at reaching out to Muslim constituencies.[6]

Islamic Relief and Muslim Aid are often invited to participate in governmental committees and advisory councils, and their work frequently receives public praise from governmental authorities. As part of this development, Islamic personalities such as the trustees of the two organisations have become increasingly involved in British society, occupying prominent positions as British and Western Muslim dignitaries.[7] The most obvious example is Hani al-Banna, founder of Islamic Relief.

Increasingly involved in a wide range of interfaith initiatives after 9/11, al-Banna came to be widely known as a voice of dialogue and moderation. In 2003, he was awarded the Order of the British Empire (OBE) for 'outstanding contribution to worldwide humanitarian work'.[8] Another example is Iqbal Sacranie, Muslim Aid's former chair. Sacranie was the founding secretary general of the Muslim Council of Britain, and is now chair of a number of Muslim centres, mosque committees and organisations, just as he is involved in several interfaith activities. Back in 1999, he was awarded the OBE 'in recognition of his efforts in the community, including his work for race relations, charity and in a former advisory role to the Home Office', and in 2005, he received the Queen's Birthday Honours, a knighthood for 'services to the Muslim community, to charities and to community relations' (BBC News 2005).[9]

Parallel to this attention from British authorities, Muslim Aid and Islamic Relief have also become the object of attention of governmental and intergovernmental development agencies, and both organisations have experienced a veritable explosion in institutional funding.[10] Thus, Islamic Relief's institutional funding has grown from close to zero before 9/11 to almost 25 per cent in 2009 (Khan 2012:92). And in Muslim Aid, institutional funding today makes up more than one-third of the total budget.[11] Some of this money comes from Middle Eastern and Islamic donors; many of them the same organisations which also support IIROSA and IICO.[12] In 2011, for instance, US$ 19 million of Islamic Relief's budget came from Middle Eastern and Muslim donors, with the largest donor being the Islamic Development Bank with a donation of almost US$ 7 million.[13] In 2009, Muslim Aid had been selected as partner in an Islamic Development Bank microfinance project, receiving a US$ 3 million grant, and in February 2011, the organisation signed a memorandum with both the Islamic Development Bank and the OIC, with the purpose of establishing a 'strategic partnership'.[14] But, unlike IIROSA and IICO, a large portion of funding actually comes from Western development donors, reflecting trends in the culture of development aid of a burgeoning interest in so-called faith-based organisations, as described in Chapter 3. One of Islamic Relief's first institutional donors was DFID, offering Islamic Relief a US$ 42,000 grant for relief work after flooding in Bangladesh in 1998. In 2001, cooperation intensified with funding for projects in Pakistan, Mali and Afghanistan, worth more than US$ 4 million. In 2006, a three-year Partnership Programme Arrangement was agreed upon, securing Islamic Relief approximately US$ 4 million funding for the period 2008 to 2011.[15] Other major donors are the European Commission for Humanitarian Operations (ECHO), the Spanish Aid Agency, the Swedish International Development Agency (SIDA) and UNDP. Entering the development donor scene a few years later than Islamic Relief, Muslim Aid got its first grant from Oxfam after the tsunami in 2005, financing a US$ 2 million housing project in Indonesia. The project received a lot of attention, opening up funding from ECHO, the World Bank, DFID, UNDP, the Asian Development Bank, and others. In 2007, Muslim Aid was awarded its first mini-grant of US$ 50,000 from DFID for a three-year development awareness project in Britain (James 2009:9), and, like Islamic Relief, the organisation is listed as a 'pre-qualified partner' in DFID's Rapid Response Facility. Other large institutional donors include the World Bank, ECHO, and the Asian Development Bank.

Table 6.1: Islamic Relief, annual growth 2003–11 (million US$)[16]

Year	2003	2004	2005	2006	2007	2008	2009	2010	2011
Income	25.4	35.9	70.3	61.4	66.2	78.8	96.0	86.6	100.8

Table 6.2: Muslim Aid, annual growth 2003–11 (million US$)[17]

Year	2003	2004	2005	2006	2007	2008	2009	2010	2011
Income	7.4	7.9	16.3	15.3	33.6	40.1	58.1	28.2	42,2

Since 2009, individual country directors have started actively approaching donors on their own, something which has resulted in many country offices now getting the major part of their budget from Western donor agencies. In Bangladesh, for instance, the then country director of Islamic Relief has actively worked to attract institutional funding, and at the time of my visit, he told me that two-thirds of the office's budget (or US$ 13.3 million) now comes from institutional donors such as ECHO, the World Food Programme, UNICEF, UNDP, and SIDA, while only US$ 6.7 million comes from individual donors, channelled through the UK headquarters. Likewise, in 2007, Muslim Aid's office in Bangladesh secured a US$ 100,000 grant from the Canadian International Development

Agency to provide assistance to victims of a big flooding. In November that same year, cyclone Sidr hit the country, 'and this was when we got our first partnership with ECHO,' a top manager recalls, referring to a US$ 450,000 grant from ECHO for distribution of food, provision of filtered water, and construction of latrines. He adds with some pride: 'Next year, we got six contracts with them.' So while 9/11 and the ensuing War on Terror resulted in decline, financial distress, and even designations for organisations such as IICO and IIROSA, for Islamic Relief and Muslim Aid it provided a whole new range of opportunities in terms of funding and cooperation. Before we look at how the two organisations present themselves and their claims to authority in this new situation, let us first take a closer look at the people working in the organisation.

Islamic personalities and young professionals

Islamic Relief was founded in Britain by two medical students in 1984. One of them was Hani al-Banna, a young Egyptian man who had migrated to Britain a few years before. A pathologist by training, al-Banna attended a medical conference in Sudan. Witnessing the hunger in the country, he returned home with the idea to establish a Muslim NGO—just like many others around that time, as we saw in Chapter 3. In 1984, al-Banna gathered a group of people, most of them Egyptians (and many of them living in Egypt), asking them to be the organisation's trustees, while he himself assumed the role of director (and later chairman). Like al-Banna, all trustees were well-educated men, many of them with degrees from North American and European universities, in disciplines such as engineering, medicine, and business administration. Many had personal or professional relations with key Muslim organisations in Europe and the Middle East, including for instance the World Assembly of Muslim Youth, the Federation of Islamic Organisations in Europe, and the Egyptian Human Relief Agency, closely related to the Muslim Brotherhood, just like some individuals were also directly involved with the Muslim Brotherhood.[18] The year after Islamic Relief was founded, in 1985, Muslim Aid was founded by the British convert and prominent folk-rock singer, Yusuf Islam (formerly known as Cat Stevens), together with representatives from twenty-three British Muslim community organisations. The majority of the founders (and later trustees) were first-generation immigrants from Bangladesh or Pakistan. As in Islamic Relief, many of them were prominent businessmen, founders of Islamic schools and community organisations, and otherwise well-known Islamic dignitaries, but unlike Islamic Relief's trustees, they lived in Britain (Benthall and Bellion-Jourdan 2003:80). And while Islamic Relief's trustees displayed connections to the Muslim Brotherhood, trustees of Muslim Aid related primarily to the Jama'at-e Islami movement and its social justice agenda. Thus, many of the founders and trustees had or have positions in different British Muslim organisations which are, to differing degrees, inspired by the Jama'at-e Islami (G. Clarke 2010:517). For instance, one of the founders of Muslim Aid is allegedly a former activist in Jama'at-e Islami in Bangladesh and co-founder of the British Dawat-ul Islam, an organisation that provides Islamic education, strongly influenced by the Jama'at (Eade and Garbin 2006:188). Likewise, several Muslim Aid trustees have enjoyed close connections to the Muslim Council of Britain and the Islamic Foundation in Leicester, both of which have also been broadly inspired by Jama'at-e Islami (Birt 2005:99; Mandaville 2009:497). Several members of Muslim Aid's board have served as secretary general of the Muslim Council of Britain, just like the director of the Islamic Foundation has served as vice chairman of Muslim Aid's board.

Historically, staff constellation in the two organisations has to a large degree reflected that of founders and trustees, with the majority being Arab and South Asian immigrant males, and all practising Muslims. The educational backgrounds of the first generations of staff were, like those of the founders and trustees, in engineering, medicine, and accounting, rather than in development studies, and many had professional experience from government or the private business sector. Many staff members had relations to other Muslim organisations. In Bangladesh, for instance, some people, especially in Muslim Aid, had sympathies for the Jama'at-e Islami—and this 'to the extent that many people thought Muslim Aid were a national organisation, not an international one,' as a person outside the organisation puts it, referring to the central position of Jama'at-e Islami in Bangladeshi politics.[19]

Today, staff in Muslim Aid and Islamic Relief no longer make up the same relatively homogenous group of pious Muslim first-generation immigrants with little development experience. While the boards of trustees are by and large unchanged, and many first generation staff members have remained in the organisations, since the mid-2000s, both Islamic Relief and Muslim Aid have increasingly incorporated a new kind of staff.[20] Contrary to the first generation of staff, many of these new staff members have relevant development education and experience. Some have a degree in development studies, others in journalism, nutrition, politics, or sociology. Many people, in particular among country office staff, have previously worked in national, non-Muslim, NGOs such as BRAC, just as others have moved on to work in transnational development NGOs such as CARE, Oxfam or Save the Children. They work in Islamic Relief and Muslim Aid because they want to work in a development NGO, not because they want to work in a religious organisation. An example of this type of staff member is Junaed who worked in Islamic Relief in Bangladesh when I visited the organisation. He was one of the first to take a degree in Development Studies in Bangladesh; later he completed an MPhil in Development and Social Change at an Australian university. Junaed is a devoted development practitioner and tells me that he insisted on having 'development practitioner' put down under 'occupation' in his passport. Today, he works in Save the Children. Interestingly, there are also examples of older staff members who have undergone a process of 'developmentalisation'. The then country director of Islamic Relief in Bangladesh, for instance, is originally a medical doctor, and has previously worked in IIROSA as well as the Brotherhood-related Human Relief Agency, but recently finished an MA in development studies at a university in Bangladesh, thus personifying the move from Islamic aid to a development-oriented professionalism.[21] Another characteristic of these new staff members is their lack of political affiliation. Encouraging a culture of political neutrality among staff, the organisations actively seek to dissociate themselves from any association with political parties and organisations. These processes of depoliticisation have been particularly pronounced in Muslim Aid's office in Bangladesh. In January 2006, a large restructuring process replaced several people who were supposedly politically biased, and in 2008, the previous country director was replaced with an expatriate to ensure political neutrality. Today, politics is strictly forbidden in the country office—to the degree that people are not even allowed to speak about politics during lunch. One person says, 'I can honestly say that Muslim Aid is very careful. [The director] has stated this very clearly. The government has suspected us for having connections, and some people still think so. But it's decreasing.'[22] Likewise, in Islamic Relief, there have been rumours that some staff members would support the Jama'at-e Islami, privileging Jama'at organisations when selecting partner organisations. The country director says that this is now a thing of the past; according to him, there might be a few people who support them, but there are also people who support the Awami League. Finally, both organisations have started employing more women and more non-Muslims. At the time of my visit, approximately half of staff were female, with the majority working at either headquarter level or at project level, and fewer working at country office level. In Islamic Relief headquarters, the first non-Muslims were employed in 2005 or 2006, and when I visited the organisation in 2008, there were approximately ten non-Muslims.[23] In Muslim Aid's headquarters, non-Muslims have been employed since 2007, and today, a couple of people are non-Muslims (for a short while there were even two non-Muslims in the management team). In country offices, the picture is more diverse. In Islamic Relief Bangladesh, there are some Hindu staff, but no Christians. 'We would like to, but they haven't applied. And you can invite people, but you can't force them,' says a staff member. In Muslim Aid, the pattern is similar. In Bangladesh, some staff members are Hindu, but like Islamic Relief, there are no Christians. 'They have their own organisations,' people repeatedly tell me.

These changes have resulted in very heterogeneous organisations. Several people speak of a divide between two different kinds of staff, the 'development professionals' and the 'religious conservatives'; a divide which often (although not always) coincides with a divide between top and bottom, old and young, and which seems to be more pronounced at country office levels than at headquarter levels. The religious conservatives, primarily older people, are in top management and board positions, as well as in the administration and fundraising departments. The young development professionals are in project departments and in country offices. As one person notes, 'you primarily find the development expertise at the bottom, and less at the top'. Many development professionals do not work for long in the organisations. As one person said during an interview in Bangladesh, considering whether to share with me some of his more critical views on the organisation: 'When are you going to publish this? In one year? Well, then there's no problem, then I probably won't be here anymore.' And he was right—a few months after, he wrote me and said that he had gotten a job in CARE. Disappointed with the lack of professionalism, people apply for positions elsewhere, often in secular development NGOs. The religious conservatives, on the other hand, tend to stay. One person says with a smile: 'You can be sure that those who have been here for more than fifteen years are not professional development people.' For management, there is no incentive to keep the young development professionals, as long as new ones keep coming. They need the development professionals to implement strategies of secular development aid, maintaining an external image of a professional development organisation. Internally, however, they have little interest in keeping the development professionals for long, insofar as this would facilitate their influence in the organisation. In other words, the employment of professional development staff ensures the kind of activities and strategies that donors want, but because these staff members do not stay for long and because they have no power in the organisations, they cannot influence internal processes and structures, thus leaving intact a conservative religious core. As such, Islamic Relief and Muslim Aid, in comparison with IIROSA and IICO, have become highly heterogeneous organisations. They are heterogeneous in terms of donors, insofar as they rely simultaneously on secular development agencies, Islamic aid organisations, and individual Muslim donors (and different kinds of individual Muslim donors). But more importantly, they are also heterogeneous in terms of their organisational constellations, divided into different generations of staff—the older religious conservatives and the young development professionals. So, put simply, whereas IICO and IIROSA are (still) firmly embedded in an Islamic culture, Islamic Relief and Muslim Aid seem to have one leg in each culture. This is a trend that is of course somewhat inherent in the organisations, insofar as they are established in Britain and not Saudi Arabia or Kuwait, but it is also a trend that has been thoroughly encouraged after 9/11. How is this double cultural identity reflected in the organisation's self-portrayal? That is the topic of the last part of this chapter, exploring organisational claims to authority.

Professional authority: 'Working towards international standards'

Unlike IIROSA and IICO, Muslim Aid and Islamic Relief do not consider themselves primarily 'Islamic' organisations: on its website, Islamic Relief calls itself 'an international relief and development charity'[24] while Muslim Aid uses the almost identical terms 'an international relief and development agency',[25] both emphasising their professional identity rather than their Islamic identity. Some people in Islamic Relief even jokingly suggest changing the name of the organisation, taking 'Islamic' out of 'relief'. Underlining this focus on professional aid provision, the organisational mottos do not refer to Islam, but to the task of providing relief and development aid. Islamic Relief is '[d]edicated to alleviating the suffering of the world's poorest people' while Muslim Aid is 'serving humanity'. In other words, Islamic Relief and Muslim Aid claim to be legitimate providers of aid because they are professional, not because they are religious. It is about the services they provide, not the values they possess (Smith and Sosin 2001:655).

Like IICO and IIROSA, Muslim Aid and Islamic Relief frame their claims to professionalism almost entirely in the language of the development culture, implicitly presenting professionalism as a condition for integration into this culture. Framing themselves as professional aid authorities, Muslim Aid and Islamic Relief emphasise professional knowledge in the form of technology, science and research. As stated by Islamic Relief in one of its research papers: 'Development work is becoming increasingly "evidence based."'[26] This scientific, research-based approach underlies all the organisations' activities. 'When we choose the field offices, we look at the level of poverty,' a Muslim Aid staff member explains. 'Then we look at the main causes for poverty in this specific context, we look into what are the needs and then finally we look at the available resources. And then we design our programme on the basis of all this.' Countries of operation are systematically presented with 'facts and stats' on poverty, health and sanitation, education and other figures. Annual reports are ripe with statistics and graphs, just as individual projects are couched in a scientific language, describing problems in terms of numbers and percentages, often quoted from the UNDP Human Development Index or other UN sources: 'Around 80% of all sickness and disease in the world is caused by inadequate water or sanitation, according to the WHO,' Islamic Relief states in an Annual Report.[27] A speech by Muslim Aid's chairman presents another typical example of this reliance on numbers and science—what Malkki (1996:390) has referred to as 'clinical humanitarianism': '22,000 children under five die every day due to lack of basic healthcare; a further 218 million children are child labourers; and only 62% complete primary education in Africa alone. Muslim Aid is determined to help eradicate this alarming problem.'[28]

Being a professional organisation also means adhering to professional practices of planning and management. While IICO and IIROSA somewhat naïvely talk about being the first NGOs to lay down a strategic basis for charitable work, Muslim Aid and Islamic Relief use terms such as 'financial management' and 'performance measurement' with frequency and great ease. By uploading their *Strategic Frameworks*, *Manuals on Accountability and Monitoring* and *Evaluation Tools* to their websites, they display and demonstrate their fluency in the language of professional development. Likewise, their decision-making procedures and structures are presented to the public in pedagogical 'organisational charts' on websites and in annual reports. Staff practices are standardised and systematised into policies and guidelines, just like projects are designed on the basis of Logical Framework Analysis, and implemented according to the Project Cycle Management tools. Activities are subject to external and internal control in the form of monitoring, audits, supervision and evaluations, aimed at ensuring 'accountability and transparency', 'measuring success' and documenting 'impact' and 'evidence of change'.[29] Both organisations have signed the Humanitarian Accountability Partnership, thus committing themselves to meeting 'the highest standards of accountability and quality management;'[30] Muslim Aid has been certified by Investors in People, 'a flexible and easy to use standard which helps organisations transform their business performance', as the company notes on its website;[31] and in July 2010, Islamic Relief was awarded second place in the Institute of Chartered Accountants in England and Wales (ICAEW) *Charities Online Financial Report and Accounts Award.*

In the claim to professional authority, strategies of association play an important role. For one, the organisations associate themselves with Britain. Islamic Relief is 'a British-based international aid agency,'[32] while Muslim Aid is 'a UK-based international relief and development agency'.[33] In this, there are, at least on the surface, some similarities with IIROSA and IICO which both emphasise their national identity. But whereas IICO and IIROSA present a national identity bound up with taking care of fellow citizens and praising the authorities, for Islamic Relief and Muslim Aid, being British is a way of signalling accountability. In a development frame of reference, Britain—and 'the West'—equals strict systems of control and monitoring. Being British is not about taking care of British citizens or praising the Queen, but about being subject to systems of control and monitoring, and by default, about being accountable. Authority is also strengthened by association with other actors, perceived to be recognised authorities of professionalism. Like IICO and IIROSA,

Islamic Relief and Muslim Aid have consultative status at the UN, but apart from that they are also members of a wide range of other networks, including BOND (the UK membership body for NGOs), the Red Cross/ Red Crescent Code of Conduct, the Sphere Standards and the Humanitarian Accountability Partnership. Furthermore, at time of writing Islamic Relief was (the only Muslim) member of the Disasters Emergency Committee (Palmer 2011), while Muslim Aid's application was being considered. Both organisations are also active in networks such as the Jubilee Debt Campaign and the Make Poverty History Campaign. On their websites, both organisations have posted the logos of these networks, institutions and organisations as a way of signalling affiliation with some of the strongest 'brands' in the international development community. Their logos serve as codes for accountability and reliability, showing that Islamic Relief and Muslim Aid are able to speak the language of the professional development culture. Likewise, in annual reports and interviews, Western development NGOs and aid agencies are highlighted over the many Middle Eastern organisations that also support the organisations. For instance, in an article published in the British NGO newsletter *ONTRAC*, Islamic Relief describes its donor base as follows: 'The organisation receives donations from multilateral and bilateral institutions and individual donors. It has entered into partnerships and cooperation agreements with Christian FBOs, such as CAFOD, as well as secular organisations' (Abuarqab 2010:7). This preference for secular and Christian partners is very explicit in Bangladesh, for instance. Neither Islamic Relief nor Muslim Aid has anything to do with IICO, IIROSA or other transnational Muslim NGOs working in the country. Instead, they are part of the so-called INGO Forum, together with Action Aid, Oxfam, CARE, Christian Aid, and other transnational NGOs.[34] Through partnerships with Western and Christian organisations, the organisations can, in their own words, 'connect ourselves with mainstream agencies'[35] and thus confirm their own status 'as a mainstream development agency working towards international standards'.[36] Cooperation with Christian organisations plays a particularly important role, and Muslim Aid and Islamic Relief each actively promote their inter-faith partnership. The most famous is without doubt the partnership between Muslim Aid and the United Methodist Committee on Relief (UMCOR), growing out of cooperation between the two organisations in Sri Lanka in 2006, and in 2007 extended into a formal partnership.[37] Around the same time, Islamic Relief entered into a similar partnership with Christian Aid, following the earthquake in Pakistan in 2005.[38] Such partnerships send strong signals of dialogue and bridge-building, making them very popular with Western donors and governments. The then treasury Minister Stephen Timms officiated at the signing of the partnership agreement between Muslim Aid and UMCOR, something which, according to G. Clarke (2010:11), reflects the British government's support for 'an innovative cross-national and trans-faith partnership'. Further reflecting the British government's support was the fact that Gordon Brown, then Prime Minister, mentioned the partnership in a speech to the UN Inter-Faith Conference in November 2008 as an example of 'the potential of faith' (G. Clarke 2010:n.52). Apart from strengthening professional authority, these relations also testify to organisational allegiance to a particular community. When Islamic Relief was awarded the ICAEW Award, as mentioned above, the PR statement on the organisation's website read: 'ahead of organisations such as Oxfam, ActionAid, World Vision, Christian Aid, NSPCC and the Prince's Trust, among others'.[39] In other words, the competition for organisational legitimacy is not a competition with IICO, IIROSA, and other Muslim NGOs, but a competition with Oxfam, ActionAid and other development NGOs. These are the organisations that Islamic Relief and Muslim Aid consider themselves comparable to.[40] Thus, whereas IIROSA and IICO's partnerships and allegiances had the character of a transnational Muslim community, a global *umma*, Islamic Relief, and Muslim Aid present themselves as part of a 'global humanitarian community.'[41] This is also evident in the two organisations' attempts to broaden their donor base to include non-Muslims.[42] Islamic Relief's 2006 Annual Report, for instance, speaks of 'attracting people of all communities, backgrounds and cultures,'[43] just like Muslim Aid expresses wishes for 'a more diversified donor base.'[44]

Just like association with certain development organisations and institutions strengthen claims to professional authority, so does dissociation from certain Muslim organisations and institutions. Epitomising this change in allegiances, Muslim Aid changed its logo in 2003: pre-2003, the organisation's logo was a globe with a flag wavering over it, with the organisation's name written in Arabic on the flag, signalling allegiance to an Arab, Islamic aid community. Today, the logo is a drop of water, underscored by a green crescent, sending signs of a more international orientation. Previously the organisation's annual reviews would often mention cooperation with various Islamic organisations, while today's reviews downplay such connections.[45] For instance, the fact that the organisations rely on Islamic institutions and personalities for religious guidance and advice is not, as in IIROSA and IICO, displayed on the front page of their websites.[46] These institutions and individuals do not have credibility as professional development authorities, and association with them will not enhance the authority of Islamic Relief and Muslim Aid. Particularly interesting for the present analysis, Gulf-based NGOs such as IIROSA and IICO are often subject to strategies of dissociation. Some people simply claim not to know the organisations. Others cast organisations such as IICO and IIROSA as 'traditional' and 'unprofessional'. A staff member bluntly states: 'They are perhaps not the most sophisticated, they don't use LogFrame and all these things.' Another person elaborates a bit more on the distinction:

> The way I see it, there are two different kinds of Islamic organisations—the traditional and the modern. The modern accept the Western system and they give it an Islamic flavour, an Islamic spirit. By Western I mean internal management systems, […] The traditional organisations depend only on personal accountability. It's about you as a spiritual person, about whether you are trustworthy or not. It's not about the system, it's about the person.

A person who used to work in IIROSA but now works in one of the UK-based NGOs tells me that he left the organisation precisely because of this: 'There was a clash between the way I needed to work as a professional and the way they worked. Their set-up is not professional.' According to some people, this lack of professionalism has to do with the role of religion in the organisations: 'The [Gulf-based NGOs] are led by religious people—not development professionals. They are good people, but they don't know,' says one person, echoing the statements of many others. In this perspective, religion—or at least a particular kind (or role) of religion—becomes the antithesis of professionalism.[47] In this perspective, Muslim Aid and Islamic Relief see themselves as much closer to non-religious or Christian NGOs such as Oxfam, Save the Children or Christian Aid than to IIROSA and IICO. Thus, whereas IIROSA and IICO defined themselves, for good and bad, in opposition to 'the West' and 'Western organisations', seeing themselves as part of a community of Muslim organisations, Muslim Aid, and Islamic Relief, define themselves in opposition to Gulf-based and other Muslim organisations, creating a dichotomy between professional and unprofessional, modern and traditional, but also between secular and religious Muslim NGOs, or—in the War on Terror terminology—between moderate and fundamentalist NGOs.

At the same time, this distinction between persons and systems points towards what is perhaps the most important difference between, on the one hand, IICO and IIROSA's conceptions of professionalism and, on the other, those of Muslim Aid and Islamic Relief. For IIROSA and IICO, professionalism is largely a question of demonstrating financial accountability, responding to allegations of terrorist financing, but for Islamic Relief and Muslim Aid it is also about relying on professional staff. Unlike in IIROSA and IICO, then, the ideal staff member is not the dedicated volunteer, but the specialised expert. A manager in Islamic Relief's headquarters says: 'If you want to be professional, and work with sustainable development, it is necessary to have paid staff.' Recruitment is determined not by religious virtues or expertise, but by 'aptitude and ability'[48] and staff are described as 'experienced' and 'professional,' presenting 'a wealth of knowledge and expertise,'[49] which is constantly improved through 'training,' 'upgrading of workforce'[50] and 'staff development'.[51] The excerpt below from a job announcement for a position as Communication Manager in Islamic Relief's US fundraising office clearly illustrates this emphasis on development expertise and specialisation, making it indistinguishable from job announcements from other mainstream development NGOs such as Oxfam and Save the Children:

Qualifications:

Three plus years of related work experience.

Bachelor's degree in English, Journalism, Communications, Public Relations or related field.

Strong Command of AP Style.

Competent in editorial principles and techniques of communicating information.

Strong editing, summary writing, and proofreading skills.

Fluent in the English language, including grammar, structure, punctuation and spelling.

Ability to work on highly technical material with strong attention to detail.

Possess strong organizational and excellent interpersonal skills.

Proficient with Microsoft Office Suite.

Able to work independently with minimal supervision, as well as in a team environment.

Must have a strong sense of ownership over projects and tasks, be able to identify new opportunities, and have the initiative to pursue them.

Knowledge of Adobe InDesign, Adobe Photoshop and layout experience a plus.

Ability to travel to Field Offices overseas to conduct interviews and compose original piece of work a plus.

Must be eligible to work in the United States.

As such, religion plays no role in the employment of staff. There are no requirements as to religious affiliation, no formal religious dress code, and people are not obliged to pray together. Illustrative of this position, Muslim Aid Bangladesh's staff manual does not mention Islam, religion or faith except when reminding staff to be respectful of other people's religion.[52] Instead, the manual explicitly states that discrimination on the grounds of religion is not tolerated:

> It is [Muslim Aid Bangladesh] policy to treat job applicants and employees in the same way regardless of their sex, race colour, religion and or ethnic origin. Any employee who acts in such a manner as to discriminate against or harass any other employee or individual with whom the employee is dealing in the course of his/her employment will be considered to have committed an act of gross misconduct.[53]

In this, Islamic Relief and Muslim Aid bear a strong resemblance to Christian NGOs such as DanChurchAid and Christian Aid, which also have religious roots but whose operations do not have a religious goal, characterised by Thaut (2009:333) as 'accommodative-humanitarian' organisations. While the religious roots of these NGOs may attract persons with a similar Christian conviction and motivation for aid provision, they will not require employees to publicly display and live by a certain kind of religious doctrine. Instead, 'the primary qualification is the professionalism of the staff' (Thaut 2009:333). This does not mean that religion has to be private, however. Inspired by traditions of multiculturalism, Muslim Aid and Islamic Relief—and Christian Aid for that matter—present themselves as organisations in which there is room, but not pressure, to cultivate one's religiosity. It is about creating a 'relaxed, Islamic environment', as one top manager formulates it. Both organisations have prayer rooms, but it is constantly underlined that there is never a pressure to use them: 'Some pray, and others don't,' says the manager of one of Islamic Relief's projects in Bangladesh. Likewise, the then country director of Muslim Aid in Bangladesh told me that he rarely prays with staff: 'Previously, the environment was more assertive—you should pray—but I think I have modified the atmosphere. I rarely pray with the staff myself, I follow a different timetable. So I think there's much less pressure now, much less attempts at forcing people.'

Islamic authority: 'The humanitarian spirit of Islam'

This emphasis on professional authority, and the inherent dichotomy between (some kinds of) religion and professionalism, does not mean that Islamic Relief and Muslim Aid do not consider Islam an important part of their organisational identity or make claims to religious authority: they both make use of hadiths and religious symbols,[54] they provide traditional Muslim aid activities such as orphan sponsorship, *Qurbani* and *ifthar* meals; they offer donors the possibility to pay their *zakat*, they inform them about Islamic practices, concepts and traditions,[55] and they engage in other religious activities with the purpose of signalling religious authority.[56] On the surface, some of these strategies for claiming religious authority are similar to those of IIROSA and IICO. But underlying them are two very different notions of religion. Whereas IICO and IIROSA promote a relatively formal or orthodox religiosity, predicated on visible collective practices and rituals, the religious authority of Islamic Relief and Muslim Aid is based on conceptions of religion that fit better with professional ideals of aid organisations. Religious authority is first and foremost understood in terms of a sharp distinction between religion and aid, echoing secular principles of the development culture. In this perspective, religion is acceptable as the source of individual values, underlying principles and motivation, but not as public rituals and collective practices influencing the ways in which aid is provided. One woman explains to me that she likes to work in an organisation 'that actually tries to transform the values of Islam into action', but in her description of organisational activities, she does not make any room for religion. This conception of religion as almost invisible is reflected in the frequent use of airy terms such as 'Islamic flavour', 'Islamic charitable values'[57] and 'the humanitarian teachings of Islam',[58] denoting an interpretation of Islam as an 'ethical reference' (Benedetti 2006:855), rather than an orthodox, visible religiosity. As Muslim Aid notes in its description of the organisation's logo: 'The drop of water that is at the centre of logo symbolizes life, underscored by the green crescent to emphasize the fact that we are driven by the humanitarian spirit of Islam.'[59]

Another dominant conception of religion in Muslim Aid and Islamic Relief ideologies is that of religion as an instrument. In this perspective, the two organisations frame themselves as legitimate religious authorities because their religion is perceived to be a useful instrument in the provision of aid. Religion is framed in terms of an instrumentalist 'added value'. As such, an organisation is religiously legitimate if—and only if—it can provide an added value on the basis of this religiosity. 'I would say that our mission is to provide innovative ways of alleviating poverty through Islamic values,' says a young development professional at Muslim Aid headquarters. 'We bring something different to the development field.' This conception of religious legitimacy resonates well with development donor expectations of an 'added value' from so-called faith-based organisations—it is not enough to simply copy secular NGOs. In this perspective, Islamic Relief and Muslim Aid have to underline their Muslim identity and the role of Islam in their activities, presenting an added value and distinguishing themselves from non-religious NGOs by promoting those religious aspects that are acceptable—and preferably even useful—to the donors.

Building on this idea of the added value of faith-based organisations, the two organisations also see themselves as having a particular responsibility and ability to build bridges between Islam and the West: 'Islamic Relief is in a unique position as an aid agency founded in the West but based on Islamic humanitarian principles,' Islamic Relief claims. 'This gives us an important role as a bridge between cultures, communities and civilisations.'[60] More specifically, it is about ensuring greater cooperation and mutual understanding between Muslim NGOs and actors in the development system, 'integrating Muslim aid agencies into the international field of humanitarian relief and development'.[61] To further this goal, Islamic Relief's founder, Hani al-Banna, together with the British Red Cross and Oxfam, has established the Humanitarian Forum as an alternative network 'which aims to build and strengthen partnerships in the worldwide humanitarian sector',[62] including non-Muslim as well as Muslim organisations, as described in the previous chapter. Likewise, Muslim Aid states that the organisation can 'play a positive role in community development and building inter-faith relations, especially in the development sector'.[63] This resonates with donors' expectations. In Islamic Relief's Partnership Programme Agreement with DFID, for instance, the objectives are not only child poverty in East Africa, but also development awareness projects among Muslims in the UK. In a similar vein, inter-faith partnerships, such as those between Islamic Relief and Christian Aid or Muslim Aid and UMCOR, are repeatedly praised by development aid agencies. Similar trends were seen in IICO and IIROSA, expressed in their engagement in various initiatives for the promotion of 'moderation'. This points to the unique expectations that Muslim NGOs, post-9/11, are subject to, compared to other organisations (whether secular or religious). As was noted in the discussion of IIROSA and IICO's claims to moderation, in order to be legitimate, Muslim NGOs cannot simply be providers of aid, but must engage in activities outside the provision of aid, contributing to building bridges between 'Islam' and 'the West', contributing to paying off the debt of collective guilt surrounding Muslim NGOs through these activities.

'In faith-based organisations, you will never get 100 per cent professionalism'

Alongside the official claims to a secularised or instrumentalised religious authority, inferior to professional authority, some segments in Islamic Relief and Muslim Aid seek to promote a religious authority that is much more conservative and formal. This way of framing religious authority clashes not only with the conceptions of religious authority outlined above, but also, and perhaps more importantly, with claims to professional authority. In essence, this is a conflict that stems from the highly heterogeneous staff constellation. In the analysis of IIROSA and IICO, we saw that attempts to merge claims to religious and professional authority were largely successful, something which can, at least in part, be ascribed to the fact that conceptions of professional authority in these two organisations is limited to questions of financial accountability, while staff remain subject to criteria of religious authority. In Islamic Relief and Muslim Aid, on the other hand, processes of professionalisation have included the employment of young development professionals alongside older and more religiously conservative staff and trustees. The young development professionals (who made up most of my informants) claim that trustees and parts of management are eager to promote an image of the organisation as 'professional' to institutional donors, but at the same time they want to maintain a certain level of religiosity internally in the organisation, satisfying their own and certain individual donors' demands for a more formal religious legitimacy. And this conflicts with young staff members' expectations of working in a professional development organisation. As one person says with regret: 'In faith-based organisations, to be honest, you will never get 100 per cent professionalism.'

The struggle between religious and professional development authority plays out in different ways. We can identify at least three strategies through which conservative religious staff seeks to subvert the official ideology of development professionalism, making space for conservative religious practices. One strategy is to prevent non-Muslim staff members from influence. Since the mid-2000s, both Islamic Relief and Muslim Aid have employed several non-Muslim staff members, emphasising their status as 'equal opportunities employers'.[64] But many people wonder whether they are being used to promote an image of organisational diversity and pluralism. A former staff member claims: 'They are driven by a need to be seen as diverse and moderate rather than a wish to actually be diverse and moderate.' In reality, some staff argue, there are few career opportunities for non-Muslims. For instance, there are no non-Muslims on the boards or among top managers. One woman says that she finds it 'very difficult' to be a non-Muslim in a Muslim organisation, and because of this, she does not see a future for herself in the organisation (in fact, she moved on to a different organisation shortly after I interviewed her).[65]

Another strategy is to exercise subtle pressure on Muslim staff in order to encourage them to comply with conservative Islamic practices. This is particularly pronounced in relation to gender practices. Reflecting norms of professionalism in mainstream development aid, Islamic Relief and Muslim Aid officially promote gender equality. However, several staff members point out that in many respects, the organisations are still dominated by conservative Islamic gender ideals. Compared to other transnational NGOs, Islamic Relief and Muslim Aid have remarkably low numbers of women employed. When I visited Bangladesh in 2009, CARE's office, for instance, had more than 30 per cent female staff,[66] while in Islamic Relief and Muslim Aid country offices, the percentage was lower than 10.[67] No trustees are women, and very few management positions are occupied by women. Instead, women are employed in bottom- and mid-level positions such as secretaries, teachers, assistants, and project coordinators. Some staff report informal and indirect pressure for women to comply with religious requirements and cover their heads. A person from one of the headquarters says that she has experienced periodic 'massive pressure' on female staff members to wear hijab. Others report more explicit demands for a 'modest dress code'. In one of the country offices, female staff members tell me that they have been specifically asked to cover: 'We are not fundamentalist, we are moderate here. So there should not be any rules for women. There are no special rules for the boys,' a woman says. 'We have said that to the management several times. But they say that it's the dress code.' In another country office, a young man tells me about an episode in which a visiting trustee from the UK asked the receptionist to put on a headscarf. 'As a professional, this is something I cannot tolerate,' he says. 'When this happened, we felt bad, we were reminded that this is a faith-based organisation.' Staff members claim that these practices challenge the organisations' image as professional development NGOs. 'We perform gender equality training, but we don't follow this ourselves,' says one person. She feels that this creates a barrier in relations to other, secular NGOs, stigmatising the organisation: 'Other organisations look at us. There might also be women from the other organisations that cover, but they do it because they have decided to do so on their own, not because they were told to do so by their organisation.' 'Donors should start enquiring about this,' her colleague says. 'Perhaps that would help.'

A third, and more radical, strategy is to simply fire or push out the people who do not allow space for or encourage conservative religious practices. The fate of Muslim Aid's previous director testifies to this: eager to move the organisation in a more professional direction, he trained old staff and hired new staff, including several women and non-Muslims. But soon trustees started expressing their scepticism with these changes, seeing them as contradictory to conservative Islamic doctrines and practices. When I interviewed the director in 2008, he knew there were problems with the board, saying that he may have implemented changes too fast: 'Internally in the organisation, there has been some reluctance. All the trustees are Muslim and they are male. And they are first-generation immigrants. They share the goals that I have, but perhaps they don't agree with the strategy.' Half a year later, he left the organisation—officially to establish his own organisation, unofficially because the board pressured him to leave. A top manager from another British organisation says flat out that he was fired: 'There was a struggle between the hardliners and the moderates. And I don't know whether it's the good or the bad that are left.' Staff members in the organisation express the same worry: 'He tried to make the organisation come out from its religious mind-set, he tried to make it secondary,' says a young development professional in Bangladesh. 'But now again we are confused. When he left, we all started thinking "wow, again we might be ..."' he says, leaving the word 'religious' unsaid.[68]

So, to sum up, Islamic Relief and Muslim Aid frame their organisational legitimacy primarily in terms of a professional authority, echoing conventional conceptions of professionalism in any Western development NGO. At the same time, both organisations make claims to a religious authority, based on conceptions of religion as a matter of personal motivation and underlying organisational values, or in terms of an instrumentalist 'added value', and as such compatible with, and inferior to, ideals of professionalism. Reflecting the highly heterogeneous staff constellations, however, there are elements in the organisations that challenge these priorities, making claims to a more formal, conservative religiosity. These different conceptions of organisational authority and NGO identity translate into ideological conflicts over conceptions of aid, as we shall see in Chapter 8. What kinds of ideologies do the organisations present and promote? How do they try to accommodate the wishes and expectations of fundamentally different actors, making their ideological frames resonate with the values and ideas of their audiences?

7

'WHAT'S SO ISLAMIC ABOUT US?'

IDEOLOGIES OF AID IN ISLAMIC RELIEF
AND MUSLIM AID

'What's so Islamic about us?' This is what a staff member, somewhat provocatively, asked me when I probed about the role of Islam in the organisation's provision of aid to the poor in Bangladesh. According to him, there was no difference between the ways in which Islamic Relief and, say, Oxfam or CARE provided aid: 'In the day-to-day programmes, there is no influence by Islamic principles. There's more of an echo of Western principles and donor wishes.' While there may be some truth to his statement, interviews with other staff members tell me that this is not all there is to it. In the following chapter, I look at the nexus between aid and Islam, giving an analysis of the ideological meaning systems formulated by Islamic Relief and Muslim Aid and exploring how ideological tensions over organisational identity and authority influence the ways in which the vision, rationale, and strategies of the organisations are formulated and presented.

Visions of aid

'A sustainable and self-reliant livelihood'

For Islamic Relief and Muslim Aid, aid provision is a response to problems of poverty and suffering, conceptualised primarily as a question of individual vulnerability and lack of capabilities: 'Many people are stuck in a poverty trap because they do not have the resources to develop their skills and work their way out of destitution,'[1] Islamic Relief notes in its strategy. Similarly, Muslim Aid conceives of poverty in terms of lack of access to basic necessities and the skills necessary to generate an income.[2] In 2008, Islamic Relief's research and policy department developed a *Policy Stance on Poverty*, giving a more detailed idea of how the organisation conceives questions of poverty, arguably also reflecting attitudes of Muslim Aid. The paper starts by asking: 'What exactly do we mean [by poverty]? Do we want to lessen the suffering of the poor, or radically reduce poverty in society? What type of poverty do we wish to alleviate?'[3] It then goes on to discuss different conceptions of and approaches to poverty, including a monetary approach, a capability approach and a rights-based approach. Against this background, the paper presents a definition of poverty as

> a multidimensional phenomenon, best understood in terms of capability deprivation, encompassing not only material deprivation (measured by income or consumption) but also other forms of deprivation, such as unemployment, ill health, lack of education, vulnerability, powerlessness, and social exclusion.[4]

This multi-dimensional understanding of poverty reflects mainstream development approaches found in organisations such as UNDP and Oxfam. But it also differs little from an Islamic understanding, the paper argues, outlining 'the Islamic perspective':[5]

> There are essentially five groups of activities and things which make up the human needs in Islam. These are: (a) Religion, (b) Physical self, (c) Intellect or Knowledge, (d) Offspring & Family, and (e) Wealth [...] necessities therefore should include the ability to perform the five pillars of Islam (Belief, Prayer, Fasting, Zakat and Pilgrimage) and calling to the way of God; protection of life (we might include here access to health services); securing food, clothing and shelter, education, the right to earn a living, to set up a family, etc.[6]

The paper goes to great lengths to align the Islamic perspective on poverty with the mainstream development culture, arguing that 'the above Islamic perspective sits comfortably within the broader consensus of opinion about poverty as a multi-dimensional issue; as it is based on human needs that cannot be reflected in monetary terms alone.'[7] 'In particular,' the paper notes, 'in as far as operational measurement is concerned; the last four types of basic activities and things that make up basic human needs in Islam are similar to the indicators in the Human

Development Indices, which stress the importance of income, education, and health.'[8] What is more problematic, is the first type of human need—that of religion, understood as the 'ability to know about and practice one's religion'. The paper states somewhat ambiguously that this is 'not commonly part of the development and relief 'package', and Islamic Relief's willingness to consider religious deprivation and its measurement warrant discussion.'[9] It is difficult to align conceptions of poverty as (at least partly) spiritual with secular development conceptions of poverty. The Millennium Development Goals, for instance, do not mention anything about the religious needs for mosques or Qur'an education. Instead, Islamic Relief discusses religion as part of poverty in the form of lack of religious freedom and discrimination against religious people; topics that do not challenge development principles of neutrality and non-confessionalism.[10] In this perspective, a multi-dimensional notion of poverty does not, as in IIROSA and IICO, refer to the equal importance of spiritual and material needs; instead, it is about including considerations as to rights and capabilities rather than relying on a strict monetary understanding of poverty. As noted in another Islamic Relief publication, *Charitable Giving in Islam*:

> The Prophet (PBUH) believed that if charity were to remain restricted only to material goods, many people, especially the poor, would be excluded. However, Islam advocates a broader approach to charity, which moves beyond the material dimension, is more inclusive and helps avoid the creation of divisions based on wealth and status in society.[11]

The solutions to the problems of poverty are formulated in the language of mainstream development rather than Islamic aid. Muslim Aid states: 'Our vision is the alleviation of poverty, education for all, and the provision of basic amenities for those in need; in order to create a world where charity and compassion produce justice, self reliance and human development,'[12] continuing:

> Our mission: Muslim Aid, a premier British Muslim relief and development agency, guided by the teachings of Islam, endeavours to tackle poverty and its causes by developing innovative and sustainable solutions that enable individuals and their communities to live with dignity and by supporting initiatives that promote economic and social justice.[13]

Islamic Relief presents its vision as: '[a] caring world where communities are empowered, social obligations are fulfilled and people respond as one to the suffering of others,' guided by 'the timeless values and teachings of the Qur'an and Prophet's example (*Sunnah*), which recognise that people with wealth have a duty to those who are less fortunate.' The organisation describes its work as follows:

> Islamic Relief works with communities to strengthen their resilience to disasters, and we provide vital emergency aid when disasters occur. We help poor people to access basic services, including education, water and sanitation, as well as healthcare. We provide lasting routes out of poverty through our sustainable livelihoods schemes. Our integrated approach to development is transforming communities worldwide. We tackle the root causes of poverty and make sure that the world's most vulnerable people have a strong voice and real influence in both our programmes and advocacy. Islamic Relief is also a policy leader on Islamic humanitarianism, and our research programmes develop distinctive, practical approaches to the key issues that are affecting our world today.[14]

Through a terminology of improvement and progress, echoing that of mainstream development, the organisations formulate their goals of 'future success' for the poor as a question of 'self-reliance' and 'sustainable livelihoods'.[15] Reflecting broader notions of poverty, it is about helping the poor to 'realise their full potential'[16] and establish 'sustainable livelihoods,'[17] 'independent of outside aid,'[18] creating 'a sustainable, brighter future for themselves and their communities.'[19] Self-help is the solution to poverty (Hattori 2003:162). In other words, the gift the beneficiaries receive is the gift of self-realisation (Stirrat and Henkel 1997:73). In this perspective, aid is about creating capacities and generating income for the individual poor; it is not about empowering the individual Muslim in order to strengthen the *umma*, as in IICO and IIROSA. Thus, whereas IICO and IIROSA's conception of aid is based on a religiously defined vision, resonating with general principles of Islamic aid, the aid of Islamic Relief and Muslim turns on a secular vision, echoing mainstream development ideals and leaving only little room for religion. Put somewhat simply, one may say that while IICO and IIROSA work to promote an Islamic culture—the *umma*—Islamic Relief and Muslim Aid work to promote a development culture, and as such, resembling secular development NGOs rather than fellow Muslim ones. In this, they also resemble certain Christian NGOs, such as DanChurchAid and Christian Aid, whose work may be based on, or inspired by, Christian values but whose vision is almost indistinguishable from those of secular organisations.

DanChurchAid, for instance, 'has a vision of a world without hunger, poverty and oppression, in which popular and political powers constantly work strongly and actively for a just distribution and use of the earth's resources',[20] while Christian Aid states that '[p]overty is an outrage against humanity. It robs people of dignity, freedom and hope, of power over their own lives. Christian Aid has a vision—an end to poverty—and we believe that vision can become a reality.'[21]

Aid for humanity

Because the vision is not religiously defined, aid can be given to all. According to both Islamic Relief and Muslim Aid, the provision of aid is not restricted to Muslims, but extended to 'disadvantaged people across the globe, irrespective of their faith, colour and race,'[22] something which is repeated numerous times on websites, in annual reports, brochures, and in interviews. Recipients are no longer understood in terms of fellow Muslim brothers and sisters in a global Muslim *umma*, but as part of a global humanity. While earlier annual reviews and reports of Islamic Relief and, especially, Muslim Aid, talked of 'the Muslim Ummah,' 'the message of Muslim brotherhood', and 'projects to improve the quality of education and skills for young Muslims,'[23] both organisations now explicitly emphasise their work with non-Muslims, distancing themselves from other Muslim organisations seen to be discriminatory and proselytising. 'We are keen to raise awareness that we work with non-Muslims,'[24] Islamic Relief states in its latest strategy, while Muslim Aid quotes a recipient for saying that '[a]t first we thought that Muslim Aid would not give us anything because we were Hindu but we were wrong—Muslim Aid helps everybody'.[25]

Emphasising phrases such as 'people from across the globe' and 'the whole of humanity,'[26] the two organisations echo mainstream aid discourses on universalism, reflecting a rationale predicated on notions of a shared humanity rather than religious solidarity. We help each other because we are all human—not because we are Muslims. Or, in the words of a staff member in Bangladesh: 'We care about humanity, we don't care about their faith.' Another staff member, also in Bangladesh, tells me: 'We tell people that we have come to work for them, whether they are Muslim, Hindu, Christian, it doesn't matter to us. The important thing is that you are a human being.' A headquarter staff member tells me about

Muslim Aid's orphan sponsorship programme, aptly termed the Rainbow Family, carrying connotations of diversity and cosmopolitanism: 'The families can be all kinds—that's why we call it the Rainbow Family. They can be black, white, Muslim, Christian, Hindu.' A photo on one of Muslim Aid's brochures hammers home the point, showing a black child wearing a big cross in his necklace and holding a Muslim Aid package (Yaylaci 2007:31). Likewise, in Muslim Aid's microfinance project in Bangladesh, staff continuously emphasise that 10 per cent of the women are Hindu, reflecting the general composition of the population. Islamic Relief's orphan's sponsorship programme includes Christian children and donors; several recipients of microfinance loans are Hindus; even Ramadan food packages are distributed to non-Muslims. Also, in recent years, both organisations have increasingly been promoting activities in non-Muslim countries. After the earthquake in Haiti in January 2010, for instance, Islamic Relief set up camps for victims of the earthquake, providing 1,100 families with accommodation, water, food and medicine. Likewise, after the earthquake in Japan in March 2011, both organisations launched emergency appeals for victims of the disaster, urging their donors to contribute. In this emphasis on universalism, there is a strong resemblance not only with secular NGOs, but also with mainstream Christian NGOs such as Christian Aid which on their website states that they give aid 'on the basis of need alone, regardless of ethnicity, religion or nationality' (cf. Thaut 2009:334f).

Both Muslim Aid and Islamic Relief seek to legitimise their universalist approach not only by reference to mainstream discourses of development aid, but also by reference to Islamic principles: 'If you look at it from the side of Islam, most instructions from the Prophet Muhammad and the Holy Qur'an are about motivating people to help others, to support and help especially the poor,' says the country director in Islamic Relief's Bangladesh office. 'And they don't mention what kinds of poor—they don't say what gender, what race, what religion.' However, despite these attempts at legitimating universalism by reference to Islam, the focus on non-Muslims as well as Muslims does conflict with some donors' (and staff members') expectations of religious authenticity. As with IIROSA and IICO, the vast majority of Muslim Aid and Islamic Relief's funds have historically come from individual Muslim donors. And despite recent increases in institutional funding, a large proportion of the two organisations' income still comes from individual donors, many of them immigrant Muslims from Pakistan, India and Bangladesh, who wish to pay their *zakat* or give donations in the form of *waqf* or *sadaqa*. Following orthodox Islamic traditions, many of these donors expect at least *zakat* donations to be used exclusively for Muslims. In his analysis of Islamic Relief's individual donors, Khan (2012:98) finds that more than one-third of donors, or 37.5 per cent, strongly believed that at least *zakat* donations should be restricted to Muslims.[27] He quotes one donor, allegedly echoing statements of many others: 'I do not support other charities because I want my donations to go towards helping Muslims' (Khan 2012:98).

Just as IICO and IIROSA would align their focus on Muslims with mainstream demands for universalism by way of pragmatic arguments, claiming that the majority of the world's poor are Muslim, so Islamic Relief and Muslim Aid try to align their universalist focus on Muslim and non-Muslim poor with individual donor expectations of religious solidarity with fellow Muslims. A common strategy is ambivalence. When directly asked about whether the organisation uses *zakat* donations for non-Muslims, most staff members say that they are not sure of this, referring to management for clarification. In one of the organisations, a high-level staff member writes to me, somewhat vaguely responding to my question on whether the organisation uses *zakat* for non-Muslims: '[T] here has been some debate about this issue among Muslim scholars, and as I mentioned in one of my emails to you that Zakat has 8 categories and it varies from one to another. Therefore, you will not find a Yes or No answer from any party.' A high-level staff member from the other organisation says:

> We support both Muslims and non-Muslims, we interpret the verses in the Qur'an like that. But practically, we work primarily in Muslim areas and zakat is only 3–4 million out of our 40 million budget, so we can tell people that their zakat money goes to Muslims if that's what they want.

Even in official documents, this ambiguity is maintained. In Islamic Relief's 2009 Annual Report, for instance, it says: 'Islamic Relief Worldwide applies the Zakat in accordance with the legislative usage as specified in the Qur'an. Thus, it is primarily applied to humanitarian programmes that benefit poor and needy beneficiaries with basic needs.'[28] Such statements illustrate how the organisations attempt, if only temporarily, to merge mainstream development's demands for universalist inclusion with (some) Muslim donors' demands for religiously defined particularism.

Another way of satisfying individual donor expectations of a focus on fellow Muslim is to maintain a strong emphasis on Muslim majority countries, mirroring the approach of IIROSA and IICO. Reflecting the composition of the organisations' founders and donors, Islamic Relief and Muslim Aid have historically focused on countries such as Pakistan, Palestine, and Bangladesh, a focus that has been maintained throughout the years, parallel to the inclusion of other countries (see Tables 7.1 and 7.2 for an overview of Islamic Relief and Muslim Aid's top ten countries in 2012). An Islamic Relief staff member says: '[B]roadly speaking I think priority countries have always been those that feature strongly in the media and those with whom their donors are likely to have some affinity. Therefore, Pakistan and Palestine/Gaza have always featured strongly.' This priority is in turn justified to secular development donors such as DFID by reference to pragmatic arguments, similar to those heard in IICO and IIROSA. As Muslim Aid states on its FAQ section on the website, answering the question 'Do you only help Muslim countries?': 'Although we work in countries with a large Muslim population, these are countries that are affected by conflict and natural disasters. We strive to work where the need is greatest.'[29] An Islamic Relief staff member agrees: '[A] lot of the countries in which there is poverty are in fact Muslim,' she says.

Table 7.1: Islamic Relief, top five countries (2012)[30]

Country	Percentage
Palestine	22
Pakistan	14
Somalia	8
Bangladesh	5
Kenya	4

A somewhat more sophisticated argument that can at once satisfy these expectations as well as individual donor demands for a focus on fellow Muslims is what we may call the religious proximity argument (Palmer 2011; Benthall 2008b; Benedetti 2006). According to this line of thought, a common religion (much like a common culture) creates a symbolic sense of community among beneficiaries, NGOs, and other actors in the aid chain, something which in turn brings about 'added

value' through, for instance, ease of access and provision of more culturally appropriate services (Palmer 2011:97). In the sense that this approach
builds on an understanding of religion as a source of community, it resonates with IICO and IIROSA's conceptions of the *umma*, with the
important difference that in Islamic Relief and Muslim Aid, the *umma*
comes to be an instrument, not a goal in itself. In this perspective, Muslim
NGOs are better suited to work in Muslim areas because they know the
culture and the religion; therefore it makes sense for Islamic Relief and
Muslim Aid to work primarily in Muslim countries. Adhering to this
logic, an Islamic Relief staff member says: 'We have an understanding of
the culture and religion that gives us an advantage.' Another staff member notes: 'I think in the future [the organisation] will also focus increasingly on Afghanistan, Iraq and Yemen where perhaps it can claim to have
"privileged access" and therefore be able to receive greater institutional
donor funds.' Thus, in this perspective, the religious proximity argument
serves at once to satisfy individual donor demands for a focus on countries in which they have religious affiliations, and institutional donor
demands of added value and enhanced development efforts.

Table 7.2: Muslim Aid, top five countries (2012)[31]

Country	Percentage
Bangladesh	28
Somalia	20
Pakistan	10
Indonesia	7
Sri Lanka	2

The rationale of aid

Islamic morality and the Millennium Development Goals

The vision of sustainable livelihoods is based on a particular rationale,
presenting different 'vocabularies of motive' (Snow and Byrd 2007) for
engaging in the realisation of this vision. Like IICO and IIROSA, both
Muslim Aid and Islamic Relief emphasise the religious duty to help as
an important element in their organisational rationale. Providing aid is,
as an Islamic Relief publication puts it, an 'Islamic duty of care'[32] and a

'moral duty of Muslims to continuously and fervently work for a more just and humane society.'[33] In an Annual Report Muslim Aid notes that 'Islam, under the institution of Zakah, makes it a duty on its adherents to work towards the removal of poverty.'[34] And elsewhere: 'Muslim Aid works to alleviate human suffering as part of Islamic duty to all mankind.'[35] 'It's a faith responsibility,' says a Muslim Aid trustee. 'It's not just a job.' Similarly, Islamic Relief presents its underlying values of sincerity, excellence, compassion, social justice and custodianship as explicitly Islamic, listing their Arabic translations and declaring that the organisation 'remain[s] guided by the timeless values and teachings provided by the revelations contained within the Qur'an and prophetic example'.[36] The two organisations also sometimes refer to the religious rewards gained by supporting the provision of aid, using the same hadith and Qur'an quotes as those used by IIROSA and IICO.

However, Islamic Relief and Muslim Aid also present substantial differences from IICO and IIROSA. In their perspective, the duty to provide aid may be Islamic, but it is not uniquely so; the values of trust and solidarity are not particular to Islam or even to religion, but simply 'common values which underpin a healthy society',[37] as a Muslim Aid publication notes. These common values are expressed in, for instance, the UN Millennium Development Goals, which make up a core element in both organisations' motivational framing. Printed on the back of each of Islamic Relief's Partnership magazines and posted on the walls in the most remote of Muslim Aid's field offices, the Millennium Development Goals sometimes seem to have taken the place that the quotes from the Qur'an and hadith occupy in IICO and IIROSA. 'Our work with the world's poorest is guided by the Millennium Development Goals',[38] Islamic Relief declares in one of its annual reports, and the organisation is actively involved in lobbying for the new Sustainable Development Goals at UN level.[39] And Muslim Aid's chairman writes in the organisation's *25th Anniversary Souvenir* brochure, outlining the focus areas of the organisation:

> We are now focused on capacity building, disaster mitigation, microfinance for development and helping local communities achieve the underperformed targets in the UN Millennium Development Goals, especially in educating the girl child, women health and maternity and poverty eradication.[40]

This emphasis on the moral duty to aid others is closely connected to notions of rights. As fellow human beings, the poor have a right to receive aid: 'Our work is founded on enabling people and institutions to fulfill the rights of the poor and vulnerable',[41] Islamic Relief declares. 'We work from the perspective that the Prophet taught—that the poor have a right to this help. You are not really helping them, they are entitled to this assistance,' says Muslim Aid's country director in Bangladesh. Combining religious references to poor people's right to *zakat* with a mainstream discourse on human rights, both organisations quote the Qur'an: 'And those in whose wealth there is a recognised right for the beggar who asks and for the unlucky who has lost his property and wealth.'[42] Muslim Aid then declares: 'Islam teaches the equality of all humanity and actively promotes individual rights such as the right to life and freedom, the right to justice, the right to freedom of thought and religion and the right to education [...] Muslim Aid believes that all humans have the right to development.'[43] The right to aid may be outlined in the Qur'an, but it is not a right that is unique to Muslims. In other words, the right to aid is conditioned not so much on religious reciprocity and solidarity, but on a common humanity, echoing mainstream human rights discourses. Unlike IIROSA and IICO, Muslim Aid and Islamic Relief do not consider the human rights discourse to be problematic, using it instead as a way to align development discourses with discourses of Islam.

Guaranteeing the rights of the poor

IICO and IIROSA's rationale, building on notions of solidarity, encouraged conceptions of the relationship between giver and recipient as a personal and intimate relationship, expressed in terms of brotherhood and family, and resonating with the prominent position of individual donors. Muslim Aid and Islamic Relief's more abstract rationale, based on notions of a common humanity and the rights of the poor and aimed not only at individual donors but also, and increasingly so, at development agencies, has different consequences for the ways in which the aid chain is conceptualised.[44] In particular three aspects are worth mentioning: the agency of recipients, the prominence of the NGO, and the invisibility of individual donors.

First, the notion of aid as predicated on a contractual relationship of rights and duties encourages a conception of recipients as proactive agents rather than grateful beneficiaries. In both Islamic Relief and Muslim Aid, recipients are portrayed as individuals who are capable and willing to change their lives. For instance, Islamic Relief's 2009 Annual Report front page shows a picture of a woman harvesting fruit, smiling at the camera. The text reads: 'Ismeta Hutinovic tending her crop of fruit trees in Bosnia-Herzegovina. Ismeta and her husband took out an interest-free loan from Islamic Relief to start up a fruit-growing business.'[45] Through a 'people-centred', 'inclusive', and 'beneficiary-led [...] approach'[46] 'involving communities in their own development',[47] recipients are interpellated as active agents of change, entering into partnerships on equal terms with the NGOs in order 'to identify their needs and collectively find ways of overcoming their problems'.[48] Unlike IICO and IIROSA, Muslim Aid and Islamic Relief do not see their role as one of 'rescuing', 'liberating', and 'saving' the poor, but instead as one of 'enabling', 'assisting', and 'mobilising' them.[49] At the same time, however, there is a clear limit to the agency of recipients. They are never entirely autonomous, capable of changing their fate themselves, but have to be assisted by the NGOs, facilitating their change. Case stories printed in annual reports and on websites all describe this process, following roughly the same pattern of change from misery and suffering to relief, through organisational intervention. On its website, Muslim Aid posts a story about Anis: '"I couldn't see clearly and my eyes used to tear a lot if I read for too long. Now I can see much better than before," said Anis, who was diagnosed with long-sightedness at Muslim Aid Sri Lanka's eye camp and prescribed glasses by the doctor.'[50] Almost resembling a religious conversion, the meeting with Islamic Relief and Muslim Aid is described as a turning point, leaving recipients empowered and capable of changing their own lives—but also grateful and somehow obliged to pay back this gift of self-realisation, as in Islamic Relief's story about Piyara: 'Piyara is so happy with the help she has received that she is now committed to spreading the message of disaster preparedness to other communities.'[51]

Interestingly, recipients' gratitude is not directed at the individual donor, as in IICO and IIROSA. When aid is a moral duty rather than an act of solidarity, there is no sense in praising the giver. This is reflected first and foremost in the fact that donors are not mentioned very often—neither in interviews nor in PR material—compared to IICO and IIROSA where discourses are often, implicitly or explicitly, directed at 'the generous donors'. Secondly, donors are not praised, but addressed in much more pragmatic terms, through an instructive and sometimes slightly lecturing language. 'What will YOU sacrifice this Eid?'[52] Muslim Aid asks its donors, using a straightforward approach far from IICO and

IIROSA's admiration and reverence towards its 'generous donors'. And further, addressing its orphan sponsors: 'Your sponsorship is not a substitute for a loving caring family.'[53] Similarly, Islamic Relief UK encourages donors to support the organisation with the somewhat patronising: 'Just help one.'[54] Unlike in IIROSA and IICO, for Islamic Relief and Muslim Aid individual donors are not the ultimate givers of aid, but merely 'supporters' and 'facilitators' of the aid that the organisations have chosen to give. They are not treated as masters to be served by the organisations, but as students who can learn from the organisations. In a brochure promoting donations through *waqf*, Islamic Relief presents a number of short stories about fictional donors, neatly illustrating this educational function. All stories provide examples of people who, after having been educated by Islamic Relief, decide to support the organisation. One story tells about Abdullah who, after hearing about the work of Islamic Relief through a friend, 'decided that participating in the Waqf Future Fund would be more beneficial for him [than buying a car] in the long term.'[55] Another example of this educational function is Muslim Aid's orphan sponsorship programme. As one donor says, after having visited his sponsor child: 'The visit has given me an insight into the life of Bosnian children after the war as well as a real feel for the people of Bosnia. I will Insha'Allah try my best to inform and educate other brothers, family and friends.'[56]

Instead, gratitude is directed at Islamic Relief and Muslim Aid, and, more abstractly, to 'the message of disaster preparedness' (or the message of development more generally). When aid is a question of rights, the NGO becomes important as the guarantor that this right is upheld. Thus, the aid chain is not so much a direct and personal relation between donor and recipient, with the NGO serving as facilitator (as we saw in IIROSA and IICO) as it is an institutional relation between NGO and recipient, with the donor serving as the facilitator. Islamic Relief's Accountability Framework, with the title *Enabling Poor People to Shape their Future*, aptly expresses this relationship, emphasising the organisation's accountability towards recipients rather than towards donors: 'In order to create [a] quality relationship with our beneficiaries and to be responsible for the burden given to us by donors, we must start by increasing our accountability to them.'[57] This rationale resonates well with (and is encouraged by) institutional donor expectations. They do not have the same explicit demands or expectations of gratitude, and their institutionalised, de-personalised support gives the NGOs a possibility to maintain an illusion of independence and sovereignty (all the while they are of course subjected to a wide range of other demands and expectations). According to staff, the increase in institutional funding has enabled the organisation to work more freely. A person from Islamic Relief's headquarters says: 'In 1999, less than 5 per cent of our funds came from institutional donors and the majority from private donors. This restricted us, as donors push the work in a certain direction. Now, 30 per cent are from institutional donors, which allows us to do more development-oriented, demanding work.' His colleague says: 'Our support from institutional donors such as DFID, UN and others paid for the activities that the individual donors wouldn't pay for.' As such, the individual donor is increasingly marginalised and scorned as the one who ties down the NGO, preventing it from engaging in professional development activities, while the institutional donor is idealised as facilitator of the NGO's (albeit illusory) position as independent from donor demands. At the same time, however, segments in both organisations are sceptical of these changes in the aid chain, preferring aid provision to remain a direct relation between recipient and donor, and the organisations to be merely 'a channel for the faithful, who wish to perform their religious duty to the poor and give to charity', as described in one of Muslim Aid's publications from the pre-institutional funding era.[58] A Muslim Aid staff member in Britain notes: 'Until some years ago the organisation perceived itself as the administrator of other people's zakat. They would collect money, find local partners and distribute the money as grants through them.' Another staff member explains: '[The religious conservatives] see sending grants as the best way to fight poverty. In their view, our duty is to get the money to the people in need as soon as possible. There are religious arguments for this. You cannot keep the money for the poor for long.' We shall discuss this further in the section on strategies below.

Strategies of aid

Now, how is the vision and the underlying rationale manifested in concrete strategies? In order to reach their vision of 'sustainable livelihoods' for the poor, Islamic Relief and Muslim Aid engage in a wide range of concrete activities, in Islamic Relief clustered under almost lyrical headings such as 'Protecting life and dignity', 'Empowering communities', and 'Campaigning for change' while Muslim Aid sticks to more prosaic ones such as 'Emergency relief', 'Healthcare and nutrition', 'Economic empowerment' and '*Qurbani/Ramadan*'. See Tables 7.3 and 7.4 for an overview of activities and budgets. These activities can be organised under three different headings, presenting three different strategies that each expresses slightly different ways of merging Islam and mainstream development aid: long-term development, Islamic traditions, and Islamic development, each representing different ways of merging aid and religion. These strategies should be understood in general terms, as tendencies and repertoires of action rather than in the sense of concrete organisational activities.

Table 7.3: Islamic Relief, overview of activities (2011)[59]

Activity	Percentage
Protecting life and dignity	47
Providing access to healthcare & water	19
Sustainable livelihoods	14
Caring for orphans and children in need	13
Supporting education	5
Campaigning for change	1
Total	99*

*Numbers have been rounded up/down which is why the totals do not equal 100 per cent.

Table 7.4: Muslim Aid, overview of activities (2011)[60]

Activities	Percentage
Emergency relief	64
Healthcare and nutrition	9
Economic empowerment	7
Education	6
Qurbani/Ramadan	5
Water and sanitation	5
Rainbow family	5
Total	101*

*Numbers have been rounded up/down which is why the totals do not equal 100 per cent.

Aid as long-term development: Empowering the poor

In order to solve problems of poverty, Islamic Relief and Muslim Aid introduce the strategy of what we may call 'long-term development', reflecting their vision of 'sustainable livelihoods' and echoing the mainstream vocabulary in the development culture. This is the dominant strategy in the two organisations, encompassing and shaping almost all activities. In defining this strategy, the organisations rely on a now common dichotomy between, on the one hand, 'development', and on the other, 'charity' and 'hand-outs'. 'Development' as a strategy is about long-term, sustainable activities, empowering poor individuals to change their lives, while charity and hand-outs are short-term, providing immediate relief but not contributing to any real change in the lives of the poor. In the publication *Translating Faith into Development*, Islamic Relief notes that

> the focus of Muslim charities' activities has generally been quite paternalistic and centred in particular on providing relief and basic services—there has been only limited involvement in longer-term development projects that focus on empowering the poor. Involvement in advocacy campaigns that address the root causes of poverty has been almost entirely absent. This contrasts with the activities of western secular and non-Muslim faith based organisations.[61]

Both organisations often emphasise their own progress from a focus on short-term emergency relief and traditional Islamic charity to long-term development activities, reflecting an increase in expenses for activities such as 'education and vocational training' and 'sustainable livelihoods' (even though they do in fact still spend a much larger part of their budget on relief activities). One person says: 'Now, we are starting to explore other ways of combating poverty.' As noted in an Islamic Relief Annual Report:

> When Islamic Relief was initially set up we responded to natural and manmade disasters. As the scope and scale of our activities increased, we began to address the long-term requirements of people in need and started tackling the underlying causes of poverty by promoting sustainable development.[62]

Muslim Aid describes its organisational history in similar terms:

> Muslim Aid was founded in 1985 when leading British Muslim organisations joined together to respond to endemic humanitarian crises in Africa [...] As the charity grew, the scope of its work expanded. Whilst continuing to fulfil its commitment to emergency relief work Muslim Aid also began to

implement long-term development programmes. Today, Muslim Aid is tackling the root causes of poverty through education and skills training, economic empowerment, orphan care, women development, water, healthcare and shelter and construction programmes.[63]

This hierarchisation of strategies is not uncommon among NGOs. Especially since the 1990s, the mainstream aid field has seen an increasing obsession with 'sustainable development', reflecting an almost paradigmatic shift in conceptions of aid (Benthall 2008a:88). For many NGOs, aid has changed from being about the provision of immediate relief to the suffering, handing out food and building shelters, to a focus on 'sustainability,' 'participation' and 'capacity building', aimed at 'empowering' people to become self-reliant and productive, active agents of their own development (Stirrat and Henkel 1997:73).[64] In this process, the provision of immediate relief came to be seen as somewhat misguided and even suspect, placing the poor as passive recipients of charity, locked in positions of dependency. At the same time, this paradigmatic shift represents an increased emphasis on issues of planning, management, and organisation—in short, the professionalisation of aid—forged in opposition to the immediacy and spontaneity of charity and relief. With the increasing popularity of the discourse of sustainable development, it has come to encompass a broad range of activities. Both organisations distinguish between relief and development, but maintain that the overall approach is development-oriented, integrating relief efforts into an overall development strategy to tackle 'the root causes of poverty'.[65] Downplaying the random, short-term, and immediate character of emergency relief, the organisations insert such activities in a long-term, planned-for framework under the heading of 'disaster preparedness programmes' and 'disaster management schemes', aimed at 'empower[ing] communities to deal proactively with emergency situations.'[66]

The strategy of sustainable development leaves little room for religion. Islamic Relief and Muslim Aid both claim that 'Islamic values […] are embedded and integrated into our programmes,'[67] but in concrete terms, religion is almost invisible in most activities. This is particularly emphasised among country office staff, where people rarely mentioned religion: 'We have no intention to use Islam in our work. We feel no need to tell people about Islam,' says a manager of one of Muslim Aid's projects in Bangladesh, adding with a smile: 'And honestly, how much information do we have about Islam?' Another person, from Islamic Relief's headquarters, says: 'These are all standard programmes, there are no specific Islamic elements in this.' There is no mention of mosques, Qur'an schools, or religious tapes—neither when staff members talk about activities, nor in annual reports or at project sites. At one of Islamic Relief's project sites in Bangladesh, we meet with a group of women, the 'beneficiaries' of the project. In the middle of their weekly meeting with the 'village motivator', all the women are gathered in the village centre—a square of maybe 50 m², surrounded by mud huts and palm trees. Here, they learn about topics such as 'group dynamics', 'income generation activities', and 'disaster preparedness', all of them (stereo)typical activities of mainstream development aid. 'This way, we try to develop their capacity, so they can join the development mainstream,' one staff member explains to me. I ask the women if they talked about Islam at their weekly meetings and they all laugh and shake their heads. 'We talk more about practical things,' a woman says. A staff member adds: 'Our main objective is to provide an input to beneficiaries—what they are doing in relation to Allah, to their God, that's their own business, that's not really our business.'

In fact, religious activities and development activities are, at least to a certain degree, seen as opposites, and the activities of visibly religious organisations such as IICO and IIROSA are considered as 'old-fashioned charity' and 'hand-outs'. 'The classical Muslim way of doing charity is about building a mosque, digging a well, distributing food,' one person explains. 'This is fine, it is helpful. But in Islamic Relief, we have decided not to build mosques. We find that funds can be used to something more important such as reducing poverty, building capacity.' 'When we work, we don't go to the Qur'an to see what to do. We work from a development perspective,' says a project manager in Muslim Aid, responsible for a health project in Bangladesh. Islam is irrelevant to the installation of water pumps in the villages; to the training of young, unemployed electricians in the slums; and to the running of health clinics in refugee camps. In fact, it might even be an obstacle to long-term sustainability. As a person from one of the country's offices says: 'The IICO and the IIROSA, I don't know much about them, but I would assume that they are traditional. They spend a lot of money slaughtering sheep for *Qurbani* and the next day, it's all gone. It doesn't last. They need to think more strategically, they need strategic support.' Or as another staff member puts it: 'The Middle Eastern NGOs are very narrow-minded in their approach. Its only relief, only about *Qurbani*, distribution of food, those kinds of things. We do that as well, of course, but only as a small part of our programme. Our main focus is development.'

This secularisation of activities is closely related to the increase in institutional funding from development aid agencies such as DFID and ECHO. As the Islamic Relief staff member quoted in the introduction to the chapter says, the day-to-day activities of the organisation are shaped much more by 'Western principles and donor wishes' than by Islamic principles. This process of secularisation concurrent with increased funding from development agencies has been noted by other researchers studying religious organisations, arguing that the influence of religion tends to decline over time as organisations adapt to donor conditions and imperatives (Chambre 2001:452), and that organisations that accept government funds may struggle to maintain their religious values and goals (Thaut 2009)—what Kuzma (2000:39) refers to as the 'mission creep' problem. Thus, Ebaugh et al. (2006:2269) as well as Smith and Sosin (2001:654) both find a negative correlation between religiosity and institutional funding, concluding that activities are fundamentally altered in a secular direction when NGOs get institutional funding. Or as Green et al. (2010) put it, in contexts of externally driven development agendas, faith-based organisations are not fundamentally different from other, secular, NGOs. Reflecting this process of homogenisation, a staff member in Muslim Aid Bangladesh says, comparing activities in his organisation with those of secular NGOs: '[T]he donor funding is the same, the reporting mechanisms are the same, the places we work are the same, the way we implement projects is the same. So how could there be any differences?'

Aid as Islamic tradition: Ramadan meals and *Qurbani* slaughters

Parallel to this secularised development strategy, in part shaped by and directed at institutional donors, we find another strategy, much more explicitly religious. This strategy may not be as dominant as the development strategy, but it is older and can be traced back to the early years of the organisations. At least on the surface this strategy is coined in terms quite different from the development strategy—here, aid is not about 'vocational training' or 'health clinics', but about '*Qurbani* sacrifices', 'Ramadan meals', and 'orphan sponsorships'. It is, in other words, about activities that are defined by and growing out of Islamic traditions of charity. Apart from paying *zakat* and giving *sadaqa*, there are a number

155

of specific traditions related to charitable giving in Islam. Some of them are part of annual holidays, such as serving *ifthar* meals and paying *zakat al fitr* to the poor during Ramadan, slaughtering goats and cows for *Qurbani* and giving a part to the poor; others relate to life events, such as *akeekah*, the slaughtering of animals on the seventh day after a child's birth and giving parts to the poor; and yet others are thematic, such as supporting orphans because the Prophet Muhammed himself was an orphan. Through different activities, Islamic Relief and Muslim Aid seek to uphold some of these traditions; during Ramadan, for instance, they distribute food packages, and for *Qurbani*, they slaughter cows and distribute the meat. In Muslim Aid, these activities make up 5 per cent of the budget. Islamic Relief no longer specifies its expenditure on *Qurbani* and Ramadan (in itself an interesting point), but in 2009, the organisation spent more than 10 per cent of its budget on these activities.[68]

Different aspects shape this strategy. First, and most obviously, the religious activities are a way for the organisations to facilitate individual donors' wish to uphold religious rituals and traditions, and through these, to be a good Muslim, honour God, and collect religious rewards. A staff member from Muslim Aid's office in Bangladesh says: 'Muslims donate to charity. They donate when they have a child, if they cannot fast during Ramadan, and so on. So these sorts of religious funds keep coming.' This function becomes particularly important in a context such as the British one, where Muslims are a minority. As one person says, it is not really possible to slaughter a goat in your backyard in Birmingham in order to celebrate the birth of your son. Secondly, these religious traditions do not only serve to facilitate religious rewards for individual donors, they also function as a way to establish and maintain bonds between immigrants and their country of origin. Many Muslims in Britain still have relatives in their country of origin, they go on vacation there, and some find their husband or wife there. Giving to Muslim Aid or Islamic Relief can be a way for donors to support their country of origin. As a staff member in Muslim Aid's office in Bangladesh explains to me:

> The Muslims in UK they know about the people in their villages, they are in the back of their minds, so they want to send them something. It's a spiritual thing, a mental thing. It's not development, it's a divine feeling. One person from here, one person from there—they are thinking about each other. Family bonds are very strong here.

Some staff members, in particular among trustees and older staff, consider these religious activities to be the authentic and original activities of the organisation and the individual donors to be the core sources of funding. They are sceptical of the more recent development-oriented strategies and the institutional funding, fearing that this will lead the organisation to forget its responsibilities as a Muslim organisation and alienation of individual donors. In their perspective, individual donors come to be equated with religiously defined aid, institutional with secular aid. Others—in particular the young, country office staff—are more critical of the *Qurbani* sacrifices and the Ramadan meals. While accepting their historical and religious legacy in the organisations, many are uncomfortable with the potential challenges to mainstream development that these activities present, threatening the reputation of the organisations among institutional donors as 'moderate' development-oriented NGOs.

In order to overcome the schism between mainstream development ideals and religious wishes of donors (and certain staff and trustees), there is a constant attempt on the part of the organisations to adjust the religious activities to development strategies through ideological negotiations. One way of doing this is to compartmentalise these activities as 'special', 'not normal', and 'seasonal', restricted to specific times of the year. In publications, these activities are often relegated to the last pages. In Muslim Aid's *25th Anniversary Souvenir* brochure, for instance, the section on 'Seasonal programmes' is placed at the far end, after the sections on 'Partners' and 'Your contributions'.[69] Thus, rather than seeing these religious activities as an integrated part of aid provision (as IICO and IIROSA do), Islamic Relief and Muslim Aid present a compartmentalised and isolated religiosity, relegated to the sphere of religious holidays. A different way of adjusting seasonal activities to mainstream development is to align them through slight reformulations and reinventions. An example is the annual celebration of *Qurbani*. Each year, both Islamic Relief and Muslim Aid slaughter thousands of cows and goats and distribute the meat to the poor. In 2009, Islamic Relief slaughtered 360 cows in Bangladesh alone, distributing the meat in packages of 1–2 kg to more than 20,000 families. But rather than legitimising these 'seasonal' activities by reference to religious traditions, they are often explained in terms of development principles, described as regular food distribution or combined with vocational training and economic empowerment projects. In a similar vein, and aligning Islamic traditions with principles of universalism, both Islamic Relief and Muslim Aid attempt to include non-Muslims, at least in their Ramadan activities: 'The *Qurbani* distribution is only for Muslims, other religions don't like it. The Hindus don't eat cow meat, you know [...] For Ramadan, it's different. Our food package includes 13 kg of rice, flour, sugar, many basic things. So it's for everyone, other religions are interested in this as well,' the person responsible for Islamic Relief's seasonal activities in Bangladesh explains to me.

Another example is the orphan sponsorship programme, a highly popular activity with both organisations. As noted above, care of orphans is an old Islamic tradition. The Prophet Muhammad was an orphan, and it is said that he who supports an orphan will be close to Muhammad in heaven. 'The orphans are very special in our religion,' says one staff member from Muslim Aid's headquarters. Islamic Relief supports 27,000 orphan children in twenty-three different countries, 6,000 of these in Pakistan which is the biggest programme. In Bangladesh, the organisation supports more than 450 orphans. Muslim Aid supports more than 1,400 children, around 100 of them in Bangladesh. The organisations offer the children financial support, education, and health check-ups until they are eighteen years old (girls in some cases until they get married). Staff members often note that in itself the orphan sponsorship programme cannot be characterised as 'sustainable development': 'In my opinion, the sponsorship programme does not contribute to development in the sense of teaching people to fish. It just gives people a fish,' says a top manager from Islamic Relief's headquarters, continuing: 'I'm not saying that we should abandon the sponsorship programme, it plays an important religious role and it's important for the donors, but we need to complement it with other programmes, such as microfinance.' Instead of cancelling the programme, which would upset thousands of donors, the organisation tries to combine it with education and vocational training for the children, teaching them about human rights, HIV/AIDS, gender equality and other mainstream development topics, thus satisfying both religious and institutional donors. In Bangladesh, I visited one group of adolescent orphans and their teachers, two young women—one of them was Mona who I mentioned in Chapter 1. The teachers meet with the young people five times a month, sometimes in their homes, sometimes in the local resource centre, or in the schools. Listing their main activities, one of the teachers says: 'We teach them about life skills, reproductive health, HIV/AIDS, sexually transmitted diseases, adoles-

cent life, sexual behaviour, general health, social behaviour, early marriage—if you marry early, your life will be ruined, you know.' On the day
of my visit, the teachers have organised an event on the occasion of the
international HIV/AIDS day, inviting local politicians and public figures to speak. A small booklet has been produced by Islamic Relief for
the event, listing scientific facts about the disease as well as giving advice
on how to avoid the disease, get treatment and treat people who are
infected. 'This is a donor requirement, it's part of government curricula,'
the project manager tells me. Based on the booklet, the speakers talked
about the importance of staying with one partner, and if that is not possible, to use condoms. All the adolescents sit on wooden benches, listen-
ing to the speeches. There is no gender segregation, and many of the girls
are unveiled. After the speeches, all participants form a procession, walk-
ing to the city centre while shouting slogans such as 'Access for everyone to human rights' and 'Support the international HIV/AIDS day'.
Compared with IIROSA's orphan education, described above, this kind
of education is thoroughly embedded in a development culture.

Aid as Islamic development: 'Translating faith into development'

Now, the analysis of Islamic Relief and Muslim Aid has presented us
with two kinds of strategies: One—the most dominant, in terms of discourses, if not in terms of funding—is a secular strategy reflecting mainstream development discourses and activities, and building on a secularised notion of religion. The other, perhaps less dominant but older,
strategy turns on 'seasonal' activities, legitimated in and defined by religious traditions, albeit increasingly adjusted to development ideals. There
is, however, a group of activities that cannot easily be placed under the
rubric of either 'secular development' or 'seasonal activities'. Instead, these
activities—including for instance Islamic microfinance projects and disaster preparedness training in mosques—can be seen as expressions of a
third strategy, seeking to Islamise development, presenting concepts of
development, universalism and human rights as truly Islamic. This strategy builds on the idea of the added value of Muslim aid organisations,
echoing an instrumentalist religious authority and arguments about religious proximity, as laid out above: religion is useful, because it can improve
the concrete implementation of mainstream development activities. Staff
members tell me how religion can be a helpful tool in countries such as

Bangladesh and Somalia, facilitating communication of development principles to a pious population: 'We tell them, in Islam, education is important,' a top manager in Muslim Aid's headquarters says. 'If you don't send your children to school, you are not fulfilling your religious duties.' Another person, likewise a top manager, but in Islamic Relief's headquarters, says: 'The effect is much stronger if Islamic Relief says the Prophet Muhammad encouraged breast feeding than if someone says that professor so and so encourages it.' Likewise, many people note that religious organisations are more aware of beneficiaries' religious demands and traditions, winning over people and gaining access. One person from the headquarters tells me about the work of Islamic Relief in Pakistan:

> South East Asians are more conservative than Africans. So when we work there, we respect for instance gender separation and we have to make sure that only women teach women. We worked in South Pakistan, which is very very conservative, and we first worked with the male community organisation and it took two years before we were allowed to work with the women. I don't think other organisations would have been allowed.

Finally, religious structures and leaders can be used to further development projects and ideas. In Muslim Aid, for instance, there are plans to implement a non-formal education programme in Somalia together with UNICEF, and the person responsible for this project tells me that he has suggested that the education be based in local mosques: 'There's no education infrastructure there. So we said, why don't we use the mosques for education? They are only used five times a day for prayer, the rest of the time they are empty. The Prophet himself used the mosque as a school.'

One of Islamic Relief's first attempts to integrate religion into its development activities was a project implemented in Bangladesh in 1996. Bringing together forty imams from rural areas, the purpose of the project was to teach these religious leaders about development issues and encourage them to talk about this in their Friday sermons. The training lasted for a week, and the first two days were spent arguing, the project manager (who now works in the headquarters) tells me: 'But in the end, we agreed on almost everything—except for the issues related to family planning. So we said, let's leave that and focus on the other things.' The group decided to focus on children's rights and drafted ten sermons, based on UNICEF's educational material, *Facts for Life*. Of the forty people participating, thirty-five pledged to be 'social mobilisers', using these texts in their Friday sermons. When I visited Islamic Relief in Bangladesh, the country director was considering a similar idea—training imams in disaster preparedness: 'Because you know, the mosques are the first places people go to when there's a disaster, and the mosque is the first charity to help people,' he explains. 'So maybe if we trained the people, we could improve and enhance their capacities to tackle this situation. And working with the mosques, you get access to all locations.' Despite the obvious focus on a particular religious group, he maintains that this would not be a 'religious activity' but an activity that would benefit 'the whole community'. This comment displays the inherent tensions in the strategy of Islamised development, on the one hand promoting the strengths of a particular religious identity and on the other hand claiming to be based on universalist principles.

Another example of the strategy of Islamic development is the microfinance loans that both Islamic Relief and Muslim Aid offer, reinventing Islamic principles and integrating them into a mainstream development project. These activities are frequently promoted by staff and in PR material as 'Islamic', and as such, as something that distinguishes the organisations from others. Today, most international NGOs run some form of microfinance activities, and in this perspective, there is not necessarily anything particularly 'Islamic' about Islamic Relief and Muslim Aid's microfinance projects. Their microfinance projects are organised the same way that most other microfinance projects are, and at first sight, it is difficult to find any signs that they should be particularly Islamic. Muslim Aid's training material on cattle rearing talks about beef fattening, cow weight tables, and vaccinations, and in Islamic Relief's community group meetings, the women discuss fertilisers, insects, and harvest times. Nobody mentions anything about Islamic principles and practices. The only visible signs of a religious identity I find in Muslim Aid are on the back of the pink booklet in which the women write down their weekly instalments. Here, a number of principles are listed, echoing the Grameen Bank's sixteen decisions but slightly reformulating them and integrating religious sayings.[70] Quoting the Qur'an, one principle reads 'We will obey our religious beliefs and rules and encourage other people to practice their own religion,' another 'We will send our children to school and madrasa' and a third 'We will grow garden vegetables in the land of our home.'[71] But for the two organisations, the particular Islamicness of their microfinance projects lies elsewhere. Staff members frequently point out that unlike other organisations, their microfinance projects have an almost 100 per cent pay-back rate; repayment rates being the main indicator for success in microfinance projects (Cons and Paprocki 2010). And this success is ascribed to a specific Islamic approach. For Islamic Relief, the particular Islamicness of their microfinance activities lies in the fact that the organisation gives loans in kind, based on Islamic economic principles: 'We don't charge interests, we don't give them cash, Instead we talk to them about what they would like to do, give them training and then we buy them a cow or what ever they want. This way, they don't spend the money on other things. This is the Islamic way,' says a manager of one of the projects in Bangladesh. For Muslim Aid, what makes the organisation's activities Islamic is also the fact that there are no interests on the loans, in Islam considered *haram* (sinful). As one person in Muslim Aid's country office explains: 'This is the home of micro finance, but I think you'll find that our projects are a bit different. We only charge a minimum of service charges. Some organisations charge more than 15 per cent in interests, for them it's more like a business. For us, it's only about covering costs'. In both cases, Islam is what makes the Muslim organisations' microfinance more successful, fair and sincere. Thus, based on Islamic economic principles, the microfinance programme has a distinct religious character (at least on the surface), but is at the same time in line with mainstream development ideals of sustainability and capacity building, and as such serves as a perfect example of the added value that religious NGOs can bring to development aid.

A secularised aid?

A secularised aid. This is, at least at a first glance, what Islamic Relief and Muslim Aid seem to be presenting. Compared to IIROSA and IICO's sacralised aid, Islamic Relief and Muslim Aid both try to promote an aid that resonates with the values of the development aid culture, more specifically those of institutional donors such as DFID, and ECHO, framing themselves as highly professional organisations, based on a vision of sustainable livelihoods for the poor, a universalist approach to recipients, and a strategy of long-term development. As such, the two organisations seem to have accommodated their ideology to the culture of development aid without major modifications: it is an ideology that may have religious roots but whose strategies are not designed to fulfil a religious vision or assist a religiously defined target group, whose donors are not religiously defined and whose staff are chosen for professional rather than religious qualifications (Thaut 2009:333, G. Clarke 2008:32). In this, they are fundamentally different from IICO and IIROSA, resembling instead many contemporary Christian NGOs—something which hints at the analytical point that differences between different conceptions of aid and religion may in fact be of much greater importance than differences between Muslim and Christian organisations, or religious and secular organisations. Having undergone much the same secularisation processes in their attempts to integrate into the mainstream development culture, NGOs such as Christian Aid and DanChurchAid today present an understanding of aid as thoroughly secular. Roots, motivation and values may be religious, but the provision of aid in itself may not. This is what Thaut (2009:333) in her typology of Christian NGOs calls 'the accommodative-humanitarian agency'.

In aid ideologies such as those presented by Islamic Relief, Muslim Aid, and many Christian NGOs, religion cannot be an all-encompassing element, as in IIROSA and IICO, as it would violate fundamental principles of a distinction between aid and religion. Instead, religion is confined to specific and well-defined functions and spaces, acceptable primarily in the form of underlying values and 'ethical references' (Benedetti 2006:855), inspiring and motivating people rather than shaping organisational activities and structures in concrete and visible ways. In this perspective, Islam is primarily about individual, or perhaps interpersonal, spirituality, thus resembling what Lincoln (2003) has called a 'minimalist religiosity'. This type of religiosity is particularly pronounced among the young development professionals in the two organisations. Paraphrasing Nagel and Staeheli (2009:101), for these staff members, religion remains intensely personal and private, even as it shapes the way they view the world and their motivations for working in an NGO. Disillusioned with their parents' version of Islam which they see as an introverted and culturally tainted 'village Islam,' they search for a more universalist Islam, more compatible with modernity and the lives they lead in Britain (P. Lewis 2007). This is 'a worldly religion that talks about inner peace and spiritual well-being and rejects religious observance in which rite is an end in itself' (Tammam and Haenni 2003, cf. Mandaville 2007:329).

This conception of religion and aid does not remain uncontested, however. Chapter 7 showed that, unlike IIROSA and IICO, Islamic Relief and Muslim Aid are strongly heterogeneous organisations: not only are their audiences heterogeneous, including individual Muslim donors (in itself a diverse group of people) as well as mainstream development agencies and NGOs such as DFID, ECHO, and Oxfam; their organisational constellation is also highly heterogeneous, roughly divided into religious conservatives (among trustees, management and older staff members) and development professionals (among the young staff members and in country offices). This heterogeneity is reflected in organisational ideologies, characterised by continuous conflicts and negotiations. Although dominant in organisational discourses, the ideological interpretation of aid as secularised is constantly challenged by some trustees and older staff members. Basing their understanding of aid on the values of a traditional Islamic aid culture rather than those of the mainstream development culture, they seek to present an aid ideology that resonates with their own religiosity as well as that of conservative Muslim donors. For them, Islam is a collectively oriented social practice, visibly manifested in social activism through rituals, traditions and dogma (and as such, in many ways similar to the religiosity of many people in IIROSA and IICO). They want an aid ideology in which the religious character remains distinct; an organisation which maintains a clear religious orientation as the primary motivation for its work, with closer ties to religious authorities and donors, more religious staff and an explicitly religious working culture, as well as a religiously influenced approach to identifying and working with beneficiaries (Thaut 2009:337, G. Clarke 2008:32).

At the same time, the secularised aid ideology is also challenged from other sides, insofar as development agencies such as DFID do not simply want to support yet another secularised NGO. They expect Islamic Relief and Muslim Aid to present an 'added value' as faith-based organisations, distinguishing themselves from non-religious NGOs and promoting the strengths and unique qualities of being a Muslim organisation. They expect Muslim NGOs to be able to facilitate access and improved communication with recipients, using their religious identity as a tool to enhance development efforts without ever compromising development principles of neutrality, universalism and non-confessionalism.

Juggling with these different expectations from within and without the organisation, Islamic Relief and Muslim Aid present attempts at merging the cultures of development and Islamic aid by Islamising development aid in different ways. Compared to IIROSA and IICO, and somewhat simplifying, one may say that this is an ideology which builds primarily on the culture of development aid, while integrating elements from the Islamic aid culture, whereas IICO and IIROSA's ideology of developmentalised Islamic aid builds on the culture of Islamic aid, integrating elements from development aid. In IIROSA and IICO, the two cultures were merged through strategies of adoption, pragmatic alignment and integration. Islamic Relief and Muslim Aid present their own ways of merging cultural frames, although in some respects mirroring those of IICO and IIROSA. Perhaps the most controversial approach to merging elements of development and Islamic aid is an approach that we may term subversive merging. This is an approach that seeks to maintain one type of frame unofficially while promoting another officially. An example of subversive merging is found internally in both organisations where trustees and older staff attempt to maintain conservative religious practices. Although the board has encouraged the increasing secularisation of aid activities as a way of attracting institutional funding, trustees still expect a certain level of religiosity among their staff members. This is particularly evident in relation to issues of gender practices. Despite official adherence to mainstream development ideals of gender equality, the organisations employ fewer women than men, women are rarely employed in top management positions and they are often subject to indirect or direct pressure to comply with religious rules such as covering. Another approach is ambiguity. As noted above, a constructive ambiguity about core terms (Hammack and Heydemann 2009:22) can conceal ideological differences (Dahl 2001:20; cf. Mosse 2005:36). This approach has proven particularly useful in relation to issues of *zakat* where individual donor expectations of *zakat* as an exclusively Muslim mechanism of redistribution clash with institutional development donor demands for universalism. Avoiding any definitive or categorical statements, Islamic Relief and Muslim Aid maintain a constructive ambiguity, opening up for different interpretations. This approach is closely related to that of pragmatic alignment (described in Chapter 6). In IIROSA and IICO, pragmatic alignment served as a way for the organisations to align their religious solidarity with development principles of universality. In Muslim Aid and Islamic Relief, it also works the other way around to align the organisation's universalist approach with donors' expectations of a religious solidarity. Finally, Islamic Relief and Muslim Aid rely on integration as an approach to merging different cultural frames. Like IIROSA and IICO integrated aspects of the development culture into the culture of Islamic aid, Muslim Aid and Islamic Relief integrate elements of Islamic aid into the culture of development aid. Examples of this approach abound, as can be inferred from the above. One example is the inclusion of imams in disaster management training, using religious structures to promote the message of development. Another example is the microfinance programmes that both organisations run. Based on Islamic economic principles, the microfinance programme has a distinct religious character, but is at the same time in line with mainstream development ideals of empowerment and self-reliance, and as such serves as a perfect example of the added value that Muslim NGOs are expected to bring to development aid.

While the analysis of IIROSA and IICO demonstrated that these organisations cannot simply be understood as 'fundamentalist' or 'traditional' Muslim organisations that completely reject the culture of development aid, the present analysis has in turn showed that Islamic Relief and Muslim Aid must be understood more broadly than as 'moderate' faith-based organisations, firmly embedded in the culture of development aid. Instead, they are highly complex and hybrid organisations, constantly balancing multiple expectations of widely differing audiences. A former Islamic Relief staff member says, somewhat frustratedly, that he thinks all these expectations of Islamic Relief are sometimes unfair: '[A] fter all it is simply a humanitarian aid organisation.' But the point is precisely this: in the contemporary aid field, transnational Muslim NGOs can never simply be humanitarian aid organisations; they have to simultaneously be secular development NGOs, faith-based organisations and Islamic charities.

8

CONCLUSION

Studying transnational Muslim NGOs

It is all about raising 'good, Muslim citizens'. This is how Hanin, quoted in the 'Introduction' to this book, explained IIROSA's provision of aid to poor orphans in Jordan. Her fellow aid worker, Mona, from Islamic Relief's office in Bangladesh had a different view. For her, providing aid to orphans was about raising awareness of the dangers of HIV/AIDS and early marriage. This book grew out of a wish to better understand the underlying aid ideologies guiding and motivating people like Hanin and Mona and the organisations they work in. What are the visions, rationale, and strategies for transnational Muslim aid provision—and what is the role of Islam in this? What are the factors and conditions that have shaped their aid ideologies? And where do transnational Muslim NGOs position themselves in the broader context of aid provision? Based on case studies of four transnational Muslim NGOs—Islamic Relief, Muslim Aid, the International Islamic Relief Organisation and the International Islamic Charitable Organisation—I have sought to answer these questions, analysing the ways in which meanings associated with aid and Islam are produced, expressed, contested and reworked in certain ways, how historical processes have led to those particular meaning constructions, and how they are redefined in the light of changing social, economic and political contexts (Deneulin and Rakodi 2011:51).

In this, I have tried to rethink conventional approaches to the study of transnational Muslim NGOs. As was discussed in Chapter 1, transnational Muslim NGOs have traditionally been studied as political actors or as faith-based organisations, often with a view to determine their positive or negative contributions to respectively politics and aid. While both of these literatures have contributed to bringing to the fore a kind of organisation that is often overlooked, they also present a number of weaknesses insofar as they are characterised by an instrumentalist, and often normative, understanding of transnational Muslim NGOs, exploring their potential as tools for the implementation of development projects or in a political struggle for the Islamisation of society. Without neglecting this instrumentalist role of certain organisations, the present book has sought to nuance the picture of transnational Muslim NGOs by broadening the scope of the analysis, based on explorative and empirical case studies.

For one, I have approached transnational Muslim NGOs first and foremost as NGOs engaged in aid provision rather than as tools in political struggles for the Islamisation of society. As such, I have sought to challenge not only conventional analyses of transnational Muslim NGOs, but also broader tendencies to view all things Muslim or Islamic through the lenses of the political. Quoting Melucci (1989), I have argued that we must put aside old habits of viewing social processes solely through the lenses of the political, reducing the social to matters of the political, and instead pay attention to those discourses and practices that may seem invisible, irrelevant or simply uninteresting in terms of formal political power but which perhaps play an important role at other levels of society, informing and shaping the production of social norms, values and morality. In other words, 'social' expressions of Islam are not interesting only or even primarily because of their potential influence on the formal political system, but because they might influence and change what is outside the formal political system—civil societies, behaviour, attitudes, cultural symbols, and value systems (Bayat 2005:898). With this analysis, I hope to have contributed to conceptualising and thinking about public Islam such that its significance exists in something other (or at least something more) than an interest in influencing the formal political system (Mandaville 2008)—in shaping conceptions and cultures of aid, for instance.

Second, I have approached transnational Muslim NGOs as NGOs rather than as faith-based organisations, seeking to challenge some of the conceptions underlying contemporary studies of faith-based organisations. As has been discussed above, much literature on faith-based organisations is based on preconceived and rather static notions of 'religion' as well as 'aid'. Very little research seems to open itself up to the question of what such terms mean for these NGOs. Against this, I have conceptualised religion not as a static or single variable, but as processes of religionisation, as an aspect of meaning construction, on a par with constructions of 'aid'. Instead of discussing pros and cons of the integration of faith-based organisations in development, this approach has opened up to broader explorations of the ways in which religion and aid are signified and practiced in these organisations, and thereby allowing for more flexible, multifaceted and subjective conceptions of the nexus between aid and religion. To grasp these processes and systems of meaning construction, I have used the concept of ideology, here defined as a meaning system or a world view that is formulated and shared by a group of people, with the purpose of guiding and motivating them in their quest for what they perceive to be the common good or the ideal society, as well as promoting and justifying their agenda, garnering support and ensuring legitimacy (Snow and Benford 1988:198; Williams 1995:125). As such, the analysis focused on the ways in which transnational Muslim NGOs conceptualise what they are doing and why they are doing it, imagine what they are trying to accomplish, and understand what constitutes the available sets of acceptable or legitimate discourses on aid and Islam (Hammack and Heydemann 2009:8).

Cultures of aid: Development and Islamic aid

Much literature has conceptualised the field of aid provision in terms of a largely Western system of development aid, at the expense of other, more periphery forms of aid provision, thus downplaying the fact that aid provision is a site of struggle between different aid paradigms (Tvedt 2002:370). Seeking to decentre such mainstream conceptions of aid provision, Chapter 3 of the book put forth the argument that transnational Muslim NGOs and their ideologies are best contextualised as part of two different aid cultures; namely a, largely Western, culture of development aid, and a, largely Middle Eastern, culture of Islamic aid, shaped by different historical trajectories: the development culture has grown out of an experience of power and hegemony, of colonising, but also out of sentiments of collective guilt and a sense of complicity in the creation of 'the distant sufferer', stemming from the same colonial legacy (Chouraliaki 2010:111). The Middle Eastern Islamic aid culture, on the other hand, is shaped by experiences of marginalisation, of being colonised, and of the poor not as a distant sufferer, but as a fellow member of the (religious) community. Against this background, the development culture, promoted by actors such as the United Nations, the World Bank, Western governmental aid agencies, and transnational NGOs, emphasises concepts such as universalism and neutrality, assuming a strictly secularised conception of religion. The Islamic aid culture, promoted by the Muslim Brotherhood, the Muslim World League, Islamic personalities, and local charity associations, emphasises notions of solidarity and justice, closely intertwined with a visible, pervasive religiosity.

Again, I should emphasise that this division into an Islamic aid culture and a (largely) Western aid culture was not meant as a repetition of Huntington's clash of civilisations thesis, insofar as I do not see the two cultures as inherently oppositional, just like I do not consider them to be generic but temporary and historically specific, constantly changing and over time merging into new cultures. In this perspective, and echoing Arce and Long (2000:24), the analysis of the ways in which transnational Muslim NGOs navigate in relation to these two cultures should be understood as an attempt at abandoning binary oppositions, and instead focusing on the interplay, joint appropriation, and transformation of different bodies of knowledge that takes place at the intersection of different cultures.

Trajectories of transnational Muslim NGOs

The historical trajectories of the organisations, outlined in Chapter 3, testified to this constant interplay between the two cultures of aid, in different ways and with differing intensity shaping the organisations and the ways in which they conceptualise aid. Overall, transnational Muslim NGOs can be seen as expressions of two parallel phenomena: the surge of transnational development NGOs and the increase in transnational Muslim organisations as part of the Islamic resurgence in the 1980s. Throughout the 1980s and 1990s, however, transnational Muslim NGOs positioned themselves as part of an Islamic aid culture rather than a culture of development aid, focusing their aid on fellow Muslim recipients. Getting most of their funding from Muslim individuals, businesses and sometimes governments in the Middle East, they did not need European or North American donors; they cooperated little with UN and other international institutions; and they did not participate in transnational networks for NGO cooperation. Even Muslim NGOs in the West focused primarily, if not entirely, on fellow Muslim donors and recipients, serving mainly as vehicles for the distribution of *zakat* from immigrants to poor people in their villages of origin. As such, transnational Muslim NGOs lived largely parallel lives to those of actors in the culture of development aid, primarily relating to these actors by way of competition, conflict or at best parallel co-existence.

This parallel existence came to an end with 9/11 and the War on Terror, at once forcing and encouraging transnational Muslim NGOs to relate explicitly to the culture of development aid, thus transforming them into sites of cultural meetings. Within a year of the attacks, several transnational Muslim NGOs were closed down or banned from working, suspected of cooperating with Al-Qaeda or other militant networks. Later, governments and inter-governmental organisations introduced a range of new laws, policies, and regulations, aimed at preventing and obstructing NGO involvement in terrorist activities. These 'hard' measures to crack down on 'terrorist' NGOs have been coupled with 'softer' approaches seeking to encourage cooperation with Muslim NGOs in order to prevent radicalisation (Howell and Lind 2009:47) and to strengthen relations with potential bridge builders. This focus on Muslim NGOs has coincided with a general interest in faith-based NGOs among development aid agencies and NGOs, considering the religious identity of organisations an instrument and an added value in the effective implementation of development aid. Thus, after 9/11, transnational Muslim NGOs were now navigating in an environment of increasing regulation and control, but with simultaneous possibilities for cooperation and funding, opening up for new repertoires of action.

Against this background, transnational Muslim NGOs came to be positioned in different ways: Some were hailed as 'moderate' (that is, adhering to the norms of Western development aid), while others came to be seen as 'fundamentalist' and 'traditional' (that is, embedded in a Middle Eastern Islamic aid culture). Exploring the ways in which four concrete Muslim NGOs position themselves in the contemporary aid field, the different ways in which they draw on different cultures of aid in their formulation of aid ideologies, I have sought to go beyond these simplistic categorisations of transnational Muslim NGOs, challenging or at least softening such dichotomies. More specifically, I identified two different types of organisations; namely the UK-based and the Gulf-based NGOs, constituting paradigmatic examples of transnational Muslim NGOs. Through studies of these two types of organisations, Chapters 4 to 7 provided in-depth analyses of the ways in which the post-9/11 situation has contributed to shaping their organisational identities and ideologies.

Sacralised or secularised aid?

Overall, the ideologies of these transnational Muslim NGOs can be divided into two different kinds, turning on two different conceptualisations of the nexus between Islam and aid: one ideology, presented by the two Gulf-based NGOs, rests on an understanding of Islam and aid as closely intertwined and inseparable—a sacralised aid—while the other, presented by the two UK-based NGOs, understands Islam and aid as two separate categories—a secularised aid. This conceptualisation, illustrating characteristics of transnational Muslim NGOs by way of a dichotomy between sacralised and secularised aid, is of course merely an analytical abstraction. In reality, the four NGOs I have studied are not as easily categorised, and as such, the dichotomy I have presented here should perhaps be seen as an illustration of different ways of conceptualising aid and Islam rather than different kinds of Muslim NGOs, making room for the possibility that organisations find new ways of conceptualising aid—something which they, as the analysis has also demonstrated, constantly do (and which shall be discussed further below).

The sacralised aid ideology, as found in IIROSA and IICO, builds on a conception of Islam and aid as indivisible. Underlying this ideology of sacralised aid is an understanding of Islam as an all-encompassing, or, to use Lincoln's (2003:59) terms, a maximalist religion, manifested in all aspects of life, and potentially relevant to all aspects of aid (in practice, this does not necessarily mean that Islam is part of all aspects of aid, but it means that there is no systematic or principled division between aid and Islam). This ideology is often expressed in an emotional, moral language, with claims to a religious authority that turns on notions of morality and compliance with religious doctrines. Arguing that aid is Islam and Islam is aid, this ideology formulates a vision of aid as simultaneously contributing to satisfying individual Muslim needs and strengthening the *umma*, with strategies responding to a conception of poverty as both spiritual and material. Based on an ideological rationale of Islamic solidarity among members of the *umma*, the ideology obliges Muslims to take care of people in need, idealising intimate and personal bonds of brotherhood between giver and receiver, and prioritising fellow Muslims over non-Muslims. This is, in other words, aid for the *umma* rather than for humanity.

The secularised aid ideology, found in Islamic Relief and Muslim Aid, promotes a conception of aid and Islam as two distinct categories, reflecting secular principles of mainstream development aid. This is aid for humanity, not for the *umma*. Contrary to the all-encompassing Islam that underlies the sacralised aid ideology, this ideology rests on a conception of Islam as compartmentalised and primarily relegated to the sphere of values and individual motivation; what Lincoln (2003:59) refers to as a minimalist religion. Often expressed in a technocratic, bureaucratic jargon, this ideology relies on a strongly professional authority, emphasising notions of accountability, expertise, and neutrality. Aid is about responding to material poverty, not about spiritually strengthening the Muslim *umma*, and as such, there is no need for strategies to be religiously defined. Poverty is best fought through economic development projects, not through Islamic education. In this, religion may serve as an underlying rationale, an 'ethical reference' (Benedetti 2006:855), but the obligation to provide aid is not uniquely Muslim. It is a human duty, based on the Millennium Development Goals and the Universal Declaration of Human Rights as much as on the Qur'an. Contrary to the religious solidarity underlying the sacralised aid ideology, this abstract notion of humanity leads to a universalist understanding of recipients as fellow human beings rather than fellow Muslim brothers and sisters.

On a side note, this is not only a relevant dichotomy in relation to Muslim organisations, but is mirrored among Christian NGOs. In her typology of Christian aid organisations, Thaut (2009) places so-called accomodative-humanitarian organisations such as Christian Aid at one end of her spectrum, and evangelistic-humanitarian organisations such as Samaritarian Purse at the other. While Christian Aid and other accomodative-humanitarian organisations argue for a sharp distinction between aid and religious mission, Samaritan Purse and other evangelistic-humanitarian organisations have an express goal to save lives and souls through their work (Thaut 2009:325). This raises the question whether differences between degrees or kinds of religiosity internally among Christian or Muslim organisations are in fact more important than differences between Muslim and Christian NGOs, or between religious and secular NGOs, for that matter?

Developmentalising Islamic aid and Islamising development aid

As hinted at above, this dichotomy between sacralised and secularised aid does not fully capture the ways in which the four transnational Muslim NGOs conceptualise aid and Islam, leaving the reader with the impression that IICO and IIROSA with their sacralised aid ideology are embedded in a Middle Eastern Islamic aid culture, while Islamic Relief and Muslim Aid, promoting a secularised aid ideology, are completely integrated into a Western culture of development aid. However, as the analysis has shown, things are in effect much more complicated. IIROSA and IICO may be firmly embedded in an Islamic aid culture, but they are simultaneously trying to approach the UN and other 'international' donors. Likewise, Islamic Relief and Muslim Aid might be the new darlings of Western development donors such as DFID and ECHO, but they also have to attend to individual Muslim donors, staff, and trustees' demands for an authentic Islamic aid as well as development donors' expectations of an added value of faith-based organisations. Thus, all four organisations are—albeit to differing degrees—positioned between two aid cultures, trying to satisfy expectations of different audiences. Merging, translating and appropriating elements from the two aid cultures, they seek to construct ideologies that are simultaneously legitimate to these widely different audiences.

Speaking from within the Islamic aid culture, IIROSA and IICO increasingly seek to align themselves with the culture of mainstream development aid, thereby hoping to create resonance with the UN and Western aid organisations. While it may be premature to speak of an actual secularisation, we can characterise this move towards the mainstream development culture as a process of 'developmentalisation', witnessed for instance in the adoption of mainstream development ideals of accountability, transparency and neutrality, and the simultaneous rejection not only of Islamic traditions of donor anonymity, but also of conceptions of aid as a tool in political struggles for justice. Another example of this is the pragmatic alignment of the organisations' solidarity-driven focus on fellow Muslims and mainstream principles of universality, central to the culture of development aid. Claiming their principled support for a universalist approach, IIROSA and IICO state that they focus primarily on Muslims out of pragmatic reasons, as such ensuring resonance with mainstream development ideals. And a third example is the introduction of *tawkeel* as an Islamic form of empowerment, testifying to the developmentalisation of an Islamic concept.

Islamic Relief and Muslim Aid, on the other hand, speak primarily from within the culture of development aid, but attempt to Islamise their conceptions of aid in order to meet not only the demands for an authentic religiosity among individual Muslim donors, trustees, and older staff members, but also development aid agencies' demands for an 'added value' of religion. Juggling with these different expectations, Islamic Relief and Muslim Aid present different ways of Islamising their secularised aid. For instance, by avoiding any definitive or categorical statements with regard to the use of *zakat*, Islamic Relief and Muslim Aid maintain a constructive ambiguity, remaining open to Muslim donor wishes for an exclusively Muslim mechanism of redistribution while not rejecting secular development agencies' demands for universalism. Similarly, the organisations attempt to maintain conservative religious practices internally, while promoting gender equality externally. Finally, and perhaps most importantly, Islamic Relief and Muslim Aid take elements from the culture of Islamic aid and use them to promote the culture of development aid, thus seeking to satisfy institutional development donors' requests for an added value of Muslim NGOs, as is done for instance in microfinance projects and the inclusion of imams in disaster management training.

The emergence of new aid cultures?

Do transnational Muslim NGOs provide aid for humanity or for the *umma*? Put differently, do they see themselves primarily as part of mainstream development traditions or in relation to a global Muslim community? With this book I hope to have shown that it is not a question of either one or the other, but that organisations can simultaneously, and with differing degrees of intensity, incorporate and reject elements from different cultures, constructing and adjusting their own aid ideologies.

In this process, they break down the boundaries between the cultures of development and Islamic aid, contributing to the creation of new cultures. Through their ideological negotiations and repertoires of appropriation, the four organisations have drawn the contours of such new cultures. By rejecting certain cultural elements and emphasising others, they have told us something about what kinds of aid are seen as legitimate today, and by extension, what contemporary aid cultures look like.

Returning to the dichotomies of aid outlined in Chapter 2, we may take a first step into describing these emerging aid cultures. I have argued that, pre-9/11, the cultures of development and Islamic aid could be conceived in terms of dichotomies between universalism and solidarity, neutrality and justice, and secularism and religion, often played out within an overall dichotomy between the West and the Middle East. With these dichotomies in mind, a number of points can be put forth, giving some indications as to the characteristics of the post-9/11 aid field. Overall, the cultures of development and Islamic aid no longer seem predicated on a sharp geographical distinction between the West and the Middle East. This is of course a process that began already with the establishment of Western Muslim NGOs such as Islamic Relief and Muslim Aid, but recent years have witnessed further blurring of these boundaries; most notably with the inclusion of young, British-born Muslim and non-Muslim staff as well as Western donors in these two organisations, but also with IICO and IIROSA's increasing internationalisation of their boards of trustees and cooperation partners. At the same time, some Western Muslim NGOs seem to return to a re-sacralisation of their aid, reaching out to the Islamic aid culture, while some Gulf-based NGOs seek to developmentalise their aid, aligning it with principles of the mainstream development culture.

More specifically, the contemporary aid field is characterised by three trends: the prominence of professionalism as a core source of legitimacy; the instrumentalisation of religion; and the introduction of the notion of religious proximity. Each of these trends points in its own way to new characteristics of—and potential problems for—the contemporary aid field, testifying to the ever-changing and contested nature of the field. First, the analysis has drawn the contours of an aid field in which the paradigm of professionalism is increasingly dominant. Especially since 9/11, conceptions of aid as justice are no longer legitimate for Muslim NGOs, and political neutrality has become an obligatory and indispensable condition for legitimacy. Making claims to a professional authority, the transnational Muslim NGOs studied here all unanimously emphasise their allegiance to principles of accountability and transparency as the only legitimate way to respond to allegations of terrorist financing. In other words, to be an NGO in today's aid field is to be a professional NGO, primarily understood in terms of financial professionalism. At the same time, some NGOs increasingly adhere to broader notions of professionalism, including not only financial systems, but also the professionalisation of staff and activities, often as a response to expectations from governmental and intergovernmental aid agencies. While the professionalisation of financial systems may be easily aligned with claims to religious authority, such broader processes of professionalisation are not entirely unproblematic for the organisations, challenging core aspects of organisational identity. In the context of aid provision, professionalism is bound with notions of institutionalisation and expertise, while religious authority turns on notions of personal care and morality. Thus, as was seen in Muslim Aid and Islamic Relief, professionalisation of staff and activities inevitably leads to a perceived loss of religious authenticity and distinctiveness. Barnett (2005:733) aptly describes this dilemma, when he says that religious organisations which increasingly drift toward rational principles as a way of defending their legitimacy might not only have difficulty competing with commercial firms but may also undermine their moral authority: 'The presumed difference between the Wal-Marts and the World Vision is that the former does not have moral authority while the latter does.' In this, the trajectories of Muslim NGOs echo not only those of contemporary Christian NGOs, as has been hinted at above, but also those of secular NGOs in the 1980s and 1990s, perhaps pointing to more deep-seated contradictions between NGOs, predicated on a moral authority, and the institutionalised aid system, predicated on a professional authority.

Second, the analysis has demonstrated how the aid field is no longer predicated on a strict dichotomy between the secular and the religious, distinguishing instead between different, and more or less acceptable, kinds of religiosity. Since 9/11, the contemporary development culture has increasingly opened up towards so-called faith-based organisations. However, this opening only includes certain organisations. Development aid agencies want a religiosity that complies with secular development principles, that is, either a personalised moral religiosity, relegated to the sphere of individual motivations, or an instrumentalised religiosity, used as a tool to enhance development efforts. In other words, it is a religiosity that is compatible with, but fundamentally subsidiary to, development aid. In practice, then, the dichotomy between religious and secular is replaced with a dichotomy between confessional and non-confessional aid. Today's NGOs can be religious, and they may even use this religiosity as a tool to meet the material needs of recipients, but they cannot use it to meet their religious needs. However, this may be exactly what recipients expect from religious organisations. Judging from Palmer's (2011) analysis of Islamic Relief's work among Rohingya refugees in Bangladesh, there are indications that the kind of Islam promoted by this organisation, avoiding overtly or explicitly religious activities such as mosque building or Qur'an classes, may very well resonate with development aid agencies' expectations of a non-confessional, non-discriminatory aid, but not with expectations of individual Muslim recipients. According to Palmer (2011:103), religious leaders in the refugee camp claimed that their religious needs were not being met by Islamic Relief, referring to the lack of key religious facilities, including graveyards, madrasas, and mosques. She quotes a Rohingya refugee as saying: 'We want Islamic Relief to establish a mosque inside the camp as we think they are Muslim and they should understand our needs. We can live without food but we can't live without our religion...' (cf. Palmer 2011:103). Thus, from the perspective of (some) recipients, a missionary religiosity such as that found in IIROSA and IICO may in fact be preferred over the non-confessional religiosity of Islamic Relief and Muslim Aid.

Third, the introduction of the argument of religious proximity points to the emergence of a position between that of solidarity and universalism. As has been described, this argument posits that a common religion (much like a common culture) creates a symbolic sense of community among recipients and NGOs, which in turn brings about 'added value' through, for instance, ease of access and provision of more appropriate services (Palmer 2011:97). Nursing ideas of 'cultural rights', 'cultural authenticity' and 'cultural relativism', this position echoes recent development ideas of cultural sensitivity, respect and understanding, inspired by trends in anthropology and multiculturalism (G. Clarke 2008, Palmer 2011). In this perspective, NGOs can, if only temporarily, maintain claims to religious solidarity without violating development principles of universality. However, there are at least two fundamental problems with the religious proximity approach: first, underlying the argument is an under-standing of religion as a source of community and solidarity (Palmer 2011:98), a coherent language that all adherents speak and understand. But, as has been demonstrated with all clarity in the above, religion is as much a source of conflict and division as of community. Second, albeit related, the religious proximity argument prioritises the religious iden-tity of recipients and NGO staff over the myriad of other possible iden-tities, such as class, nationality, political stance or gender. In the words of de Kadt (2009:784): 'Taking religion seriously is one matter, but it becomes seriously problematic when it is promoted as the only identity that counts, disregarding the many other components of identity that should be salient in different situations, thereby truncating a broader sense of self.'

The success of these new trends is predicated on at least two factors: one is the continuing interest in faith-based organisations among devel-opment aid agencies. The culture of development aid has a history of infatuation with buzzwords (Cornwall 2007), 'faith-based organisations' being only the latest of many. Will the interest in transnational Muslim NGOs fade, as the interest in NGOs arguably has, once development aid agencies realise that they are not the 'magic bullet' of development? Adding to this risk of re-marginalisation is a continuous scepticism of the inclusion of religion in development among staff in many aid agen-cies. When interviewing staff at DFID, for instance, G. Clarke (2007) noted significant concerns about the erosion of the agency's historical secularism. Similarly, the history of the World Faiths Development Dialogue reflects a weariness of religious organisations among World Bank staff. According to Marshall (2005:4), the launch of the initiative was met with 'widely varying and fundamental objections' among staff and board members, a scepticism that has never completely gone away. The other factor is the emergence of new donors in the Islamic aid cul-ture. The OIC is increasingly engaged in aid provision and cooperation with NGOs, opening up the possibility that transnational Muslim NGOs may turn towards this organisation for resources and cooperation, min-imising their need for acceptance by, for example, the UN, DFID and Western NGOs.[1] Likewise, the Saudi and Kuwaiti governments have in recent years been increasing their contributions to aid provision. According to the OECD's Development Assistance Committee, Kuwait's official development assistance increased from US$ 160.9 million in 2004 to

US$ 283.2 million in 2008, and Saudi aid increased from US$1.7 billion to US$ 5.6 billion, making Saudi Arabia one of the largest non-DAC donors (Coghlan, McCabe and Thornton 2010:209). Likewise, recent years have seen an increase in these countries' funding of relief efforts; in 2010, for instance, Saudi Arabia pledged US$ 220 million to Pakistan, surpassing the pledges of all European donors together (Al-Yahya and Fustier 2011:4). And in 2013, the Kuwaiti government pledged US$ 300 million in humanitarian support for Syrian refugees and internally displaced people.[2] Depending on the direction taken by the aid ideologies of these new donors, this may mean that Muslim NGOs will have greater room for manoeuvre in defining the role of Islam in their work and identity in the future.

APPENDIX A

METHODOLOGY

Collection of data

Data for the analysis of the four transnational Muslim NGOs has been collected by way of a three-pronged approach, inspired by ethnographic, journalistic, and micro-sociological methods: gathering of documents, semi-structured interviews, and so-called presentations, the former expressing official representational discourses and the two latter more individualised representational discourses. All data has been collected in the period from 2007 to 2013, the majority in the years 2008 to 2010, and as such, they (re)present the four organisations at a particular moment in history.

First, I have collected documents about and by the organisations, including most importantly website information, annual reports, financial statements, policies, brochures, project documents, and photos.[1] These documents reflect and express official representational discourses; they are negotiated and agreed-upon discourses presented by the organisations rather than by individuals in the organisations. A few documents have an identifiable author, but most do not, presenting instead the organisation as the authoritative author. As such, these documents reflect the official ideology of the organisations, conveying the image the organisations want their audiences to see.[2] But ideologies are not only expressed in texts, as deterritorialised and disembodied official representations; they are also expressed in and through concrete people and the ways in which they present themselves, their organisation, and their activities. Therefore, my case studies also rely on data collected through visits to the four organisations. Although the official representations are per definition more coherent and consistent, the individualised representations play an equally important role in the maintenance and development of ideologies, formulating links between discourse and practice and ensuring the continued relevance of the ideology. Thus, rather than competing kinds of representations, they should be seen as complementary aspects of the same ideology, describing different aspects. Geographically, my fieldwork included visits to all four headquarters, located in respectively Britain, Kuwait, and Saudi Arabia, and to selected country offices in Bangladesh and Jordan as well as a brief trip to Lebanon. The visits were carried out in 2008 and 2009, each lasting between one and five weeks, altogether a period of approximately four months. During my visits to the four NGO headquarters and country offices, I conducted almost 100 interviews, attempting to cover a broad range of different representatives from the organisations and including headquarter staff, country office staff, trustees, management, and regular staff as well as male and female staff. In addition to staff in the four organisations, I have conducted more than 30 interviews with representatives of other national and transnational aid organisations, Muslim as well as non-Muslim, as well as other resource persons, serving as background and context information to the analysis.[3] Finally, apart from interviews, I would also collect organisational material through what we may call presentations: staff would present their organisation to me, they would present other staff, and, most importantly, they would present organisational project sites. In total, I have visited more than 30 project sites, including orphanages and day-care centres, vocational training centres, microfinance projects, HIV/AIDS campaigns, and dyke construction sites, to mention only a few. Often, I would visit several projects in one day, spending an hour or two at each site, conducting short interviews with staff and recipients and getting a tour of the facilities.

The challenges of multi-sited fieldwork

This particular fieldwork design, including visits to different geographical sites carries some inherent challenges. In principle, multi-sited fieldwork can of course be exactly as in-depth and long as single-sited fieldwork, but in practice it will most often be much shorter since the researcher has to visit several different sites in the same time other researchers visit one. In my case, I remember looking enviously at my fellow PhD student's one-year return ticket to Pakistan, while desperately trying to squeeze my own trips to Britain, Bangladesh, Jordan, Kuwait, Lebanon, Saudi Arabia (and then Britain once more) into the same time period. Such a large number of sites combined with a restricted timeframe meant that I was not able to spend more than a few weeks in each site, something which naturally had some consequences for the kinds of data I was able to collect.

First, the short visits of multi-sited fieldwork had implications for my understanding of context. Logically, with shorter visits comes a loss of descriptive details (Nadai and Maeder 2005), not only of the organisational discourses and practices, but also of their immediate context. In other words, with visits to six different countries, my knowledge of each national context is substantially less detailed than if I had only visited one country. Does this lack of contextualisation mean that multi-sited research such as the present study is 'rushed' or indeed 'bad' research? (Nadai and Maeder 2005). Two responses to this can be advanced: one is pragmatic, arguing that it is simply a question of focus. Thus, while a single-site study of the headquarters of one transnational NGO would perhaps be based on a more detailed description of the local or national context, it would most likely lack information on international or transnational aspects such as relations to country offices, project site activities and cooperation with intergovernmental institutions—aspects which the present study includes. Another response would question more fundamentally the notion of 'context', challenging expectations of complete contextualisation. Nadai and Maeder (2005) argue that this ideal of contextualisation stems from the classic anthropological fieldwork tradition, focusing on a particular and clearly bounded culture in a single place (ideally an island), and encouraging holistic representations of this entity. In this perspective, the 'context' is a relatively easily defined and delimited thing, and complete contextualisation is a tenable ideal. But contemporary ethnographic research takes place in increasingly complex societies, aiming not to describe society in its entirety, but particular social forms and expressions. This means that the boundaries of a particular 'context' are no longer an empirical reality, but must be constructed by the researcher. This perspective underlines an attention to gaps and lacks and blind angles in any contextualisation, but at the same time opens up alternative ways of contextualising. In the present analysis, then, transnational Muslim NGOs are contextualised on a number of different levels: overall, they are seen as part of, and shaped by, global and transnational aid cultures. At the same time, they are situated in relation to particular historical trajectories. And finally, individual NGOs are placed in concrete national and local contexts, exploring their specific organisational constellations and audiences.

Another consequence of the fieldwork design centres more specifically on my interaction with staff in the organisations. Due to the short duration of my visits, I would only interview people once (or, in some cases, twice), and most often on the organisation's own premises (that is, in an office or a meeting room). Likewise, my visits to project sites would often be relatively short and always accompanied by country office staff. With little time to build up mutual confidence, to observe other than the most visible practices or to explore alternative interpretations, visits of this length and kind generate a certain kind of data, centring on external (re)presentations. Thus, I did not witness any fights or gossip between staff members, nor did I hear much about financial problems or visit any failed projects, just as I did not read internal memos or staff meeting minutes. Instead I was presented with annual reports on glossy paper, I visited what management considered the most successful projects, and I talked to the most competent and eloquent staff members. I did, in other words, by and large see the organisations as they wanted me to see them. As such, one could argue that I did not get a 'real' picture of the organisations; I did not scrape the surface to find out what was underneath this image I was presented with. Is it really true what they say? Do their strategies work? Are their recipients as happy as they say they are? While it is certainly true that this picture shows only a certain part of the organisations, such criticism misses the point of the present study. The purpose of this study has never been to present complete ethnographies of the four organisations in question, covering all aspects of their work and identity (insofar as that is even possible). Instead, the analysis focuses on a very specific aspect of these organisations, namely their construction, expression, and presentation of ideologies of aid. In this perspective, it does not matter whether the information I get is 'real' or not—what matters is that this is what the organisational representatives have chosen to present, thus to some degree expressing the self-image and (re)presentations of the organisation. In the words of Hilhorst (2003:4), NGOs present different faces to different stakeholders and in different situations, and one face is not more 'real' than the other. My interest lies in what face people present to me, how they present it, and why they choose to present me with precisely this face.

Questions of positioning: Studying the familiar and the foreign

For me, to study Muslim NGOs was in many ways to study the familiar (Alvesson 2003); in particular when I was studying strongly development-oriented NGOs such as Muslim Aid and Islamic Relief. I am a former NGO employee myself; I have worked in Save the Children and in Danish Red Cross. I know about empowerment, capacity building, and rights-based approaches. I have been a project manager and I have taken courses in LogFrame Approaches. I have been to coordination meetings, written tender applications, and I have reported, monitored, and evaluated. In short, I know the 'NGO speak' (Tvedt 1998). This familiarity with the field was further strengthened by two things: one, when setting up interviews with staff, my contacts in Muslim Aid and Islamic Relief would often select young development professionals rather than older, more religiously conservative staff. Whether this was part of a conscious strategy to present me with the organisations' most 'development-friendly' face, an attempt to couple me with people they thought would be sympathetic to my project, or simply a coincidence, I do not know. Two, when choosing to study Islamic Relief and Muslim Aid's country offices in Bangladesh over say, Pakistan, I (unknowingly at the time) chose two country offices that are, according to many staff members, among the more liberal ones in terms of organisational religiosity. A former staff member of Islamic Relief says: 'There is quite some variation in staff opinions depending upon where you visit—there are more religious offices and less religious ones. Bangladesh is one of the less religious ones. Opinions and therefore impressions of the organisation would differ greatly if you went to, say, Pakistan.'

This has a number of methodological ramifications, including—but not restricted to—questions of rapport and analytical distance. First, my identity as a former NGO employee shaped meetings with people in different ways. With many, it would contribute to strengthening rapport, creating a sense of intimacy and bonding. 'Hey, we are almost colleagues!' In some cases, this connection was further strengthened by the fact that we would be of more or less the same age, share almost the same educational background, and be at roughly the same level in the job hierarchy. The fact that I was 'studying over' rather than 'up' or 'down' (Markowitz 2001) contributed to creating a collegial atmosphere which not only meant that people would feel comfortable using insider jargon and share technical and professional details, knowing that I would understand; it also meant that they would sometimes voice their criticisms of the organisation to me, complaining about low salaries, bossy managers and work overload or voicing alternative visions for the organisation. However, as in any conversation with a colleague from a different organisation, there were limits to this honesty, shaped not only by conceptions of organisational loyalty but also concerns as to the trustworthiness of the colleague.

Second, being familiar to the field not only has consequences for how one is received by actors in this field; it also shapes one's views and understanding of the field. Because I know the field, there may be things I do not see, things I take for granted, things I do not problematise. Speaking the NGO speak, in other words, does not only potentially enable and facilitate research; it is also potentially delimiting. This situation, common to all researchers studying the familiar, raises the question of how to create analytical distance, allowing for a new look at the field. An obvious strategy is the adoption of an analytical language to describe the field. However, this is particularly tricky for students of NGOs insofar as the language used in the NGOs often overlaps with the analytical language used to study the NGOs. Concepts such as 'civil society', 'faith-based organisation' and 'development' are simultaneously analytical terms and part of NGO practices and discourses. They are, in other words, at once emic and etic, creating what Cunningham (1999) calls a representational conundrum. In order to overcome this, I avoid the analytical use of these terms, introducing instead a set of alternative, and hopefully more neutral, terms. For instance, the choice of 'aid culture' over 'development system' is grounded in a desire to introduce a relatively neutral term into a field loaded with normative and ideological terminology. Picking a neutral point from where to describe the field makes it possible to analyse more loaded terms and concepts as part of the normative and ideological struggles of the field. Thus, in this perspective, rather than analytical concepts, terms such as 'civil society', 'faith-based organisation', and 'development' are considered empirical categories to be explored—part of a specific aid culture's ideologies, values and rules rather than generic and universally valid categories.

If studying NGOs was for me to study the familiar, studying Muslims and Islam was in some ways to study the foreign. This was particularly clear in my studies of the two Gulf-based NGOs, IICO and IIROSA, based in Kuwait and Saudi Arabia. In particular since 9/11, Muslims and Islam have come to be the significant 'Other' in contemporary Western society, in part constituted through what we may call the War on Terror discourse, resting on a sharp dichotomy between 'Islam' and 'the West'. This highly politicised environment has had different consequences for the present study. In concrete terms, the War on Terror discourse has framed and shaped many of my interviews. Attempting to study Muslim NGOs as something else than potential fronts for terrorist activity, I would initially seek to place my analysis firmly outside the War on Terror discourse. Before each interview, I would explicitly state that I was interested in the relationship between Islam and aid; not the relationship between Islam and terrorism. However, rather than sidestepping or overcoming the War on Terror discourse, this statement of course expressed the impossibility of escaping the discourse. The mere fact that I felt it necessary to distance myself and the study from the War on Terror discourse underlined its all-encompassing presence. Responses to my statement further confirmed the importance and inescapability of this discourse. People would often explain their own involvement and the purpose of their organisation in terms of a global struggle to promote 'moderate' interpretations of Islam, combating on the one hand stereotypical Western images of Islam, and on the other, militant and extremist expressions of Islam.

The War on Terror discourse and its underlying dichotomy dividing the world into 'Islam' and 'the West' also shaped some people's perceptions of me. Within this logic, a few people would see me as a 'bad Westerner', an agent or a spy, perhaps even working for 'the Jews'. My nationality would only add to their scepticism, evoking memories of the infamous cartoon crisis in 2005. They would be reluctant to speak, clearly fearing my misrepresentations of their work and religion (Bolognani 2007:282), and only telling me the most basic information.[4] Most people, however, positioned me as the 'Good Westerner' or the 'Good Non-Muslim'; as someone who was dedicated to conveying a true image of Islam and Muslim organisations to the Western public (as opposed to 'bad Westerners' whose research focuses on terrorism and fundamentalism). In their perspective, I was a bridge-builder and potential spokesperson for Muslim NGOs, and many would explicitly thank me for carrying out the study, which they saw as a chance for them to 'get the record straight' and 'tell it like it is' to a Western, non-Muslim audience (Bolognani 2007:288). While I would try to make sure not to create false expectations as to my ability to and interest in functioning as a mouthpiece of transnational Muslim NGOs, I would not object to being positioned as the 'Good Non-Muslim' or 'Good Westerner'. In fact, I would sometimes actively seek to place myself in this position, distancing myself from what I see as stereotypical or discriminating treatment of Muslims and Islam in the Western media and the public, just like I would question the tendency within academic studies of Islam to prioritise studies of terrorism, fundamentalism and extremism over other topics.

Accessing transnational Muslim NGOs

Naturally, the different ways in which I was positioned and positioned myself in relation to the four organisations shaped my study in myriad ways, many of which I am probably not even aware of myself. However, in particular one point is important to underline, insofar as it has very concrete consequences for the analysis, and that is the question of access to material. As noted above, the case studies build on organisational texts as well as interviews with and presentations by staff in organisational headquarters and country offices. But due, at least in part, to my position as respectively a foreigner and a familiar face, my access to material differed widely in the Gulf-based and UK-based organisations. Influenced by traditions of secrecy, hierarchy, and, not least, scepticism towards the West (and, by extension, me), IIROSA and IICO would not share much material with me.[5] This unwillingness was, at least among some people, further strengthened by unfamiliarity on the part of IIROSA and IICO staff with the sociological methods underlying my study (and, not least, my own incapacity to communicate this approach to people), due to different educational traditions. For instance, while management were generally welcoming and willing to participate in interviews, some were somewhat uncomprehending to my requests to speak with regular staff. As one manager noted with surprise when I asked him whether he could arrange an interview with one or two of his staff members: 'Why do you need to talk to them?' implying that he had just told me all there was to know about the organisation. Likewise, many people did not see the point in lengthy interviews, considering them to be primarily for the communication of facts, prioritising quantitative information over qualitative. Finally, many were wary of sharing information and taking me to visit their project sites without explicit approval from top management. This was the case with the IICO office in Bangladesh. Despite several attempts at obtaining permission from the organisation's top management, I did not succeed in getting full access to the organisation; I was only allowed two interviews with representatives from IICO, and did not visit any of the organisation's project sites.

In comparison, I interviewed more than 30 people from Islamic Relief and Muslim Aid in Bangladesh, visiting several of their project sites and activities. In general, Islamic Relief and Muslim Aid were willing to share with me much of their material. Educated in the same research traditions as me, most people would immediately understand the methods I used, setting up interviews with people from different organisational layers, expecting interviews to last at least one hour, and organising two- and three-day trips to project sites. Further contributing to this openness, Muslim Aid and Islamic Relief, being based in Britain, operate in a context in which demands for accountability are legally consolidated, meaning that they are obliged to share organisational information. All this means that the analysis of Islamic Relief and Muslim Aid builds on much more extensive material than IICO and IIROSA, including not only far more interviews and project visits, but also more written material in the form of website text, reports, PR material, policy papers, and project documents, reflecting a fundamental difference between the two kinds of organisations. This in turn may have resulted in more detailed analyses of Islamic Relief and Muslim Aid. A further consequence is that the wealth of available material on Islamic Relief and Muslim Aid allowed for much greater insights into ideological conflicts and negotiations than the more sparse material on IIROSA and IICO. This is not to say that the analysis of IICO and IIROSA is invalid, as it still builds on a substantial amount of material. Furthermore, insofar as the analysis centers on representational discourses, these issues of transparency and access are not only methodological obstacles; they tell us important things about the ways in which the two Gulf-based organisations relate (or do not relate) to the culture of development aid, and how they differ from the British-based ones in this, as is discussed throughout the book.

APPENDIX B

ORGANISATIONAL MATERIAL[1]

For documents that are available online, references to websites have been included. All websites referenced in the following were last accessed August 2015.

B1. Organisational material, IIROSA

Websites

www.egatha.org (Arabic and English).[2]
www.iirosa.org (Arabic and English).

Annual reports and strategies

Annual Report for the Fiscal Year 2003–2004.
Annual Report for the Fiscal Year 2005/2006.
Operational Plan for IIROSA's Programs and Projects 2007–2008 Referred to as *Annual Report 2007–2008.*
Development Obstacles in the Muslim World and Efforts of the International Islamic Relief Organisation to Address Them. Report presented to the 11th Islamic Summit Conference, 2008. Referred to as *ISC Report.*
Overall Performance Report of the Int'l Islamic Relief Organization, Saudi Arabia (IIROSA) Projects & Programs for the Year 2010/2011. Referred to as *Overall Performance Report 2010/2011.* Available at http://www. egatha.org/pdf/annualreport/iirosa_annualreport_3132_en.pdf.
Overall Performance Report of the Int'l Islamic Relief Organization, Saudi Arabia (IIROSA). Projects & Programs for the Year 2011/2012. Referred to as *Annual Report 2011–2012.*

http://www.egatha.org/pdf/annualreport/iirosa_annualreport_3233_ en.pdf.

Report of the General Performance of the International Islamic Relief Organization Programs 2009–2010. Referred to as *Annual Report 2009–2010.* Available at http://www.egatha.org/pdf/annualreport/ iirosa_annualreport_3031_en.pdf.

Magazines and newsletters

Bulletin vol. 1, no. 26, 2006.
Bulletin, vol. 1, no. 27, 2006.
Bulletin, vol. 1, no. 28, 2007.
Bulletin vol. 1, no. 33, 2009.
Bulletin, vol. 1, no. 34, 2010.
Bulletin, vol. 1, no. 36, 2010.
IIROSA Magazine, n.d.

Brochures

Program for Health Welfare (Arabic), n.d.
Social Welfare: Muslim World League, International Islamic Relief Organisation, the Kingdom of Saudi Arabia (Arabic), n.d.
Sponsor an Orphan (Arabic), n.d.
Reporting Format for Orphan Sponsorship (Arabic), n.d.
The Waqf Projects (Arabic), n.d.

B2. Organisational material, IICO

Websites

www.iico.org (Arabic).
http://www.iico.org/AxCMSweblive/enIndex.cms (English). This link is not longer accessible.

Annual reports and strategies

Activity Report for Six Months from September 2010–February 2011.
Administrative and Financial Report 2010–2011.
Annual Report 2008 (Arabic).
http://www.iico.org/AxCMSweblive/upload/2008_581_325.pdf.
Annual Report 2009 (Arabic).
http://www.iico.org/AxCMSweblive/upload/2009_582_373.pdf.

Annual Report 2010 (Arabic).
Special Publication: Introduction to the International Islamic Charitable Organisation (Arabic), n.d.
Management Report for IICO Activities for 1425–1426, 2005. Referred to as *Management Report.*

Magazines and newsletters

al-Alamiya, no. 242, 2010.
al-Alamiya, no. 243, 2010.
al-Alamiya (Arabic), no. 246, 2010.
al-Alamiya (Arabic), no. 247, 2010.
All al-Alamiya magazines can be found here: http://www.iico.org/axc-msweblive/en_alalamiya_magazine.cms

Brochures

Their Relief ... Is Our Duty, 2012
Pioneering in Charity, n.d.
Charitable Studies Center Reality and Ambition, n.d.
Firm International Regional and Local Relations, n.d.
Our Waqf Projects Give Life (English), n.d.
Your Zakat Gives Life (English), n.d.

B3. Organisational material, Islamic Relief

Websites

http://www.islamic-relief.com.
http://www.islamic-relief.me/index.php/home (Arabic).
http://www.islamic-relief.org.uk.
http://www.islamicreliefusa.org.

Annual reports and strategies

Annual Report and Financial Statements 2011.
Annual Report 2009.
Annual Report and Financial Statements 2008.
Islamic Relief Strategy 2007–2009.
Annual Report and Summary Financial Statements 2007.

Annual Report 2006.
Annual Report and Financial Statements 2006.
Annual Report 2005.
Annual Report and Financial Statements 2005.
Annual Review 2004.
Financial Statements 2004.
Annual Review 2003.

Some of the above are available here: http://www.islamic-relief.org.uk/
about-us/annual-reports/ otherwise they are no longer available online.

Research and policy papers

Islamic Relief: Faith and Identity in Practice, ONTRAC, 2010. Available
at http://www.intrac.org/data/files/resources/694/ONTRAC-46.pdf.
Khan, Ajaz Ahmed and Isabel Philips: *The Influence of Faith on Islamic
Microfinance Programmes,* 2010. Available at http://www.islamic-relief.
org.uk/content/uploads/2013/09/Policy_Microfinance_Influence_
Faith.pdf.
ten Veen, Rianne C.: *Charitable Giving in Islam,* 2009. Available at http://
policy.islamic-relief.com/wp-content/uploads/2014/05/Charitable-
Giving-in-Islam-Sep-09.pdf.
Abuarqub, Mamoun and Isabel Phillips: *A Brief History of Humanitarianism
in the Muslim World,* 2009. Available at http://policy.islamic-relief.
com/portfolio/a-brief-history-of-humanitarianism-in-the-muslim-
world/
Khan, Ajaz Ahmed, Ismayil Tahmazov and Mamoun Abuarqub:
Translating Faith into Development, 2009. Available at http://relief-
web.int/sites/reliefweb.int/files/resources/2508C161FA9D528BC12
575D5006DCFC9-IR-May2009.pdf.
Definitions of Poverty, 2008. Available at http://policy.islamic-relief.com/
wp-content/uploads/2014/05/Definitions-of-Poverty.pdf.
Reproductive Health Policy, 2008. Available at http://policy.islamic-relief.
com/wp-content/uploads/2014/05/Reproductive-Health-Policy.pdf.
Enabling Poor People to Shape their Future: IR's Accountability Framework,
2008. http://www.islamic-relief.com/InDepth/downloads/IR%20
Accountability%20Framework.pdf. This publication is no longer avail-
able online.
IR Beliefs, Values and Code of Conduct, 2008. http://www.islamic-relief.

com/InDepth/downloads/IRs%20Beliefs,%20Values%20and%20
Code%20of%20Conduct.pdf. This publication is no longer available
online.
Gender Analysis in Programme Design, n.d. http://www.islamic-relief.com/
InDepth/downloads/Gender%20Analysis%20in%20Programme%20
Design%202.pdf.

Project material

PPA Self-Assessment Review, Reporting Year 2008/2009. Available at
http://www.dfid.gov.uk/Documents/ppas/200809selfassessrevs/self-
assess-rev-isl-rel-wdwde.pdf. This publication is no longer available
online.
Information Booklet on HIV/AIDS, Child Welfare Programme, Islamic
Relief Bangladesh, n.d.
Text book, Integrated Community Action Programme, Islamic Relief
Bangladesh, n.d.

Brochures

Waqf Brochure, n.d.

B4. Organisational material, Muslim Aid

Websites

http://www.muslimaid.org.
http://www.muslimaidbd.org.
http://www.muslimaid.org.pk.

Annual reports and strategies

Trustees' Report and Financial Statements 2009.
Trustees' Report and Financial Statements 2008.
Trustees' Report and Financial Statements 2007.
Financial Statements 2006. This publication is no longer available online.
Trustees' Report and Financial Statements 2005. This publication is no lon-
ger available online.
Annual Review 2011.
Annual Review 2010.

Annual Review 2009.
Annual Review 2008.
Annual Review 2007.
Annual Review 2006.
Annual Review 2005.
Annual Review 2004.
Annual Review 2003.
Annual Review 2002.
Annual Review 2001.
Annual Review 2000.
Annual Review 1999.

Some of the above are available here: https://www.muslimaid.org/about-us/finance, while others are no longer available online.

Research and policy papers

Bullying and Harassment Policy, 2007.
Capability and Conduct Policy, 2008.
Code of Conduct Policy, 2008.
Disciplinary Procedure Policy, 2007.
Equal Opportunities & Diversity Policy, 2007.
Grievance Policy, 2008.
Health and Safety Policy, 2007.
Maternity Leave Policy & Procedures, 2007.
Policy Statement on the Recruitment of Ex-offenders, 2008.
Staff Manual, Muslim Aid Bangladesh, n.d.
Training and Development Policy, 2008.
Volunteer Policy, 2007.

Internal memos

Measures to Combat Fraud and Corruption, Memo, Muslim Aid Bangladesh, 2009.
Procedures for Reporting Allegations of Fraud and Corruption, Memo, Muslim Aid Bangladesh, 2009.
Preventing Fraud and Corruption in Muslim Aid Bangladesh Field Office Projects. A Guide for Staff, n.d.

Project material

Application form, Fael Khair Microfinance Programme, Muslim Aid
Bangladesh, 2009.

Booklet for Instalments, Fael Khair Microfinance Programme, Muslim Aid
Bangladesh, 2009

Booklet for Cattle Rearing and Vegetable Growth, Muslim Aid Bangladesh,
n.d.

Brochures

25ᵗʰ Anniversary Souvenir, 2010. http://www.muslimaid.org/images/sto-
ries/pdfs/MA_25_Booklet_A4L_Aug10_FINAL_LOWRES.pdf.
This publication is no longer available online.

Love Water, Love Life, n.d. http://www.muslimaid.org/images/stories/
pdfs/waterleaflet.pdf. This publication is no longer available online.

Working together. UMCOR/Muslim Aid Partnership Brochure, n.d.

APPENDIX C

FIELD TRIPS, INTERVIEWS AND PROJECT VISITS

C1. Field Trips

Birmingham and London, Britain, three weeks, May 2008 (Islamic Relief and Muslim Aid headquarters).

Kuwait City, Kuwait, ten days, June 2008 (IICO headquarters).

Amman, Jordan, five days, April 2009 (IICO, IIROSA and Islamic Relief country offices).

Beirut, Lebanon, eight days, April 2009 (Muslim Aid's country office and an Islamic Relief partner organisation).

Jeddah, Saudi Arabia, ten days, October 2009 (IIROSA headquarters).

Dhaka, Bangladesh, one month, November–December 2009 (IIROSA, IICO/KJRC, Muslim Aid and Islamic Relief country offices).

Furthermore, data collected during a two-month trip to Jordan (March–May 2007) for an independent research project on Jordanian Muslim charities has been included in the analysis.

C2. Interviews

Islamic Relief

13 interviews, Islamic Relief headquarters, Birmingham, Britain, May 2008

18 interviews, Islamic Relief country office, Dhaka, Bangladesh, November–December 2009

1 interview, POSKK, Islamic Relief partner organisation, Tangail, Bangladesh, November 2009

1 interview, Islamic Relief country office, Amman, Jordan, April 2009
3 interviews, Islamic Welfare Association, Islamic Relief partner organisation, Saida, Lebanon, April 2009

Muslim Aid

8 interviews, Muslim Aid headquarters, London, Britain, May 2008
15 interviews, Muslim Aid country office, Dhaka, Bangladesh, December 2009
1 interview, Muslim Aid country office, Beirut, Lebanon, April 2009

IIROSA

11 interviews, IIROSA headquarters, Jeddah, Saudi Arabia, October 2009
1 interview, IIROSA country office, Dhaka, Bangladesh, December 2009
2 interviews, IIROSA country office, Amman, Jordan, April 2009

IICO

6 interviews, IICO headquarters, Kuwait City, Kuwait, June 2008
2 interviews, IICO/KJRC country office, Dhaka, Bangladesh, December 2009
4 interviews, IICO country office, Amman, Jordan, April 2007 and April 2009
1 interview, Islamic Center Charity Society office, IICO partner organisation, Zarqa, Jordan, April 2009
4 interviews, Islamic Center Charity Society office, IICO partner organisation, Amman, Jordan, April 2007

Interviews with other Muslim NGOs

1 interview, Aga Khan Foundation, London, Britain, May 2008
9 interviews, Muslim Hands headquarters, Nottingham, Britain, May 2008
1 interview, Muslim Hands country office, Dhaka, Bangladesh, December 2009
1 interview, Direct Aid headquarters, Kuwait City, Kuwait, June 2008
1 interview, Revival of the Islamic Heritage Society headquarters, Kuwait City, Kuwait, June 2008

1 interview, Islam Presentation Committee, Kuwait City, Kuwait, June 2008

1 interview, Women's Committee, Society for Social Reform, Kuwait City, Kuwait, June 2008

1 interview, World Assembly of Muslim Youth, Jeddah, Saudi Arabia, October 2009

1 interview, Al Rahma Center, Saida, Lebanon, April 2009

Interviews with non-Muslim NGOs

2 interviews, Christian Aid, Dhaka, Bangladesh, December 2009

1 interview, CARE, Dhaka, Bangladesh, December 2009

1 interview, Save the Children Denmark, Dhaka, Bangladesh, December 2009

Interviews with donors

3 interviews, DFID, Glasgow, Britain, May 2008

1 interview, Kuwait Zakat House, Kuwait City, Kuwait, June 2008

3 interviews, Organisation of Islamic Conference, Jeddah, Saudi Arabia, October 2009

1 interview, Islamic Development Bank, Jeddah, Saudi Arabia, October 2009

1 interview, ECHO, Dhaka, Bangladesh, December 2009

1 interview, USAID, Dhaka, Bangladesh, December 2009

1 interview, Fael Khair Program, Islamic Development Bank, Dhaka, Bangladesh, December 2009

1 interview, NGO Affairs Bureau, Dhaka, Bangladesh, December 2009

C3. Project Visits

Islamic Relief

Hospital, Tripoli, Lebanon, April 2009
Centre for vocational training, Saida, Lebanon, April 2009
Qurbani celebration, Tangail, Bangladesh, November 2009
Vocational centre, Dhaka, Bangladesh, November 2009
Vocational centre, Dhaka, Bangladesh, November 2009
Islamic Relief Rangpur area office, Rangpur, Bangladesh, December 2009
Health and Education for the Ultra-Poor (HELP-UP), project office, Rangpur, Bangladesh, December 2009

Community group meetings, HELP-UP, Rangpur, Bangladesh, December 2009
Goat-herd training, HELP-UP, Rangpur, Bangladesh, December 2009
Community Action Project (CAP) and Integrated Community Action Project (ICAP), branch office, Rangpur, Bangladesh, December 2009
Community group, CAP, Rangpur, Bangladesh, December 2009
Community groups, ICAP, Rangpur, Bangladesh, December 2009
HIV/AIDS training, ICAP, Rangpur, Bangladesh, December 2009
Tailor training, ICAP, Rangpur, Bangladesh, December 2009
Adolescent Reproductive Healthcare, Child Welfare Program, Rangpur, Bangladesh, December 2009

Muslim Aid

Women's Development Project, Dhaka, Bangladesh, December 2009
Institute of Technology, Dhaka, Bangladesh, December 2009
School, Dhaka, Bangladesh, December 2009
Shelter and Sanitation Project, Sakhtira, Bangladesh, December 2009 (several locations)
Cash for Work, Satkhira, Bangladesh, December 2009
Climate Change Event, National Press Club, Dhaka, Bangladesh, December 2009
Fael Khair Microfinance Project, Kalaroa office, Satkhira, Bangladesh, December 2009
Fael Khair Microfinance Project, Tala office, Satkhira, Bangladesh, December 2009
Emergency and Early Recovery Project, Satkhira, Bangladesh, December 2009

IIROSA

Day-care center, IIROSA, Amman, Jordan, April 2009
Medical clinic, Dhaka, Bangladesh, December 2009

IICO

Islamic Center Charity Society community center, Amman, Jordan, April 2007
Islamic Center Charity Society community center, Zarqa, Jordan, April 2009
Productive Projects, Zarqa, Jordan, April 2009

NOTES

1. INTRODUCTION: STUDYING TRANSNATIONAL MUSLIM NGOS

1. With the term 'NGO' I refer to non-profit organisations that are not formally part of governmental structures (although some of them may receive funding from government). While NGOs do of course engage in a wide range of different activities, my focus here is solely on those engaged in aid provision. The term 'transnational' refers to the fact that these organisations engage in aid activities and relations across the borders and spaces of nations (Mandaville 2007:276). There are no comprehensive overviews of transnational Muslim NGOs, and the number presented here is thus only a rough estimate, based on different sources, including numbers drawn from the Union of International Associations database (www.uia.be), the number of organisations participating in the OIC annual civil society conferences, and interviews with various people.

2. Among others, Al Haramain and Benevolence International, the Holy Land Foundation and the Global Relief Foundation. The International Islamic Relief Organisation, subject of the present analysis, has also had its branches in Indonesia and the Philippines designated. To date, only one NGO (the Holy Land Foundation) has been convicted for contributing to militant activism (Guinane 2006:11).

3. One of the most well-known books in this regard has been Burr and Collins' now withdrawn *Alms for Jihad* (2006), providing examples on the ways in which some of the funds made available to and managed by Muslim NGOs have been chan- nelled to militant Islamic groups and organisations. Other examples include Ly (2007), Flanigan (2006), Kohlman (2006), Levitt (2006), and Napoleoni (2005).

4. An example is Alterman and von Hippel (2007). Other, somewhat more nuanced, analyses of Muslim NGOs and their role in formal politics are Benthall and Bellion-Jourdan (2003), Schaeublin (2009), Clark (2008), Bellion-Jourdan (2007), Hamzeh (2007), Soares and Otayek (2007), Solberg (2007), Salih (2002) and Wiktorowicz (2001).

5. When not directly referring to the particular literature on faith-based organisa-

tions, I will use the term 'religious' instead of 'faith-based'. The term faith-based indicates that non-religious NGOs are not faith-based, while I would argue that all NGOs are, to some degree, faith-based insofar as they are ideological, promoting a certain 'faith' over others, whether that faith is human rights, development, secularism or Islam. See Benthall (2008c) for a discussion of secular NGOs as religious. For more general discussions of development as a religious belief, see Giri et al. (2004) and Quarles van Ufford and Schoeffeleers (1988).

6. This 'religious turn' in what has historically been a strongly secularist field has in part been prompted by an increase in the actual number and visibility of religious organisations involved in development-related activities. Today, some of the largest NGOs are religious; the number of Muslim NGOs seems to be growing rapidly; and in Sub-Saharan African, the World Bank estimates that as many as 50 per cent of all health and education services are provided by religious organisations (James 2009:7). Studies such as the World Bank's *Voices of the Poor* (2000) have underlined the importance of such religious organisations for the poor, concluding that many people have more trust in religious organisations than in secular NGOs, government or other societal institutions.

7. For literature on religion and development, including the role of faith-based organisations, see, among others, Haynes (2007), Marshall and van Saanen (2007), G. Clarke and Jennings (2008), Deneulin and Bano (2009), M. Clarke (2011), and Haar (2011). For a critical review of this and other literature on religion and development, see Jones and Juul Petersen (2011).

8. Recently, other students of transnational Muslim NGOs, many of them anthropologists, have presented similarly alternative approaches, including Benthall (2006, 2011), Ahmed (2009), Yaylaci (2007, 2008) and Kaag (2007). Furthermore, there is an emerging literature on local and national Muslim NGOs, focusing on the provision of social welfare in the context of the state. See, for example, Jawad (2009), Harmsen (2008), and Clark (2004).

9. In this, I am particularly inspired by writers such as Mosse (2005), Hilhorst (2003), Bornstein (2003), and D. Lewis (2001) who, each in their own way, direct attention to the discourses and practices of NGOs, exploring their meaning systems in terms of the actors, institutions, organisations and social relationships through which they are articulated (Mosse 2005:10).

10. It is difficult, if not impossible, to determine beforehand whether a given case has prototypical value, and as such, the selection of cases is necessarily a dialectic process. I started out with a much larger number of organisations, a pool of potential cases, which was then gradually reduced to four organisations as my knowledge and understanding of the field increased. Arguably, a number of other NGOs could have been interesting to study. For instance, Iranian Shi'ite NGOs, often in the form of semi-governmental foundations, are obvious examples of transnational Muslim NGOs that have remained squarely outside the culture of development aid. Likewise, as home to one of the largest groups of Muslim NGOs in terms of numbers, the USA is severely underrepresented in the analysis.

Although many North American Muslim NGOs were forced to close down as a consequence of new anti-terror legislation and declining popular support after 9/11, the country still hosts more than thirty active organisations. Finally, recent years have seen the emergence of several Muslim NGOs in Turkey, including the Deniz Feneri Association and the Human Rights and Liberties Humanitarian Relief Foundation.

11. For a more detailed description of my methodological approach, including a discussion of some of the problems and limitations of this approach, see appendix A. For a list of all organisational material, see appendix B. For a detailed overview of trips, interviews, and presentations, see appendix C.

12. The table builds on the following sources: Information on IIROSA from IIROSA, *IIROSA Annual Report 2011/2012*, IIROSA *Annual Report 2003/2004*, as well as communication with staff. Information on largest country programmes is from 2004, as information from later years could not be obtained. Information on IICO from IICO, *Management Report 2005, Administrative and Financial Report 2010–2011*, as well as communication with staff. Information on Islamic Relief from Islamic Relief, *Annual Report 2011*, as well as communication with staff. Information on Muslim Aid from Muslim Aid, *Annual Review 2011*, as well as communication with staff. All budgets refer to expenses, not total income.

13. See, for example, Benedetti (2006) or Marranci (2008) for similar definitions. This means that organisations such as the Aga Khan Foundation and the Red Crescent societies are not included here, since they do not self-define as 'Muslim' but claim to be non-denominational. Nonetheless, some of these organisations display characteristics that would traditionally be considered religious (the Aga Khan Foundation, for instance, is headed by a religious leader, and funded by a religiously defined donor constituency), pointing to the potential problems with complete reliance on self-definitions.

14. With 'ideology' I do not refer to formal political ideologies such as liberalism or socialism, nor to ideology as class-motivated bourgeois deceptions and false consciousness in a Marxist, materialist sense of the word (see Thompson 1984, 1990). Instead, I understand ideology more broadly, based on a conception of the social as having a hermeneutic, in the sense of interpretive, dimension (Purvis and Hunt 1993:474). More specifically, and building on social movement traditions (for instance Heberle 1951; Wilson 1973; McAdam, McCarthy and Zald 1996; Snow 2004) and cultural anthropology (for instance Geertz 1973), I understand ideology as referring to sets of references that frame the way actors understand, categorise and act upon the world; as ensembles of ideas, concepts, and categories through which actors organise and give meaning to their observed, experienced and/or recorded 'reality' (Hilhorst 2003:8; Gasper and Apthorpe 1996:2). In this perspective, ideology is not necessarily the tool of the dominant powers, used to legitimise their domination. Rather, these are tools that are available to all, to be used in the signifying work and struggles for fixation of social meaning.

15. It is important to note that this book is not an attempt to reject or cast suspicion on the genuine desire that people have to help others. What concerns me here are the ideologies that the organisations publicly display and promote; not the individual motivations people have for providing aid.

16. This does not mean that practices and structures are irrelevant to the study of ideologies. In the words of Lincoln (2003:6), practices operationalise the ideology, moving it from the sphere of conscious speech to that of embodied material action, while structures, regulating discourse and practice, sediment the ideology in institutions and organisations, thus securing (or attempting to secure) ideological coherence and continuity. However, insofar as I am primarily interested in intentional representations, I study these practices and structures mainly as they are presented to me through discourses, as 'reported reality' (Nauta 2006:150).

17. My understanding of culture is in large part consistent with Foucault's notion of discursive formation (e.g. Foucault 1970), understood as a large and relatively stable (although flexible) body of knowledge, a framework outlining rules and norms for what can be said and done. Likewise, my understanding of ideology has some similarities with the underlying understanding of discourse, insofar as they both, as noted by Purvis and Hunt (1993:474), refer to 'the idea that human individuals participate in forms of understanding, comprehension or consciousness of the relations and activities in which they are involved' and further, that this understanding is 'borne through language and other systems of signs, it is transmitted between people and institutions, and, perhaps most importantly, it makes a difference; that is, the way in which people comprehend and make sense of the social world has consequences for the direction and character of their action and inaction'. However, rather than seeing the two as interchangeable, I conceptualise ideology as a particular form of discourse. In this perspective, cultures and discursive formations are made up by a wide range of different kinds of discourse, including, for example, ideologies, traditions, common sense, and histories, each with their specific characteristics. As such, my choice to use the term ideology should not be understood as a rejection of discourse theory in the Foucaultian sense, but rather as a supplement. To make matters more complicated, in the following I do not use the term discourse in a broad, Foucaultian sense, but as referring more specifically to the texts, statements, and narratives produced and expressed by staff in the four NGOs.

18. I use the term 'the West' geographically to refer to the North American and European countries, but also culturally to refer to those traditions, ideologies and ideas that have grown out of these countries' particular histories. Naturally, I do not consider 'the West' in the cultural sense to be a static and unchanging entity, but to be constantly changing, interacting, and merging with other cultures.

19. Echoing Howell and Lind (2009:2), I use quotation marks to stress my misgivings with respect to the War on Terror, as a discourse and as an assemblage of counter-terrorism structures introduced after 9/11, as well as to underline the

deeply politicised nature of the phrase. To enhance readability, however, I will not use quotation marks from this point onwards.

20. In their edited volume on faith and humanitarianism, Barnett and Stein (2012) present a distinction between 'secularised' and 'sanctified' aid. While the authors share my interest in exploring the role of religion and religious actors in contemporary aid provision, decentring mainstream conceptions of aid, their distinction is nonetheless slightly different from my distinction between 'secularised' and 'sacralised' aid. They use the term 'sanctified' to describe the ways in which aid 'is viewed as pure and separate from the profane', that is, as an innocent and altruistic space free of politics, emphasising values and ethics over instruments and interests (Barnett and Stein 2012:8). Against this, 'secularisation' denotes the processes by which elements of the profane become integrated into aid provision, evident in 'the growing role of states and commercial enterprises, the centrality of fundraising, encroachment of earthly matters such as governance, processes of bureaucratization and professionalization' (Barnett and Stein 2012:8). As such, their distinction is concerned not solely with the role and pervasiveness of religion in aid provision, but more broadly with the differences between normative conceptions of aid (religious as well as non-religious) and more technical, bureaucratic ones. This is an interesting and useful distinction which—as we shall see—is also relevant in relation to the two kinds of organisations I describe here.

21. For a useful discussion of the shifting boundaries between the secular and the religious, see Lynch (2011).

22. I use the terms 'secularisation', 'secular' and 'secularism' to denote different things. With 'secularisation' I refer to the process of separation of religion from other spheres of life, not to the elimination of religion (Roy 2004:334). Similarly, I use the term 'secular' to refer to cultures, societies, institutions and organisations based on this distinction between religion and other spheres of life. Finally, with 'secularism' I refer to the underlying ideology promoting the separation of religion from other spheres of life.

2. THE CULTURES OF DEVELOPMENT AND ISLAMIC AID

1. For a comprehensive analysis of the history of development, see Rist (2008) or Escobar (1995). The present analysis includes development and humanitarian aid under the same heading (that of development aid), although they could arguably be considered two distinct approaches to the provision of aid, insofar as they have grown out of slightly different historical trajectories and are based on different conceptions of aid (see, for example, Bornstein and Redfield 2007). While I agree that there are substantial differences between development and humanitarian aid meriting closer attention, I nonetheless argue that for the purpose of the present analysis it makes sense to approach them as part of the same overall aid culture. In practice most aid actors—be they NGOs, governmental aid agencies or intergovernmental organisations—are simultaneously involved in both development

and humanitarian aid. Their—slightly different—conceptions of aid rest on the same core values, use many of the same discourses and practices, and depend on the same economic structures.

2. Insofar as the culture of transnational Islamic aid grew out of a primarily Middle Eastern context, the analysis focuses on this geographic area. This does not mean, however, that Muslim countries outside the Arab world did not experience similar trends and developments. In fact, countries such as Indonesia and Malaysia both have strong traditions of Islamic aid. However, these aid cultures have tended to remain largely national, with few links to other countries.

3. For an in-depth historical analysis of Islamic charity, see Singer (2008) or Bonner, Ener and Singer (2003). For more specific historical analyses of the concept of *zakat*, see Bonner (2005) or Benthall (1999).

4. For literature on the Islamic resurgence, see Roy (2004), Wiktorowicz (2004), Schulze (2000) or Esposito (1998).

5. Other organisations shared the overall ideology and language of the Islamic movement, but did not relate themselves explicitly to the Muslim Brotherhood. The Lebanese Shi'a organisation Hezbollah, for instance, established in 1982 as a direct response to the Israeli occupation of Lebanon, oriented itself much more towards Iran, which since the 1979 Islamic revolution had become for many the symbol of an ideal Islamic society. And in Turkey, the *Milli Görüs* movement (in English, National Outlook), established in 1969 by right-wing nationalists and supported by prominent Sufi sheikhs, came to be an important actor in the Islamic movement, serving as the ideological and organisational backbone of a range of Islamic parties in the following decades (Solberg 2007:432; see also Yıldız 2003).

6. For a history of the emergence of Islamic banks, see also Maurer (2005).

7. Backed by the ruling house of Saudi Arabia, led by King Faisal, and financially supported by a number of Saudi business men, forty Muslim states established the Islamic Development Bank (IsDB) in 1973 (Pripp 2006:137), some fourteen years after the first regional development bank—the Inter-American Development Bank—was established. While the IsDB was specifically charged with directing funds towards poor countries, other, more profit-oriented, banks soon emerged, with Dubai Islamic Bank as the first in 1975 (Pripp 2006:137). In 1977, the International Association of Islamic Banks was set up. Parallel to the establishment of private Islamic banks, several governments—including those of Pakistan, Iran and Sudan—brought in measures to Islamise the national economy. As a side note, this was also the period in which new governmental aid agencies started emerging in the Middle East. The Kuwait Fund for Arab Economic Development had been the first in 1961, followed by the Abu Dhabi Fund for Arab Economic Development in 1971. The Saudi Fund for Development and the Iraqi Fund for External Development were set up in 1974.

8. According to the Qur'an (9:60), *zakat* should be distributed to one of eight groups of recipients: 'Alms are for the poor and the needy, and those employed to administer (the funds); for those whose hearts have been (recently) reconciled (to Truth); for

those in bondage and in debt; in the cause of Allah; and for the wayfarer.' Naturally, the precise meaning of these categories has been widely discussed throughout the history of Islam. Most importantly for the present analysis is the question of whether *zakat* should be given to Muslims, or if it can, as the more general alms of *sadaqa*, be given to non-Muslims as well; a question which, as we shall see, continues to trouble contemporary Muslim scholars and organisations.

9. In some countries, the payment of *zakat* is obligatory (such as Pakistan), in some obligatory for businesses and voluntary for individuals (such as Saudi Arabia and Kuwait), in others entirely voluntary (such as Jordan); and in yet others, there are no official *zakat* systems (such as Oman and Morocco). These differences reflect the lack of scholarly consensus on the topic. Whereas some scholars, such as Muhammad Baqir Al-Sadr and M. Umer Chapra, interpret *zakat* as a voluntary tax that should be administered through the mosques (Pfeifer 1997:158), others—Mawdudi, Syed Naqvi, Qutb, and Qaradawi, place a much stronger emphasis on the compulsory state tax and the public responsibility to pay it (Weiss 2002:16).

10. The organisation later changed its name to Organisation of Islamic Cooperation. See Pultz (2008), Kayaoglu (forthcoming) and Khan (2001) for a history of the OIC.

11. Many Egyptian, Iraqi, and Syrian members of the Brotherhood who had fled persecution in their own countries in the 1950s and 1960s were offered positions in Muslim World League (Hegghammer 2010:18; Roy 2004:67).

12. At its foundation, the Saudi government donated US$ 250,000 to the League. By the 1980s, this had reportedly grown to US$ 13 million (Mandaville et al. 2009:28).

13. The World Assembly of Muslim Youth (in Arabic, *al-Nadwa al-'alamiyya li al-shabab al-islami*), established in Saudi Arabia in 1972, was also part of this trend. The International Islamic Council for Da'wa and Relief, established in Egypt in 1988, also deserves mention. With more than 100 members, primarily from the Middle East, the International Islamic Council for Da'wa and Relief is today perhaps the most extensive network of Muslim NGOs and governmental institutions involved in *da'wa* and relief. Members include the Jordan Hashemite Charity Organisation, IICO, IIROSA, Muslim World League, World Assembly of Muslim Youth, Federation of Islamic Organisations in Europe, Qatar Charity, Kuwait Zakah House as well as the Ministries of Awqaf in Egypt, Iraq, Jordan, Kuwait, Morocco, Qatar, and the United Arab Emirates.

14. Although they may not share the same interpretations of Islam, the European branches of the Brotherhood and the Muslim World League have become increasingly intertwined. Many senior members of the Muslim Brotherhood, for instance, served in leadership positions in the Muslim World League. Likewise, distinctions between Brotherhood and Jama'at-e Islami affiliated organisations are increasingly blurred (Mandaville et al. 2009:24f).

15. *Qurbani* is a religious sacrifice, often a cow or a goat, made in relation to *Eid al-adha*, an important religious holiday in Islam, commemorating the willingness of Ibrahim (in Christianity, Abraham) to sacrifice his son.

16. Naturally, and as can be inferred from the above, this does not mean that the Islamic aid culture has not fostered any organisations or institutions; it just means that historically, the legitimacy of these organisations and institutions has, in large part, sprung from the individuals leading them, predicated on notions of personal morality, virtues, and merits rather than systems and structures.

17. Underlying these relationships is a somewhat chequered history of relations between the Gulf States and the UN, including over sanctions against some Arab states and the UN Security Council's position on the Israeli-Palestinian conflict (Cotterrell and Harmer 2005:14).

18. With this description of the values underlying the two aid cultures I do not pretend to say anything about how aid is in fact provided within the cultures of Islamic aid and development; instead, these values say something about how aid should be provided. In other words, these are the values that actors need to adhere to in order to appear legitimate within a given aid culture. Thus, for instance, when I posit that neutrality is a core value in the culture of development aid, I do not mean to say that development aid is always provided in a neutral manner—history has shown otherwise countless times—but simply that actors need to claim adherence to the value of neutrality in order to gain legitimacy within this culture.

3. TRAJECTORIES OF TRANSNATIONAL MUSLIM NGOs

1. Of course, there are many other events of importance in the history of transnational Muslim NGOs; most importantly perhaps the ongoing conflict between Israel and Palestine. With the Islamisation of the Palestinian resistance and the emergence of Hamas in 1987, Palestine became a prime site for the development of local Muslim NGOs (Ghandour 2004:329), many of them supported by transnational Muslim NGOs. Organisations established as a response to the conflicts in Palestine include the Holy Land Foundation (established in the USA, 1988), Interpal (UK, 1994), Kinder USA (USA, 2002) and KindHearts (USA, 2002).

2. Later renamed African Muslims Agency and now Direct Aid International.

3. The role of the media in spurring organised aid goes back in time. Barnett (2005:733), for instance, writes that the establishment of the International Red Cross in 1862 and other relief organisations at that time can be seen partly as a result of the emergence of war reporting as a profession, giving the public access to stories and pictures from the increasingly gruesome wars. For discussions of the relationship between aid and media, see Chouliaraki (2010) and Benthall (1993).

4. In the early 1990s, Abdullah Azzam, then director of the Office for Services to the Mujahedeen, clearly expressed this general suspicion of Western organisations

in a publication dealing with the health of Afghan refugees: 'Who is facing this dramatic situation [in Afghanistan]? It is the missionaries, because wherever poverty, ignorance and illness are to be found, missionaries are there. And so groups of missionaries (*al-mubashirun*) bearing different names have come to settle in Peshawar' (cf. Benthall and Bellion-Jourdan 2003:74). Likewise, in 1997, Ahmed Sonoussi, then head of the Afghan office of the Kuwaiti Islamic Call Committee (in Arabic, *Lajnat al-Da'wa al-Islamiya*), wrote a widely disseminated memo criticising what he called 'the malicious activity of the crusaders' who, through relief work in Afghanistan, were seeking to 'poison the minds of Afghans and gradually convert them to Christianity'. He later admitted that this was a deliberate exaggeration designed to mobilise public opinion in the Muslim world and obtain more funds for his organisation (Ghandour 2003:n.p.).

5. This fear of proselytisation remains present among staff in many Muslim NGOs. In his analysis of three transnational Muslim NGOs in sub-Saharan Africa, Ahmed (2009:427) speaks of a widespread conspiracy theory among Muslim NGOs portraying the aid of Red Cross and Western NGOs as means to convert Muslims to Christianity and exercise political control over them.

6. These organisations were supported by people such as the (self-proclaimed) Islamic scholar Hassan Makki Mohamed Ahmed, writing for the UK-based Islamic Foundation, which is closely connected to the Jama'at-e Islami. In his publication *The Christian Design* (1989), Ahmed studied the impact of missionary activities in Sudan from 1843 to 1986, arguing that missionary humanitarian organisations have historically been agents of Western influence over Sudanese society; a pattern which is now repeated in the form of Western NGOs using aid as a weapon to impose Christianity or Western secularism on the populations of South Sudan (Ahmed 1989).

7. Islamic Relief later became a member of the network. While relations between Muslim and Western NGOs were generally bleak, a few organisations stood out, insisting on cooperation and coordination. Here, the Sudanese organisation Islamic African Relief Agency is a case in point. From the inception in 1981, the founder of the organisation, Abdallah Suleyman al-'Awad, sought cooperation with Christian and Western organisations, declaring that he preferred 'field dialogue' over 'intellectual dialogue' between Islam and Christianity and reminding people that Muslims and Christians alike just wanted to help the poor. In concrete terms, this resulted in a range of project partnerships with organisations such as World Vision, the Lutheran World Federation, Oxfam, and the Adventist Development and Relief Agency, just as the Islamic African Relief Agency, through its American sister organisation the Islamic American Relief Agency, obtained financial support from USAID. Relations were, however, abruptly cut when in 1999, the Islamic Africa Relief Agency came under investigation for involvement in the 1993 attacks on the World Trade Center and the 1998 attacks on the US embassies in Nairobi and Dar es Salam (Benthall and Bellion-Jourdan 2003:126). In 2004, the organisation was designated by the US Treasury Department.

8. ACBAR website, www.acbar.org. Later, Islamic Relief—which only started working in Afghanistan in 1992—became a member.

9. There are no precise figures for the number of Saudi fighters in Afghanistan; Hegghammer (2010:47) suggests between 1,000 and 5,000 people.

10. Examples from Muslim Aid, *Annual Review 1999*. Available at www.muslimaid. org

11. Let me reiterate that the focus of this analysis is not to evaluate whether the measures taken against Muslim NGOs in the USA are fair or not, nor is it to judge whether the NGOs are innocent or not. Instead, the intention is, more modestly, to outline what 9/11 has meant for transnational Muslim NGOs in terms of opportunity structures and obstacles.

12. For a detailed account of the rise and fall of Al Haramain, see Bokhari, Chowdhury, and Lacey (2014). As noted in this text, Saudi concerns about terrorism financing predate 9/11 and the War on Terror. Already in 1991, King Fahd urged the country's richest families to be more careful in their donations to charity, prompted by Al-Saud's falling out with Osama Bin Laden. A few years later, a royal decree was issued, banning the collection of money for charity without official permission, and the Supreme Council of Islamic Affairs was established, allegedly with the purpose of centralizing and supervising aid requests from Islamic groups. In 1994, a number of units were established in the Ministry of Interior, in the Saudi Arabian Money Agency and in the commercial banks to track and block suspicious financial transactions (Bokhari, Chowdhury, and Lacey 2014:206).

13. The table is based on EU Council (2012), UN Security Council Committee (2015), and US Department of the Treasury (nd).

14. The designation concerns only the Philippine and Indonesia branches.

15. Defined in United States Code, title 18, §2339A(b) as 'currency or monetary instruments or financial securities, financial services, lodging, training, expert advice or assistance, safe houses, false documentation or identification, communications equipment, facilities, weapons, lethal substances, explosives, personnel, transportation, and other physical assets, except medicine or religious materials' (available on http://codes.lp.findlaw.com/uscode/18/I/113B/2339A/notes).

16. In March 2007, the Kuwaiti government introduced similar initiatives, at the same time forbidding cash collections in the street or in mosques (Benthall 2007:9).

17. For instance, in 2002, the now US-based Benevolence International Foundation was designated for alleged relations to Bin Laden. In court, the judge held that the prosecution had 'failed to connect the dots' proving a relationship between Benevolence International Foundation and Bin Laden, and the charges against the organisation were dismissed. However, 'by the time the criminal cases were resolved BIF's resources were gone and it was not able to file another civil action challenging seizure of its assets. As a result, the organisation is shut down per-

manently' (Guinane 2006:11), with all clarity illustrating the lethal consequences that even unfounded suspicion can have for transnational Muslim NGOs.

18. While there is little evidence of abuse of funds among the majority of transnational Muslim NGOs, there can be no doubt that many of these NGOs are (or were) guilty of intransparency, unprofessionalism, and lack of institutionalised structures for transfer of funds. See Bokhari, Chowdhury, and Lacey (2014) for an example of this. In a case study of the now defunct Al Haramain, the authors show how this organisation had no licence or legal mandate to operate as a charity, ran funds through the personal accounts of its founder, and did not keep accurate documentation for how, when and where funds were spent.

19. Since 2005, the initiative has been hosted as part of the Graduate Institute of International Studies, Geneva. See Benthall (2014) for further information on this initiative.

20. See James (2009), Lunn (2009), Kirmani and Khan (2008), Marshall and van Saanen (2007), Ferris (2005), and Marshall and Keough (2004).

21. Other initiatives for cooperation with Muslim NGOs includes the DFID-sponsored research programme *Religions and Development* at Birmingham University, with Islamic Relief as the only non-academic partner. Likewise, DFID was involved in the Tony Blair Foundation's seminar series, Faith and Development, hosted together with Islamic Relief, World Vision and Oxfam.

22. Some development researchers and practitioners argue that faith-based organisations can contribute to providing 'alternative visions of development', challenging narrow conceptions of development as economic growth. This understanding builds on an assumption of faith-based organisations as somehow better and more authentic than other kinds of organisations because they link up to people's moral and spiritual lives, and as such, offer a better framework for bringing about a more people-centred and sustainable development. On the surface, this approach to religious NGOs is slightly different from the one outlined above, insofar as it sees religious organisations not as tools to enhance mainstream development approaches, but as a way of challenging these approaches through their attention to 'spiritual insights about the meaning of human life' (Tyndale 2006:27) and 'positive values' (Lunn 2009:948). However, in effect the religious values praised are ones that converge with mainstream development values and principles, and as such, this literature ends up resembling the literature that focuses more narrowly on organisational features. In other words, the role of religion in development remains instrumental, not intrinsic (Deneulin and Rakodi 2011:49).

23. An interesting exception to this is the US. Here, the (also recent) attention to faith-based organisations in development activities is not predicated on a similarly strict secularist distinction between religion and aid. The 2001 *Faith-based and Community Initiatives Act* (or the Charitable Choice Act) weakened some of the rules designed to enforce separation between religion and state. Now religious organisations could use religious structures and have religious symbols on display in places where US aid is distributed. As noted by James (2009:7), they were only

encouraged, but not required, to make clear to recipients that they did not have to participate in religious activities. This was later reinforced by a 2004 USAID ruling on *Participation by Religious Orders in USAID Programmes*, stating that USAID cannot discriminate against organisations which combine development or humanitarian activity with 'inherently religious activity such as worship, religious instruction or proselytization' (cf. James 2009:7; see also Clarke 2007). However, in practice, USAID cooperates almost exclusively with Christian faith-based organisations, making this exception irrelevant to the present study. Von Hippel (2007:39f) writes that of the US\$ 1.7 billion USAID spent on faith-based organisations between 2001 and 2005, 98 per cent went to Christian organisations. Only two of the 159 recipient organisations were Jewish and only two were Muslim. In this perspective, and to put it somewhat simply, the US involvement with faith-based organisations is perhaps better understood as part of the War on Terror's hard rather than soft measures, strengthening dichotomies between Muslim and Western, Christian NGOs.

24. The table is based on the following sources, listed in the same chronological order as the table: Aga Khan Development Network website, http://www.akdn.org/faq.asp (2010 numbers); *Islamic Relief Annual Report 2011*; Forbes Middle East, http://www.forbesmiddleeast.com/en/lists/read/2012/the-most-transparent-charities-in-the/listid/15 (on Social Reform Society and Direct Aid, both 2011 numbers); IHH website, http://www.ihh.org.tr/en/main/pages/gelir-gider/86 (2011 numbers); IICO, *Administrative and Financial Report 2010–2011*; LIFE for Relief and Development, *Audited Financial Statements 2011* (available at http://www.lifeusa.org/site/DocServer/2011_AUDITED_FINANCIALS.pdf?docID=1581); Muslim Aid, *Annual Review 2011*; IIROSA, *Annual Report 2011–2012*; Forbes Middle East, http://www.forbesmiddleeast.com/en/lists/read/2012/the-most-transparent-charities-in-the/listid/15 (on Dubai Charity Association and Sheikh Al Nouri Charity Society, both 2011 numbers); Muslim Hands, *Ramadan Feed-back 2011* (available at http://muslimhands.org.uk/media/46178/feedback-report-2011.pdf); Helping Hand for Relief and Development, *Consolidated Financial Statements 2011* (available at http://www.hhrd.org/auditReport/FinancialAudit-2011_Final.pdf); Comité de Bienfaisance, *Rapport Annuel 2010* (available at http://www.cbsp.fr/notre-actualite/publications-a-communiques/download-file.html?path=Nos+rapports+annuels%2Frapport_annuel_2010.pdf); Human Concern International, *Annual Report 2011–2012* (available at http://3426.bbnc.bbcust.com/document.doc?id=8); Interpal, *Annual Report and Financial Statements 2010* (available at http://interpal.org/Files/media/Interpal%20Annual%20Report%20&%20Financial%20Statements%202010.pdf); Salam and de Waal 2004:71 (on MDI, no date on numbers); Charity Commission website, http://www.charitycommission.gov.uk/find-charities/(on Muslim Charity, 2011 numbers); Mercy USA for Aid and Development, *2011 Annual Report* (available at http://mercyusa.org/wp-content/uploads/2014/01/2011-Annual-Report-High-Res.pdf); Kroessin 2009:12 (on

Human Appeal International, 2005 numbers); Hidaya Foundation, *Financial Statements and Supplementary Information 2012* (available at http://www.hidaya. org/about-us/financials/); Kinder USA, *Financial Statements 2010–2011* (available at http://kinderusa.org/wp-content/documents/Kinder%202011%20financial%20statements.pdf).

25. I have elsewhere (Juul Petersen 2012b) presented this history of transnational Muslim NGOs in terms of four different ideal types, each related to one of the four events presented above. In this perspective, one type is the da'watist NGO, promoting an understanding of aid as simultaneously material and spiritual, and engaging in the construction of mosques, distribution of religious texts and establishment of Qur'an schools as indispensable parts of aid; another type is the jihadist NGO, relying on an understanding of aid as an important tool in the (sometimes violent) fight for justice, and engaging in moral as well as material support to the fighters; a third type is the solidarity-based NGO, rejecting notions of direct *da'wa* and armed jihad, but still seeing aid as a way to strengthen solidarity among Muslims; and finally, a fourth type is the secularised NGO, in many ways indistinguishable from mainstream, secular (or Christian) NGOs.

4. PIETY AND PROFESSIONALISM: CLAIMS TO AUTHORITY IN IIROSA AND IICO

1. At least theoretically, recipients also influence the construction of ideologies. Just as NGOs need the support of donors and partners, they also need the acceptance of recipients in order to appear legitimate. In this perspective, NGOs can be expected to adjust their ideologies to recipients in the same way they adjust their ideologies to donors and partners, opening up for spaces of negotiation (Silk 2004:236). That said, however, there can be no doubt that, compared to other types of audience, recipients' possibilities for exercising influence on organisational ideologies are severely limited. They cannot condition their support on material or other kinds of resources; all they can offer the organisations is their acceptance or rejection of aid, and insofar as there are many more poor people in need of aid than there are organisations, this resource is not worth much. Instead, the present analysis pays more attention to recipients as objects of aid, exploring the ways in which they are interpellated through ideologies. Naturally, this does not mean that recipients do not exercise agency in the ways in which they interact with the organisations. However, this aspect is not the topic of the present book. For a discussion of how recipients interact with Muslim NGOs, see Palmer (2011).

2. In June 2009, the Supreme Court turned down the case on the grounds that Saudi Arabia and its officials are immune from lawsuit for governmental acts outside the United States (Vicini 2009). A new lawsuit was filed in 2011. At the time of writing, the case was still ongoing.

3. Again, let me reiterate that I am not in a position to judge whether or to what extent these allegations were true or not.

4. A few years later, in 2009, IIROSA's office in Bangladesh was closed, although no

relations with local terrorist groups had been detected. A representative from the Bangladeshi government's NGO Affairs Bureau says: 'We got the [designation] list from the UN, and that's why the [Bangladesh Central] Bank was ready to close them down, even though they have had no negative activities in Bangladesh.' The office was re-opened in October 2010, allegedly by the request of the Bangladeshi government (IIROSA, *Bulletin* no. 36, p. 4).

5. Thus, in 1993, when the original secretary general, Farid al-Qurashi, voiced his scepticism of the government's alliance with the US during the Gulf war, he was replaced by the more government-friendly Adnan Khalil Basha.

6. At the same time, however, signals are ambiguous. For instance, although pressured by the US, the Saudi government has yet to establish the promised National Commission for Relief and Charitable Works Abroad, aimed at increasing control of Saudi NGOs. Leaving the lines of reporting and control somewhat vague, the government tries to retain maximum governmental flexibility and, at least on the surface, maintain good relations with IIROSA and other Muslim NGOs (Alterman 2007). As an observer and former volunteer notes: 'The Saudi government didn't destroy the IIROSA. This would damage their image. They live on their Islamic image. If they destroyed the organisation, it wouldn't be good for them. Instead, they neutralise it. They put someone in charge who is supportive of government.'

7. Generally, however, the Kuwaiti government seems to have been more supportive during the War on Terror. A director of another Kuwaiti NGO says: 'The government is very supportive of us and of the IICO. They know that we are not political. Because of US relations, they sometimes have to distance themselves from us, but they always excuse this.'

8. Many people I talked to in Saudi Arabia and Kuwait would interpret the allegations against Muslim NGOs as part of a long history of Western, and particularly US, hypocrisy and imperialism. This is a common perception that has roots far back in history, but in recent years it has been nourished by events such as the invasions of Afghanistan and Iraq and the boycott of the democratically elected Hamas in Palestine. In the eyes of many people, then, 'the West' is not only, or even primarily, about freedom, democracy and human rights, but also about Unmanned Armed Vehicles, or UAVs, killing civilians, waterboarding, and unjust court cases. And Osama bin Laden, Al-Qaeda and the Taleban are not simply terrorists but freedom fighters who stand up against this hypocrisy and imperialism.

9. The organisation was formally founded at the twentieth session of the Muslim World League Constituent Council in 1978. In 1979, a royal decree approved the establishment of IIROSA, allowing it to open branches abroad.

10. IIROSA *Overall Performance Report*, p. 56.

11. IICO, *al-Alamiya*, no. 243.

12. Information about IICO's and IIROSA's General Assembly and trustees has been gathered from IICO magazines, interviews, and websites (IIROSA, website,

http://www.egatha.org/ga2013/, and IICO, website, http://www.iico.org/
AxCMSwebLive/en_board_directors.cms

13. The person who served as director of the IICO at the time of my interviews, Ibrahim Hsaballah, was replaced by Suleiman Shams Al-Din in 2010.

14. The Islamic Personality of the Year Award is part of the Dubai International Holy Qur'an Awards and consists of a prize of approx. US$ 270,000. The King Faisal Award in Service to Islam consists of a prize of approx. US$ 200,000 (see King Faisal Foundation's website, www.kff.com

15. IICO, *Special Publication*, p. 15.

16. IIROSA's Islamic identity is less pronounced: the colours of the website are not green, but blue, just like the logo contains fewer overtly Islamic symbols. The logo takes the shape of a globe on a background of two red and yellow circles, thus creating two crescents. On the globe, the location of Saudi Arabia is marked with a black spot. Together, the three circles resemble an eye with the globe as the iris and Saudi Arabia as the pupil. The eye, *hamsa*, is a common symbol in Islam, referring to the Hand of Fatima.

17. IICO, website, http://www.iico.org/AxCMSwebLive/en_give_your_zakat.cms

18. IICO, website, http://www.iico.org/AxCMSwebLive/en_fatwa.cms

19. IIROSA, *Annual Report 2007/2008*, p. 10.

20. IICO, *Administrative and Financial Report*, p. 18.

21. IICO, website, http://www.iico.org/AxCMSwebLive/en_shari_board.cms

22. In both Saudi Arabia and Kuwait, businesses are required to pay *zakat*, while it is voluntary for individuals. *Zakat* can be paid either to the government or to a licensed NGO. There are no statistics on how many people give to the government and how many give to NGOs. A former IIROSA trustee explains: 'People tend to give half and half.'

23. A *waqf* is a sort of Islamic endowment, the proceeds of which are used for religious or charitable purposes. Historically, *waqf* has played an important role in the Middle East as a tool for provision of public goods and social welfare (Kuran 2001:841). For literature on the role of *waqf* in Islamic history, see Kuran (2001).

24. The IICO tries to implement what it calls 'a modernised version' of *waqf*, in cooperation with its affiliate investment company Al Safwah International Development Company. According to the Annual Report for 2006, the income from investments was more than US$ 10 million, up from US$ 7 million in 2005. In 2010, a wealthy man named Ali Saleh Allahib donated a third of his wealth as *waqf* to IICO, equalling more than US$ 31 million (IICO, *Administrative and Financial Report*, p. 31). Likewise, in 2010 IIROSA launched six *waqf* projects (housing and commercial buildings in Mecca) at a cost of more than US$ 125 million, with expected annual returns of approximately US$ 12 million (Ghafour and Shamsuddin 2010). As in IICO, the land was purchased through the help of a number of wealthy philanthropists and businessmen (IIROSA, *Bulletin* no. 34, p. 1).

25. IICO, *Pioneering in Charity*, p. 1.

26. In its Annual Reports, IIROSA has also had a somewhat similar section, including references to various authorities. The 2007/2008 Annual Report, for instance, refers to letters of appreciation from, for example, the secretary general of the Muslim World League, the secretary general of OIC and from several princes.
27. IICO, website, http://www.iico.org/AxCMSwebLive/en_testimonials.cms
28. IICO, website, http://www.iico.org/iicolive/InnerPageContent_en.aspx?Pg_id=1&Pg_dtl_id=12, last accessed February 2015.
29. For example, IIROSA, *Bulletin* no. 33; IIROSA, Annual Report 2009–2010, p. 50.
30. The Ministry of Awqaf and Religious Affairs also has a unit especially for this but the two are independent.
31. IICO, *al-Alamiya* no. 243.
32. IICO, *Management Report*, p. 4. The organisation also organised several media campaigns, including 'Moderation is Light', and the campaign 'Tolerance and Moderation are Ways for Life', under the patronage of Prince Sabah al-Ahmad. At one point, the organisation had plans to launch a satellite channel dedicated to religious moderation, but this did not happen (IICO, *Management Report*, p. 4).
33. IICO, *Pioneering in Charity*, p. 7.
34. While highly interesting in themselves, these extra-aid activities are not a central part of the analysis, insofar as it focuses more specifically on their aid ideologies.
35. See for instance, IICO, *Positive Relations at All Levels*, p. 7ff, and IIROSA, *Overall Performance Report*, p. 52.
36. IIROSA, *Overall Performance Report 2010/2011*, p. 11
37. IIROSA, *Operational Plan*, p. 35; Ibrahim 2010a.
38. Members are British Red Cross, DFID, IICO, Islamic Relief, Foundation for Human Rights and Freedoms and Humanitarian Relief (IHH), Imam Khomeini Relief Foundation, Mercy Corps, Muhammadiyah Foundation, National Rural Support Programme, Near East Foundation, Qatar Charity, Qatar Red Crescent Society, Swiss Agency for Development and Cooperation, and the World Assembly of Muslim Youth (Humanitarian Forum, website, www.humanitarianforum.org
39. Humanitarian Forum, website, http://www.humanitarianforum.com/pages/en/what-we-do.html. In 2006, a conference was held in Kuwait, organised by the IICO and gathering Kuwaiti and Gulf-based NGOs with the purpose of discussing the problems faced by Muslim NGOs after 9/11. In 2009, a workshop brought together Kuwaiti NGOs, representatives of the Kuwaiti Ministry of Social Affairs and Labour, the British Charity Commission and Islamic Relief in order to discuss possibilities for capacity building of local NGOs. Following this workshop, the Forum established a national office in Kuwait (the Humanitarian Forum Kuwait), serving as an umbrella organisation for thirty-five Kuwaiti NGOs under the leadership of IICO's secretary general and director. IICO, *al-Alamiya* no. 232;

Humanitarian Forum, website, http://www.humanitarianforum.com/countries.
php?action=view&id=5

40. UN News Centre website, http://www.un.org/apps/news/story.asp?NewsID= 42871. At the conference, a web-based Arab Humanitarian Portal was also launched, aimed at facilitating access to humanitarian information in the Arab region as well as to document Arab efforts in the field. The portal is established as a partnership between OCHA, IICO, Direct Aid, the Humanitarian Forum, OIC, Qatar Ministry of Foreign Affairs, United Arab Emirates Foreign Aid Coordination Office, International Humanitarian City, League of Arab States, the Royal Charity Organisation, Oman Charitable Organisation, and the Inter-Agency Standing Committee (Arab Humanitarian Portal, website, http:// arabhum.net

41. On IIROSA's website, there is even a reference to a World Bank conference in Chad where IIROSA was allegedly selected as 'the best Islamic Arab charity working in rural development in Chad and one of the best international organisations working in this field' (IIROSA, website, http://www.egatha.org/eportal/ index.php?option=com_content&view=article&id=12&Itemid=4. When this conference took place, and precisely by whom the IIROSA was selected, is unclear and it has been impossible to find additional information on the conference from other sources.

42. IIROSA also recently established a similar centre, the Research and Studies Centre (see IIROSA, Annual Report 2011–2012, p. 9.

43. IICO, website, https://www.iico.org/AxCMSweblive/en_charitable_studies_center.cms

44. IICO, website, http://www.iico.org/AxCMSwebLive/en_charitable_studies_center.cms

45. IIROSA, *Bulletin* no. 26, p. 5.

46. IICO, *Special Publication*, p. 27.

47. IICO, website, http://www.iico.org/AxCMSwebLive/en_mission_vision.cms

48. IICO, website, http://www.iico.org/AxCMSwebLive/en_training_programs_conferences.cms

49. These included the Muslim World League, World Assembly of Muslim Youth, Al-Muntada al-Islami, Makkah al-Mukkarama Charity Foundation, and the now defunct Al-Haramain'.

50. Since the organisation and its website no longer exist, the information is not publicly available.

51. IIROSA, *Bulletin* no. 27, p. 3.

52. IIROSA, *Bulletin* no. 28, p. 2 and 3. As part of this strategy to claim a professional authority, the secretary general accuses the US itself of lack of transparency and neutrality, claiming that most of these allegations are based on 'unfounded newspaper clippings, news statements and unsubstantiated intelligence reports' and that the allegations of terrorist funding are politically motivated, directed

by 'Zionist groups in the United States' and 'for political reasons that have nothing to do with charity work' (IIROSA, *Bulletin* no. 27, p. 3).

53. The same pattern of non-cooperation seems to be found in other countries. In Senegal, for instance, neither IIROSA nor Kuwait Joint Relief Committee is part of CONGAD, the council of Senegalese and transnational NGOs working in Senegal (Renders 2002:64). Likewise, in her analysis of transnational Muslim NGOs in Chad, Kaag (2007:101) writes that '[i]n organized forums, Muslim and Christian NGOs hardly meet each other, let alone collaborate. The NGO forum in Moundou (a large town in southern Chad), for instance, consists of Christian and lay organisations only.'

54. Royal Embassy of Saudi Arabia 2009; IIROSA, *Operational Plan*, p. 34.

55. IIROSA, *Annual Report*, p. 49.

56. IICO, *Administrative and Financial Report*, p. 22f.

57. IICO, *Administrative and Financial Report*, p. 23.

5. 'IT'S ALL IN ISLAM!' AID IDEOLOGIES IN IIROSA AND IICO

1. IICO, *Pioneering in Charity*, p. 1.

2. IICO, website, http://www.iico.org/AxCMSwebLive/en_mission_vision.cms

3. IIROSA, website, http://www.egatha.org/eportal/index.php?option=com_content&view=article&id=2&Itemid=2

4. IICO, *Pioneering in Charity*, p. 5.

5. IICO, website, http://www.iico.org/AxCMSweblive/en_objectives.cms

6. IIROSA, *ISC Report*, p. 10.

7. IICO, *Pioneering in Charity*, p. 7.

8. Speech by Yusuf al-Qaradawi, IICO *Special Publication*, p. 15.

9. IIROSA, *Bulletin* no. 28, p. 2f.

10. For instance IICO, website, http://www.iico.org/axcmsweblive/en_objectives.cms

11. IIROSA, *Annual Report*, p. 40.

12. Insofar as the vision is framed as a response not only to material, but also spiritual poverty, beneficiaries may not only include the poor but also well-off people who are in need of spiritual strengthening. For instance, IICO's initiative *Build a School, Revive a Nation* seeks to build model schools 'that attract and educate students from the upper class for high fees and distinguished students from the less-privileged members of Muslim communities for free, especially in Africa and Asia, and instil noble virtues in them' (IICO, *al-Alamiya* no. 243).

13. For instance 'impoverished Muslim countries and communities' (IICO, *Pioneering in Charity*, p. 2) and 'keep the Muslims safe and rescue them from hunger' (IICO, *Special Publication*, p. 5).

14. IIROSA, *Bulletin* no. 28, p. 6.

15. IIROSA, *ISC Report*, p. 16.

16. IIROSA, *Overall Performance Report 2010/2011*, p. 14.

17. Both IIROSA and IICO have worked in their home countries for many years (IIROSA since 1998 and IICO since the Gulf War), but they have intensified their involvement in national aid provision since 9/11 and the War on Terror, at least in part prompted by the introduction of restrictions on international transfers.
18. The table is developed on the basis of IIROSA, *Annual Report 2003/2004*. Data from later years could not be obtained.
19. IICO, *Their Relief … Is Our Duty*, p. 10ff.
20. IIROSA, *Bulletin* no. 36, p. 12.
21. An important part of ideological motivation is the motivation of staff. However, insofar as this analysis centres on external representations, focus is on motivational discourses directed externally at potential donors rather than internal motivational discourses.
22. See for instance IICO, *Pioneering in Charity*, p. 3. This duty to do good is not only religiously explained. IIROSA in particular also uses terms such as a 'humanitarian duty' (e.g. *ISC Report*, p. 4), albeit not as frequently.
23. IIROSA, *Annual Report 2011–2012*, p. 1
24. IICO, website, http://www.iico.net/home-page-eng/News-08/aug_08/iico-eng-6.htm
25. IICO, website, http://www.iico.org/AxCMSwebLive/en_our_story.cms
26. IICO, Special Publication, p. 5.
27. IICO, website, http://www.iico.org/axcmsweblive/en_objectives.cms
28. Examples from IICO and IIROSA posters and brochures.
29. The PR material is no longer available on the IICO website.
30. IICO, *Pioneering in Charity*, p. 4.
31. IIROSA, *Annual Report*, p. 6.
32. News articles on the twenty-fifth anniversary are no longer available on the IICO website.
33. In his essay *The Poor* (1908), Georg Simmel writes about charitable giving in a Christian tradition, claiming that the motive for alms resides exclusively in the significance of giving for the giver: 'When Jesus told the wealthy young man, "Give your riches to the poor", what apparently mattered to him were not the poor, but rather the soul of the wealthy man for whose salvation this sacrifice was merely a means or a symbol' (1994 19081:153, cf. Bornstein 2003:116).
34. The quote was included in a 2008 news item on IICO's website which is no longer available.
35. IIROSA, *Magazine*.
36. *Overall Performance Report 2010/2011*, p. 14.
37. IIROSA, *ISC Report*, p. 13. Another example is this: 'The IICO, with its desire to implement the message of Islamic brotherhood as referred to in the Prophet's hadith, "The relationship of the believer with another believer is like (the bricks of) a building, each strengthens the other", has managed to alleviate many problems related to poverty, hunger, illiteracy, ignorance and deprivation in many

impoverished Muslim countries and communities' (IICO, *Pioneering in Charity*, p. 2).

38. IIROSA, *Bulletin* no. 34, p. 4.
39. IIROSA, *ISC Report*, p. 16.
40. IICO, *Pioneering in Charity*, p. 2.
41. IIROSA, *ISC Report*, p. 18.
42. See Bornstein 2009 for a discussion of this dilemma in an Indian context. She writes: 'To coerce the impulse to give into rational accountability is to obliterate its freedom; to render giving into pure impulse is to reinforce social inequality' (2009:643).
43. IIROSA, *Sponsor an Orphan*.
44. IICO, website, http://www.iico.org/axcmsweblive/en_give_your_zakat.cms
45. The table builds on information from IICO's *Administrative and Financial Report 2010–2011*, p. 41.
46. The table builds on information from IIROSA's *Annual Report 2007/2008*. It has not been possible to obtain information from later years.
47. IIROSA, *Annual Report*, p. 8.
48. IICO, website, http://www.iico.org/axcmsweblive/en_activities_campaigns.cms
49. There may be an analytical point in this: it might be easier for religious organisations to relate to ideologies of humanitarianism than ideologies of development, insofar as humanitarianism emphasises the emotional, moral, and the individual whereas development is more oriented towards progress, bureaucracy, and technology.
50. IIROSA, website, http://www.egatha.org/eportal/index.php?option=com_content&view=article&id=39:iirosa-executes-285-health-projects-in-48-countries-benefiting-more-than-34-million-patients&catid=6:iirosa-news&Itemid=14
51. For instance, IICO's description of its Asia programme states that projects target 'social, educational and health problems', listing for instance mosque building, spiritual education, and Qur'an teaching alongside drilling of wells, orphan sponsorship, and disaster prevention (IICO, website, http://www.iico.org/axcmsweblive/en_asia_committee.cms).
52. IICO, *al-Alamiya* no. 218.
53. IICO, *al-Alamiya* no. 243, 2005/2006.
54. IIROSA, website, http://www.egatha.org/eportal/index.php?option=com_content&view=article&id=14&Itemid=8
55. IIROSA, *Annual Report 2011–2012*, p. 64.
56. IICO, *al-Alamiya* no. 243.
57. Speech by Yusuf al-Qaradawi, *IICO Special Publication*, p. 15.
58. IICO, website, www.iico.net/home-page-eng/news-10/jan-10/iico-eng.htm. This news item is no longer available on the IICO website.
59. These include the International Islamic University, Islamabad; Islamic University of Malaysia; Islamic University of Uganda; Islamic University of Niger; Regulatory

University of Sri Lanka; University of Chittagong, Bangladesh; Iyman University, Yemen; King Faisal University, Chad (IICO, *Special Publication*, p. 26).

60. IICO, *Pioneering in Charity*, n.d., p. 10.
61. IIROSA, website, http://www.egatha.org/eportal/index.php?option=com_cont ent&view=article&id=13&Itemid=7
62. In Sudan, for instance, IIROSA has built three educational institutions, providing education for almost 4,000 students. In Kenya, the organisation has established a teacher's college for Islamic education. In Nigeria, IIROSA established the Umm Al-Qura Institute in 1999, accommodating more than 600 students. In Senegal, IIROSA built the Dar al-Hekma Islamic Education Complex where 450 students go. And in 2009, a school in Djibouti was established, enrolling 150 students. IIROSA has also established several universities. In Thailand, for instance, IIROSA established the Jala Islamic University, where 2,500 students study Arabic, religion, public administration, finance, economy, Islamic banking, Islamic history, and other sharia subjects. Likewise, the organisation contributed to the establishment of the King Faisal University in Chad, consisting of four colleges teaching Arabic, Islamic education, computer engineering and economy. And in Pakistan, IIROSA established a women's university with colleges for Islamic studies, Arabic, and translation (Ibrahim 2010b).
63. IICO, *Annual Report*, p. 10.
64. IICO, *Pioneering in Charity*, p. 6.
65. See, for example, IICO, *al-Alamiya* no. 218.
66. IICO, *al-Alamiya* no. 243.
67. IICO, *al-Alamiya* no. 243.
68. IICO, *al-Alamiya* no. 243.
69. For example, talks about 'comprehensive development' (IIROSA, *Annual Report*, p. 34), 'comprehensive welfare' (IIROSA, ISC, p. 4), and the 'productive family program' (IIROSA, website, http://www.egatha.org/eportal/index.php?option= com_content&view=article&id=4&Itemid=6).
70. IICO, *Pioneering in Charity*, p. 4.
71. IICO, *Pioneering in Charity*, p. 1.
72. The story is also mentioned in several publications, for example: 'The Prophet Muhammad said, and Alzubair the son of Alauam said the story after him, that if you take a rope and go up the mountain and come down with a pack of wood, carrying it on your back, by which you will keep your dignity, is better than asking people for money, who might give it or not' (IICO, *Special Publication*, p. 6).
73. IICO, *Special Publication*, p. 2.
74. For example, IICO, *Special Publication*, p. 5.
75. According to Qaradawi, Muslim leaders 'have been too busy with politics and have left everything else, until the charitable work invaded them from abroad' (IICO, *Special Publication*, p. 15).

6. PROFESSIONALISM AND (A BIT OF) PIETY: CLAIMS TO AUTHORITY IN ISLAMIC RELIEF AND MUSLIM AID

1. Thaut et al's (2012) study of Islamic Relief gives a very similar analysis to the one presented here. They argue that especially after 9/11, Muslim NGOs were considered to be 'moral suspects' in the West, prompting them to initiate a range of organisational reforms, in particular in areas of financial transparency and professionalism, and that these responses, designed to increase legitimacy with a Western audience, in turn had potentially negative consequences for the organisation's legitimacy with some Islamic audiences (Thaut et al 2012:141).

2. Islamic Relief, website, http://www.islamic-relief.com/NewsRoom/NewsDetails.aspx?catID=2&newsID=146

3. Muslim Aid, *25th Anniversary Souvenir* brochure, p. 2.

4. Muslim Aid, website, https://www.muslimaid.org/media-centre/news/hrh-the-prince-of-wales-and-prime-minister-congratulate-muslim-aid-as-over-600-guests-attend-its-25th-anniversary-dinner/. Similarly, at a reception hosted by Muslim Aid at the Houses of Parliament, the MP Martin Horwood, Co-Chairman of the Liberal Democrat Committee on Foreign Affairs, International Development and Defence, said: 'Many congratulations to Muslim Aid on their twenty-fifth anniversary. This fantastic organisation has led the way in the development world in terms of building links within communities and promoting tolerance.' Muslim Aid, website, https://www.muslimaid.org/media-centre/press-release/british-mps-pay-tributes-to-muslim-aid/

5. Britain has a history of transparent and simple charity legislation and policies as compared to those of many other countries (de Cordier 2009a:611). Coupled with governmental ideologies of multiculturalism, this has encouraged the establishment of many Muslim organisations. According to the Charity Commission, there are more than 1,300 Muslim organisations (including mosques and Islamic centres) in Britain. Of these, approximately fifty are transnational NGOs, of varying size, involved in aid provision (Kroessin 2009:5).

6. In March 2010, the *Sunday Telegraph* and the *Daily Telegraph* published two articles stating that Muslim Aid had in 2005 funded several organisations that were 'allegedly linked to terrorist groups', one of them (Al Ihsan Charitable Society) an organisation that had been designated by the UK government (Charity Commission 2010:2). These accusations lead to the instigation of a Charitable Commission investigation of Muslim Aid. The month-long investigation found that Muslim Aid had, prior to the UK government's designation of Al Ihsan Charitable Society in 2005, funded the organisation through its *Qurbani* programme (approx. US$ 4,000 in 2002 and US$ 5,000 in 2003) and had set aside funds for a dentist chair (approx. US$ 21,500) but had not transferred this money, since Al Ihsan Charitable Society had in the meantime been designated by the government. The Charity Commission concluded that '[w]ithin the scope of this investigation the Commission found no evidence of irregular or improper use of

the Charity's funds or any evidence that the Charity had illegally funded any proscribed or designated entities' (quoted from Muslim Aid, Annual Review 2010, p. 28. The original Charity Commission report is no longer available on the Commission's website). In June 2014, the Charity Commission announced that Muslim Aid was again subject to statutory inquiry (Charity Commission website, https://www.gov.uk/government/news/charity-commission-names-further-charities-under-investigation). According to Muslim Aid, '[t]he Inquiry was launched as a result of Muslim Aid's own notification to the Charity Commission of non-compliance with some operational aspects in two field offices' (Muslim Aid, website, https://www.muslimaid.org/media-centre/news/muslim-aids-statement-on-charity-commission-inquiry/). The inquiry was not completed upon publication of this book.

7. Despite these developments, a former staff member notes that trustees in both Islamic Relief and Muslim Aid are still heavily involved in what he refers to as post-colonial politics. 'It's Egyptian politics, Pakistani politics that's reflected in the organisations, not British politics […] It's not about whether you are a Tory or Labour, it's about the particular types of South East Asian politics,' he says.

8. Islamic Relief, website, http://www.islamic-relief.com/NewsRoom/6–2–121-president-of-islamic-relief-awarded-obe.aspx. He has also been awarded the Ibn Khaldun Award for Excellence in Promoting Understanding between Global Cultures and Faiths, and the Muslim Power 100's Lifetime Achievement Award. Power 100s are lists of the most influential men and women in different sectors in the world, including for instance arts power, legal power, women's power and, as mentioned above, Muslim power. See www.power100.co.uk for more information.

9. In 2002, the *Guardian* newspaper listed him as one of the ten most influential Muslims in the UK (http://www.theguardian.com/world/2002/jun/17/religion.immigrationpolicy) and in 2005, he was ranked at number ten on a magazine list of the 100 most powerful men in Britain. Information from Wikipedia, http://en.wikipedia.org/wiki/Iqbal_Sacranie

10. Despite steep increases in institutional funding, much funding still comes from individual donors, the majority of them immigrant Muslims from South Asia and the Middle East. Muslim Aid has 30,000–40,000 regular individual donors (G. Clarke 2010). There are no numbers for Islamic Relief's donor base but taking into consideration that the organisation has several fundraising offices, it is estimated to be substantially higher. Islamic Relief gets 49.5 per cent of donations from Pakistani British, 16.5 per cent from Indians, 8.5 per cent from Bangladeshi, 8.5 per cent from Arab British, 5.5 per cent from White British, and the remaining 11.5 per cent from other ethnic and national groups, including Ugandans, Somalis, and Turks (Khan 2012:95). There are no detailed statistics on the composition of Muslim Aid's donors but it can be expected to reflect Islamic Relief's, albeit perhaps with a larger percentage of Pakistani and Bangladeshi donors.

11. Muslim Aid, *Annual Review 2011*, np.

12. Interestingly, while donations from organisations and institutions in the Middle East are increasing, donations from individuals in the Middle East have been decreasing steadily—from approximately US$ 6.8 million in 2007 to US$ 4.5 million in 2008 and US$ 2.8 million in 2009 (Islamic Relief, *Annual Report 2009*, p. 44). This may have to do with the emergence of new Muslim NGOs, many of them in the Gulf countries and in Turkey, presenting individual donors with other options closer to home.

13. Islamic Relief, *Annual Report 2011*, p. 75.

14. Muslim Aid, website, http://www.muslimaid.org/index.php/about-us/partners. This perhaps also testifies to the trends towards more development-oriented aid in the Islamic Development Bank and the OIC.

15. Islamic Relief, *PPA Self-Assessment Review*.

16. Information from *Annual Reports* 2003–2011, total incoming resources converted from UK£ to US$.

17. Information from *Annual Reviews* 2003–2011, total incoming resources converted from UK£ to US$.

18. This is not something that Islamic Relief publicly announces; however, several former and current staff members confirm the relation.

19. Jama'at-e Islami has been part of Bangladeshi parliament since 1986, when the party won ten seats. From 2001 to 2006, Jama'at-e Islami was part of government in a four-party alliance with, among others, the Bangladesh Nationalist Party, holding two ministries.

20. In both organisations, volunteers seem to play an increasingly important role, organising fundraising events and promoting the organisation in other ways. There is no doubt that their involvement and conceptions of the organisation's aid ideology merit further investigation; however, for lack of space, the present analysis will not deal with this particular group of staff.

21. The emergence of this new kind of Muslim staff member is mirrored by the that of a new type of Muslim donor, consisting in young, well-educated second- or third-generation immigrants who cultivate their religious identity and are active in their religious community. For them, donating to, for instance, Muslim Aid or Islamic Relief is a way of reasserting their religious identity and supporting their community. But contrary to older, more conservative donors, they are not satisfied with *Qurbani* sacrifices and Ramadan food packages: they expect Muslim NGOs to be modern, professional organisations, on a par with secular organisations such as Oxfam and CARE, but, through their religiosity, contributing to strengthening the Muslim community and modern Islam. As part of the attempts to attract these new donors, Muslim Aid and Islamic Relief have introduced new kinds of fundraising, including events such as the Allah Made me Funny stand-up show, Ramadan volunteer possibilities, spoken word poetry, and walkathons, echoing trends among secular NGOs but adding a distinctive religious flavour.

22. Interestingly, at least one person expresses scepticism as to whether the organisation will manage to separate itself from the Jama'at. In his view, managers do not

care—and do not have to care—about the criticism from government now that they have institutional funding from Western donors.

23. In an e-mail correspondence with a staff member in May 2011, I was told that the number of non-Muslims had increased significantly the last year.

24. Islamic Relief, website, http://www.islamic-relief.com/whoweare/Default. aspx?depID=2

25. Muslim Aid, *Strategic Framework 2007–2010*, p. 4.

26. Islamic Relief *Policy Stance on Poverty*, p. 2. Islamic Relief even has an entire department dedicated to research and policy-making, and both organisations cooperate frequently with British universities. Islamic Relief was part of the DFID-funded *Religions and Development Research Programme*, Birmingham University, and a member of the steering committee for the research programme Religion and AIDS in Africa at the African Studies Center in the Netherlands (*PPA Self-Assessment Review*, p. 10).

27. Islamic Relief, *Annual Report 2006*, p. 10.

28. Muslim Aid, website, http://www.muslimaid.org/index.php/media-centre/press-releases/573-muslim-aid-raises-over-p300000-for-needy-children

29. For instance Islamic Relief, *Annual Report 2008*, p. 4, and Islamic Relief, *Annual Report 2006*, p. 2.

30. Humanitarian Accountability Partnership, website, www.hapinternational.org

31. Investors in People, website, www.investorsinpeople.co.uk

32. Islamic Relief, *Annual Report 2008*, p. 72.

33. Muslim Aid, website, http://www.muslimaid.org/index.php/about-us

34. Similarly, Muslim Aid's largest partner organisation is not a Muslim organisation, but Lutheran Aid for Medicine, and other major partners are also non-Muslim organisations. Likewise, Islamic Relief cooperates with the Church of Jesus Christ of Latter-day Saints and Thengamara Mohila Sabuj Sangha, also non-Muslim, while Muslim partners are used primarily for implementation of seasonal activities such as *Qurbani* and Ramadan celebrations. Unlike IIROSA and IICO, neither of the two organisations have much cooperation with mosques or Qur'an schools; in fact, Islamic Relief only recently started considering the inclusion of imams in a project (more about this in Chapter 7). Instead, they cooperate mainly with local government representatives, school officials, and other non-religious community representatives. Similarly, they do not cooperate with the Ministry of Religious Affairs, but the NGO Affairs Bureau, the Ministry of Food and Disaster, and the governmental microfinance fund, reflecting priorities of the mainstream development community.

35. Muslim Aid, *Financial Statement 2008*, p. 7.

36. Muslim Aid, *Financial Statement 2007*, p. 8

37. For a full account of the partnership, see G. Clarke (2010).

38. At some point, there were even talks about possible cooperation between Muslim Aid and World Jewish Relief. However, this did not materialise, perhaps testifying to the limits of bridge-building and religious tolerance: many individual Muslim

donors (as well as trustees and conservative religious staff members) would not appreciate this, interpreting it as a betrayal of the Palestinian cause. Considerations by Islamic Relief as to possible cooperation with World Vision were also met with criticism, although here criticism came from young development professionals who had difficulties cooperating with an explicitly missionary organisation. As one of them says: 'Of all the religious organisations, they are some of the ones that are most different from us because they evangelise.' Despite this, Islamic Relief entered into cooperation with World Vision on a small project in Sudan in 2011.

39. First place was awarded to the British Red Cross Society (Islamic Relief, website, www.islamic-relief.com/NewsRoom/4–300-islamic-relief-is-runner-up-in-charity-finance-award.aspx).

40. Demonstrating similarly subtle signs of allegiance, Muslim Aid's Code of Conduct Policy states that: 'This document has benefited from the policies, suggestions or thinking of International Federation of the Red Cross, International Organisation for Migration, Mission Aviation Fellowship Europe, Médecins Sans Frontières Holland, Norwegian Refugee Council, PLAN International, Save the Children Sweden, World Food Program, The United Nations, and a variety of expert individuals from the NGO community such as People in Aid' (Muslim Aid, *Code of Conduct Policy*, p. 1).

41. Islamic Relief, *Annual Report 2006*, p. 2. Likewise, Muslim Aid wants to be 'a key global player' (Muslim Aid, *Strategic Framework 2007–2010*, p. 9) and 'achieve international recognition' (*Strategic Framework 2007–2010*, p. 13).

42. Khan (2012) found that 2 per cent of Islamic Relief's donors are non-Muslims (although noting that this number may be higher in relation to public collections or appeals for emergency relief).

43. Islamic Relief, *Annual Report 2006*, p. 14.

44. Muslim Aid, *Strategic Framework 2007–2010*, p. 12.

45. Compare for instance Muslim Aid's *Annual Reviews* 1999 and 2000 with the one from 2009.

46. Muslim Aid uses the vice-chairman of the Islamic Foundation in Leicester and the mufti Barakat Ullah, while Islamic Relief gets advice from the European Council of Fatwa and Research and Al Azhar University (Khan 2012:112). On a side note, their choice of religious authorities also emphasises allegiances with broader Islamic movements, as hinted at in the previous sections. The Islamic Foundation is part of a Jama'at-e Islami-inspired British movement, while the European Council of Fatwa and Research is closely affiliated with the European Muslim Brotherhood.

47. Interestingly, when the two organisations do engage with other Muslim NGOs, it is often with the explicit goal of professionalising them. For instance, Islamic Relief was a founding member of the Muslim Charities Forum, established in 2007, together with Human Appeal International, Human Relief Foundation, and Muslim Hands, with the purpose of improving the contributions of UK-based

Muslim NGOs to international development through exchange of experiences, ideas, and information, networking with governments and other international development actors. A year before, the Muslim Council of Britain launched its Charitable Foundation Project, funded by Muslim Aid and aimed at building capacity in Muslim organisations in Britain.

48. Islamic Relief, *Annual Report 2006*, p. 18.
49. Islamic Relief, *Strategic Framework 2007–2010*, p. 2.
50. Muslim Aid, *Strategic Framework 2007–2010*, p. 10.
51. Muslim Aid, *Financial Statement 2007*, p. 2.
52. Muslim Aid Bangladesh, *Staff Manual*, p. 14.
53. Muslim Aid Bangladesh, *Staff Manual*, p. 13.
54. The logo of Islamic Relief presents a globe flanked by two minarets, while that of Muslim Aid displays a drop of water and a crescent, held in green colours.
55. On Muslim Aid's website, for instance, there is a whole section explaining *zakat* and other Islamic terms (Islamic Relief, website, http://www.islamic-relief.org/zakat/zakat-faq/).
56. Muslim Aid, for instance, offers Islamic wills, in cooperation with the firm 1st Ethical (Muslim Aid, website, http://www.muslimaid.org/index.php/what-we-do/islamic-wills).
57. Islamic Relief, *Annual Report 2008*, p. 5.
58. Muslim Aid, *Strategic Framework 2007–2010*, p. 4.
59. Muslim Aid Pakistan, website, https://www.muslimaid.org/page-faq/
60. Islamic Relief, *Annual Report 2006*, p. 2.
61. Islamic Relief, *Annual Report 2006*, p. 13.
62. Islamic Relief, *Annual Report 2006*, p. 13.
63. Muslim Aid, *25th Anniversary Souvenir* brochure, p. 2.
64. All Islamic Relief's job advertisements, for instance, note that Islamic Relief is an 'equal opportunities employer' (see also Islamic Relief, *Annual Report 2006*, p. 18).
65. In 2009, when I visited Muslim Aid headquarters, two members of the management team were non-Muslims but they have since left the organisation.
66. According to a CARE staff member, 91 out of 264 are women (e-mail communication, 16 December 2009).
67. The number is higher if including staff in the field.
68. A staff member in Islamic Relief thinks that Hani al-Banna withdrew from Islamic Relief precisely because of this conflict: 'My personal opinion is that he wanted to take the organisation in a particular direction, making it more a mainstream development organisation […] However, he came up against other senior staff and trustees who were more conservative and he became frustrated and left. There was talk that he would return after a year or two, but that was over two years ago now.'

7. 'WHAT'S SO ISLAMIC ABOUT US?': IDEOLOGIES OF AID IN ISLAMIC RELIEF AND MUSLIM AID

1. Islamic Relief, *Strategy 2007–2009*, p. 19.
2. Muslim Aid, website, http://www.muslimaid.org/index.php/what-we-do
3. Islamic Relief, *Definitions of Poverty*, point 1.0.
4. Islamic Relief, *Definitions of Poverty*, point 2.8.
5. Islamic Relief, *Definitions of Poverty*, point 3.0.
6. Islamic Relief, *Definitions of Poverty*, point 3.0.
7. Islamic Relief, *Definitions of Poverty*, point 3.1.
8. Islamic Relief, *Definitions of Poverty*, point 3.1.
9. Islamic Relief, *Definitions of Poverty*, point 4.1.
10. See for instance point 3.1.
11. Islamic Relief, *Charitable Giving in Islam*, p. 4.
12. Muslim Aid, website, http://www.muslimaid.org/index.php/about-us
13. Muslim Aid, website, http://www.muslimaid.org/index.php/about-us
14. Islamic Relief, website, http://www.islamic-relief.org/about-us
15. For instance, 'give communities a real chance of future success', Muslim Aid, website, http://www.muslimaid.org/index.php/what-we-do/healthcare-a-nutrition, and 'creating successful communities', Muslim Aid, website, http://www.muslimaid.org/index.php/what-we-do/economic-empowerment
16. Islamic Relief, *Annual Report 2008*, p. 50.
17. Islamic Relief, *Annual Report 2010*, p. 4.
18. Muslim Aid, *Strategic Framework 2007–2010*, p. 17.
19. Muslim Aid, website, http://www.muslimaid.org/index.php/what-we-do/education
20. DanChurchAid, Vision and Plan 2014: 3.
21. Christian Aid, website, http://www.christianaid.org.uk/aboutus/who/aims/our_aims.aspx#vision
22. Muslim Aid, *Financial Statement 2008*, p. 11. Islamic Relief has a similar formulation: 'regardless of race, colour, political affiliation, gender or belief' (Islamic Relief, *Annual Report 2008*, p. 4). Notably, this universalism does not include sexual orientation. G. Clarke (2010:n.24) notes that Muslim Aid's Annual Review 2006 included a commitment to tackling poverty 'regardless of religion, ethnicity, nationality, disability, sexual orientation, gender or age.' According to an interviewee, this reference to sexual orientation troubled some trustees and was not likely to appear in future publications, something which has proven correct. Likewise, Islamic Relief's HIV/AIDS material does not include references to homosexuality.
23. All examples from Muslim Aid, *Annual Review 1999*.
24. Islamic Relief, *Strategy 2007–2009*, p. 21.
25. Muslim Aid, *Annual Review 2008*, p. 4.
26. Muslim Aid, *Financial Statement 2008*, p. 11.

27. This number may be higher among donors from the Middle East. In an interview with Khan, a regional fundraiser notes that 'most of the donors I deal with believe that *zakat* donations are restricted to Muslims, in fact if we used *zakat* donations to assist non-Muslims then they would cease giving to the organisation altogether' (Khan 2012:98, emphasis in the original).

28. Islamic Relief, *Annual Report 2009*, p. 58.

29. Muslim Aid, website, https://www.muslimaid.org/page-faq/. Islamic Relief and Muslim Aid do in fact share with Oxfam a focus on countries such as Kenya, Pakistan, Palestine, Bangladesh, Indonesia, and Sri Lanka. In 2010, for instance, Oxfam's ten largest programmes were in Kenya, Congo, Haiti, Zimbabwe, Pakistan, Palestine, Bangladesh, Indonesia, Sri Lanka, and the Philippines (e-mail correspondence with Oxfam's UK office, 2 August 2010).

30. Islamic Relief, Annual Report 2011, p. 71. The percentage refers to the percentage of total expenditure. Naturally, focus varies from year to year, depending on disasters, wars and other emergencies. However, there seems to be some stability insofar as the programmes in these countries have been among the largest for several years.

31. Information from Muslim Aid staff.

32. Islamic Relief, *Strategy 2007–2009*, p. 21.

33. Islamic Relief, *Translating Faith into Development*, p. 4

34. Muslim Aid, *Financial Statement 2008*, p. 11.

35. Muslim Aid, *Code of Conduct Policy*, p. 2.

36. Islamic Relief, *Annual Report 2011*, p. 3.

37. Muslim Aid, *Strategic Framework 2007–2010*, p. 17.

38. Islamic Relief, *Annual and Financial Statements 2006*.

39. Islamic Relief, website, http://policy.islamic-relief.com/portfolio/policy_influence/

40. Muslim Aid, *25th Anniversary Souvenir* brochure, p. 2.

41. Islamic Relief, *Annual Report 2011*, p. 3.

42. Muslim Aid, *Strategic Framework 2007–2010*, p. 16. See also Islamic Relief, website, http://www.islamic-relief.org.uk/resources/charity-in-islam/zakat/

43. Muslim Aid, *Strategic Framework 2007–2010*, p. 15f.

44. Interestingly, it seems that in the case of Palestine, a more emotional, solidarity-based rhetoric is often used. Muslim Aid, for instance, writes that 'When our team entered Gaza on May 19th 2009 […] the humanitarian crisis, although very real, was masked by the determination and courage of the people of Gaza to overcome the recent conflict and ongoing siege. Our projects, both new and ongoing, were progressing well and were a testament to the fact that our brothers and sisters could rebuild their lives if given the opportunity. Through their smiles and warm welcomes, it was obvious that your compassion, your commitment and your duas had been received and had made all the difference, alhamdulillah'.

45. Islamic Relief, *Annual Report 2009*, p. 1.

46. For instance, Muslim Aid, *Strategic Framework 2007–2010*, p. 16.

47. Muslim Aid, *Strategic Framework 2007–2010*, p. 17.
48. Islamic Relief, *Annual Report 2008*, p. 44.
49. For instance, 'ensure that individuals can have access to basic necessities and the skills necessary to generate an income so that they are not permanently dependent on aid agencies for food and shelter', Muslim Aid, website, https://www.muslimaid.org/what-we-do/
50. Muslim Aid, website, http://www.muslimaid.org/index.php/what-we-do/education/spectacle-distribution-in-sri-lanka
51. Islamic Relief, *Annual Report 2008*, p. 47.
52. See one of Muslim Aid's fundraising videos here: http://wn.com/Islamic_Relief_Qurbani_Appeal_What_Will_You_Sacrifice
53. Muslim Aid's Rainbow Family website, https://www.muslimaid.org/mediacentre/rainbow-family/file-900/
54. Islamic Relief UK, website, http://www.islamic-relief.org.uk/index.aspx
55. Islamic Relief, *Waqf Brochure*, p. 6.
56. Muslim Aid, *Annual Review 2007*, p. 13. This educational function of Muslim NGOs is also expressed in Islamic Relief's partnership with DFID. One of the goals of the agreement is to raise 'awareness and commitment to international development' among 'young people and the Muslim-based communities within the UK' (Islamic Relief, *PPA Self-Assessment Review*, p. 4). This is done through, for example, the organisation's Development Education Unit, which works to 'raise awareness of the root causes of poverty [and] promote an understanding of the humanitarian message of Islam in the context of international development' (Islamic Relief UK, website, http://www.islamic-relief.org.uk/resources/education/. Muslim Aid has been involved in similar projects; its first DFID grant, for instance, was for a development awareness project in Britain.
57. Islamic Relief, *Accountability Framework*, p. 5.
58. Muslim Aid, *Annual Review 2000*, p. 4.
59. Islamic Relief, *Annual Report 2011*, p. 61.
60. Muslim Aid, *Annual Review 2011*, n.p.
61. Islamic Relief, *Translating Faith into Development*, p. 6
62. Islamic Relief, *Annual Report 2006*, p. 20.
63. Muslim Aid, *25th Anniversary Souvenir* brochure, p. 4f.
64. Muslim Aid even uses the term 'customers' (see, for example, Muslim Aid, *Annual Review 2007*, p. 2), carrying strong connotations of business relations.
65. See for example Muslim Aid, *25th Anniversary Souvenir* brochure, p. 5.
66. Islamic Relief, *Annual Report 2008*, p. 6. See also Muslim Aid *25th Anniversary Souvenir* brochure, p. 8.
67. Islamic Relief, *Strategic Framework 2007–2010*, p. 21.
68. Islamic Relief, *Annual Report 2009*, p. 61.
69. Muslim Aid, *25th Anniversary Souvenir* brochure, p. 25.
70. The Grameen Bank was one of the world's first microfinance banks and its founder, Mohammed Yunis, developed a set of principles, or decisions, that all

lenders should uphold. The sixteen decisions can be found on the website of the Grameen Bank, www.grameen.com
71. Muslim Aid, *Microfinance Booklet*.

8. CONCLUSION

1. The OIC has historically been engaged in aid provision through, for example, the Islamic Development Bank (1973), and the Islamic Solidarity Fund (1974). More recently, the organisation has established an office for the coordination of member states' humanitarian relief efforts, the OIC Humanitarian Affairs Department (ICHAD), as well as a fund for long-term development programmes, the Islamic Solidarity Fund for Development, with a budget of US$ 3 billion (compared with the Islamic Solidarity Fund's annual budget of US$ 20 million). Furthermore, the OIC has introduced a range of initiatives with the purpose of strengthening relations with NGOs in the organisation's member states: in 2007, for instance, the OIC introduced annual conferences for NGOs, and in 2012 the organisation granted humanitarian NGOs the possibility to apply for observer status, just like the organisation has entered into partnerships with several individual NGOs.
2. BBC News, http://www.bbc.co.uk/news/world-middle-east-21258511

APPENDIX A: METHODOLOGY

1. In my analysis, I do not include internal organisational documents such as e-mails, minutes from staff meetings and memos, insofar as I analyse the ways in which organisations present their ideologies, not the role ideologies play internally in organisations as a way of motivating and creating internal coherence.
2. Islamic Relief and Muslim Aid's websites are in English with Arabic versions available, just like most of their organisational material. IICO and IIROSA's websites, on the other hand, are both in Arabic, with English versions. Similarly, most of the two organisations' material is in Arabic, with the exception of a few annual reports, newsletters (or parts of newsletters), and pamphlets. Since I do not speak Arabic, I had some of this material translated into English by native Arabic speakers, either in writing or orally. In order to rule out the possibility that the English language and Arabic language material presented fundamentally different ideologies, I made some random checks, but found that there were no substantial differences between the two types of material. However, there is no doubt that more systematic comparisons between Arabic and English versions of the websites could have been fruitful, displaying subtle differences in the ways in which the organisations target respectively English-speaking and Arabic-speaking audiences.
3. In the analysis, all interviewees have been anonymised. When relevant, they are presented with function and locality. Certain functions are of course difficult to anonymise, due to their uniqueness; for instance, there is only one IIROSA country director in Jordan, and people with knowledge of the organisations will know who

he is. In such cases, I have left out the title when I judged the quote to be the least bit controversial or sensitive. In other instances, I have kept the title. I have not anonymised the organisations, except in what I judged to be controversial or sensitive cases.

4. Interestingly, I never encountered any difficulties being a female researcher in religiously conservative societies such as Saudi Arabia and Kuwait. In Saudi Arabia, some men would prefer not to meet me alone (I brought along my brother), but apart from this, my gender did not seem to be an obstacle. I was once asked to wear a headscarf for a background interview with the head of a missionary organisation in Kuwait—the Revival of the Islamic Heritage Society—but staff in IICO and IIROSA never asked me to do so. For a discussion of Western female researchers in the Middle East, see Schwedler (2006).

5. Another factor is the fact that IICO and IIROSA simply do not produce as many public texts as Islamic Relief and Muslim Aid do.

APPENDIX B: ORGANISATIONAL MATERIAL

1. If not otherwise indicated, materials are in English.
2. For documents that are available online, references to websites have been included. All websites referenced in the following appendices were last accessed August 2015.

BIBLIOGRAPHY

All website references were last accessed August 2015.

Abdulhadi, Nural. 1990. *The Kuwaiti NGOs. Their Role in Aid Flows to Developing Countries.* Washington DC: Policy and Review Department, the World Bank.

Abrams, Joseph. 2008. UNICEF Partners With Islamic Charity Linked to Terror Groups. *Fox News*, 19 June 2008. http://www.foxnews.com/story/0,2933, 366319,00.html.

Abuarqab, M. 2010. Islamic Relief. Faith and Identity in Practice. *ONTRAC. The newsletter of INTRAC* 46.

Ahmed, Chanfi. 2009. Networks of Islamic NGOs in Sub-Saharan Africa: Bilal Muslim Mission, African Muslim Agency (Direct Aid) and al-Haramayn. *Journal of Eastern African Studies* 3 (3).

Ahmed, Hassan Makki Mohamed. 1989. *The Christian Design: A Study of the Missionary Factor in Sudan's Cultural and Political Integration 1943–1986.* Leicester: The Islamic Foundation.

Al-Yahya, Khalid, and Nathalie Fustier. 2011. *Saudi Arabia as a Humanitarian Donor: High Potential, Little Institutionalization.* Berlin: Global Public Policy Institute.

Ali, Abdullah Yusuf (trans.). 2000. *The Holy Qur'an.* Hertfordshire: Wordsworth Editions.

Alterman, Jon B. 2007. Saudi Charities and Support for Terror. In *Understanding Islamic Charities*, edited by J. B. Alterman and K. Von Hippel. Washington DC: Center for Strategic and International Studies.

Alterman, Jon B., and Karin von Hippel, eds. 2007. *Understanding Islamic Charities.* Washington DC: Center for Strategic and International Studies.

Alvesson, M. 2003. Beyond Neopositivists, Romantics, and Localists: A Reflexive Approach to Interviews in Organizational Research. *Academy of Management Review* 28 (1).

Arce, A., and Norman Long, eds. 2000. *Anthropology, Development and Modernities: Exploring Discourses, Counter-Tendencies and Violence.* London: Routledge.

Aziz, Afshan. 2012. IIROSA, OCHA, UNHCR Discuss Aid for Syrians. *Arab*

News, 24 October 2012. http://www.arabnews.com/iirosa-ocha-unhcr-discuss-aid-syrians.

Banna, Hassan al. 1993. *Message of the Teachings*. London: Ta-Ha Publishers.

Bano, Masooda. 2005. Review. The Charitable Crescent. *Journal of Islamic Studies* 16 (3).

Barnett, Michael. 2005. Humanitarianism Transformed. *Perspectives on Politics* 3 (4).

Barnett, Michael and Janice Gross Stein, eds. 2012. *Sacred Aid. Faith and Humanitarianism*. Oxford: Oxford University Press.

Barnett, Michael, and Thomas G. Weiss, eds. 2008. *Humanitarianism in Question: Politics, Power, Ethics*. Ithaca and London: Cornell University Press.

Bayat, Asef. 2007. *Making Islam Democratic: Social Movements and the Post-Islamist Turn*. Stanford: Stanford University Press.

BBC News. 2005. *Profile: Iqbal Sacranie*. *BBC News*, 10 June 2005. http://news.bbc.co.uk/2/hi/uk_news/4081208.stm.

Beek, Kurt ver. 2000. Spirituality. A Development Taboo. *Development in Practice* 10 (1).

Bellion-Jourdan, Jerome. 2000. Islamic Relief Organizations: Between 'Islamism' and 'Humanitarianism'. *ISIM Newsletter* 5.

———. 2007. Are Muslim Charities Purely Humanitarian? A Real but Misleading Question. In *Non-Governmental Politics*, edited by M. Feher. Cambridge MA: Zone Books.

Benedetti, Carlo. 2006. Islamic and Christian Inspired Relief NGOs: Between Tactical Collaboration and Strategic Diffidence. *Journal of International Development* 18.

Benford, Robert D., and David A. Snow. 2000. Framing Processes and Social Movements: An Overview and Assessment. *Annual Review of Sociology* 26.

Benthall, Jonathan. 1993. *Disasters, Relief and the Media*. London and New York: I.B. Tauris.

———. 1999. Financial Worship. The Quranic Injunction to Almsgiving. *Journal of the Royal Anthropological Institute* 5:27–42.

———. 2006. Islamic Aid in a North Malian Enclave. *Anthropology Today* 22 (4).

———. 2007. Islamic Charities, Faith Based Organizations, and the International Aid System. In *Understanding Islamic Charities*, edited by J. Alterman and K. Von Hippel. Washington DC: Center for Strategic and International Studies.

———. 2008a. The Palestinian Zakat Committees 1993–2007 and Their Contested Interpretations. *PSIO Occasional Paper*. Geneva: Graduate Institute of International and Development Studies.

———. 2008b. Have Islamic Charities a Privileged Relationship in Majority Muslim Societies? The Case of Post-Tsunami Reconstruction in Aceh. *Journal of Humanitarian Assistance*. http://sites.tufts.edu/jha/archives/153.

———. 2008c. *Returning to Religion: Why a Secular Age is Haunted by Faith*. London: I.B. Tauris.

———. 2011. Islamic Humanitarianism in Adversarial Context. In *Forces of Compassion. Humanitarianism Between Ethics and Politics*, edited by E. Bornstein and P. Redfield. Santa Fe: SAR Press.

———. 2014. The Islamic Charities Project. In *Gulf Charities and Islamic Philanthropy in 'The Age of Terror'—and Beyond*, edited by Robert Lacey and Jonathan Benthall. Berlin: Gerlach Press.

Benthall, Jonathan, and Jerome Bellion-Jourdan. 2003. *The Charitable Crescent: The Politics of Aid in the Muslim World*. London: I.B. Tauris.

Berger, P.L., and Thomas Luckmann. 1966. *The Social Construction of Reality: A Treatise in the Sociology of Knowledge*. New York: Anchor Books.

Birt, Jonathan. 2005. Lobbying and Marching: British Muslims and the State. In *Muslim Britain: Communities under Pressure*, edited by T. Abbas. London: Zed Books.

Bokhari, Yusra, Nasim Chowdhury and Robert Lacey. 2014. A Good Day to Bury a Bad Charity. The Rise and Fall of the Al-Haramain Islamic Foundation. In *Gulf Charities and Islamic Philanthropy in 'The Age of Terror'—and Beyond*, edited by Robert Lacey and Jonathan Benthall. Berlin: Gerlach Press.

Boli, John, and George M. Thomas. 1997. World Culture in the World Polity. *American Sociological Review* 62 (2).

Bolognani, Martha. 2007. Islam, Ethnography and Politics. Methodological Issues in Researching among West Yorkshire Pakistanis in 2005. *International Journal of Social Research Methodology* 10 (4).

Bonner, Michael. 2005. Poverty and Economics in the Qur'an. *Journal of Interdisciplinary History* 35 (3):391–406.

Bonner, Michael, Mine Ener, and Amy Singer. 2003. *Poverty and Charity in Middle Eastern Contexts*. Albany NY: State University of New York Press.

Bornstein, Erica. 2003. *The Spirit of Development: Protestant NGOs, Morality, and Economics in Zimbabwe*. New York and London: Routledge/Taylor and Francis.

———. 2009. The Impulse of Philanthropy. *Cultural Anthropology* 24 (4).

Bornstein, Erica, and Peter Redfield. 2007. A Working Paper on the Anthropology of Religion, Secularism, and Humanitarianism. *SSRC Research Papers*. New York: Social Science Research Council.

——— (eds.). 2011. *Forces of Compassion: Humanitarianism Between Ethics and Politics, Advanced Seminar Series*. Santa Fe: SAR Press.

Brenner, Louis, ed. 1993. *Muslim Identity and Social Change in Sub-Saharan Africa*. Bloomington and Indianapolis: Indiana University Press.

Burr, J. Millard, and Robert O. Collins. 2006. *Alms for Jihad: Charity and Terrorism in the Islamic World*. Cambridge: Cambridge University Press.

Caeiro, Alexandre, and Mahmoud al-Saify. 2009. Qaradawi in Europe, Europe in Qaradawi? The Global Mufti's European Politics. In *Global Mufti. The Phenomenon of Yusuf al-Qaradawi*, edited by Bettina Gräf and Jakob Skovgaard-Petersen. London: Hurst Publishers.

Calhoun, Craig. 2008. The Imperative to Reduce Suffering: Charity, Progress, and Emergencies in the Field of Humanitarian Action. In *Humanitarianism in Question. Politics, Power, Ethics*, edited by M. Barnett and T. G. Weiss. Ithaca & London: Cornell University Press.

Carroll, Thomas F. 1992. *Intermediary NGOs: The Supporting Link in Grassroots Development*. West Hartford: Kumarian Press.

Chabbott, C. 1999. Development INGOs. In *Constructing World Culture: International Nongovernmental Organisations since 1875*, edited by J. Boli and G. M. Thomas. Stanford: Stanford University Press.

Chambre, S. M. 2001. The Changing Nature of 'Faith' in Faith-Based Organizations: Secularization and Ecumenicism in Four AIDS Organizations in New York City. *Social Service Review* 75 (3).

Chouliaraki, Lilie. 2010. Post-Humanitarianism: Humanitarian Communication beyond a Politics of Pity. *International Journal of Cultural Studies* 13 (2).

Christensen, Asger 1995. *Aiding Afghanistan: The Background and Prospects for Reconstruction in a Fragmented Society*. Copenhagen: NIAS Press.

CIA. 1996. International Islamic NGOs and Links to Terrorism. http://en.wikisource.org/wiki/CIA_Report_on_NGOs_With_Terror_Links.

Clark, Janine. 2004. *Islam, Charity and Activism*. Bloomington: Indiana University Press.

———. 2008. FBOs and Change in the Context of Authoritarianism: The Islamic Center Charity Society in Jordan. In *Development, Civil Society and Faith-Based Organisations*, edited by G. Clarke and M. Jennings. Basingstoke: Palgrave Macmillan.

Clarke, Gerard. 2006. Faith Matters: Faith-Based Organisations, Civil Society and International Development. *Journal of International Development* 18 (6).

———. 2007. Agents of Transformation? Donors, Faith-Based Organizations and International Development. *Third World Quarterly* 28 (1).

———. 2010. Trans-Faith Humanitarian Partnerships: The Case of Muslim Aid and the United Methodist Committee on Relief. *European Journal of Development Research* 22 (4).

Clarke, Gerard, and Michael Jennings, eds. 2008. *Development, Civil Society and Faith-Based Organisations: Bridging the Sacred and the Secular*. Basingstoke & New York: Palgrave Macmillan.

Clarke, Matthew. 2011. *Development and Religion. Theology and Practice*. Cheltenham: Edward Elgar Publishing.

Charity Commision. 2010. *Regulatory Case Report, Muslim Aid*. London: Charity Commission. http://www.charitycommission.gov.uk/Our_regulatory_activity/Compliance_reports/RC_reports/rcr_muslim_aid.aspx.

Coghlan, Nora, Katie McCabe and Erin Thornton. 2010. *The Data Report 2010*. London: ONE. http://www.one.org/report/2010/en/downloads.

Cons, Jason, and Kasia Paprocki. 2010. Contested Credit Landscapes: Microcredit, Self-Help and Self-Determination in Rural Bangladesh. *Third World Quarterly* 31 (4).

Corbridge, Stuart. 2007. The (Im)possibility of Development Studies. *Economy and Society* 36 (2).

Cornwall, Andrea. 2007. Buzzwords and Fuzzwords. Deconstructing Development Discourse. *Development in Practice* 17 (4–5).

Cotterrell, Lin, and Adele Harmer. 2005. *Aid Donorship in the Gulf States*. London: Overseas Development Institute.

Cunningham, Hilary. 1999. The Ethnography of Transnational Social Activism: Understanding the Global as Local Practice. *American Ethnologist* 26 (3).

Dahl, Gudrun. 2001. Responsibility and Partnership in Swedish Aid Discourse. In *Discussion Paper*. Uppsala: Nordic Africa Institute.

DanChurchAid. 2014. *Global Strategy 2015–2020*. Copenhagen: DanChurchAid.

Danckaers, Tine. 2008. In the Name of Allah: Islamic Relief Organizations in Great Britain. *Mondiaal Nieuws*. http://www.mo.be/en/article/name-allah-islamic-relief-organizations-great-britain.

de Cordier, Bruno. 2009a. Faith-Based Aid, Globalization and the Humanitarian Frontline: An Analysis of Western-Based Muslim Aid Organizations. *Disasters: The Journal of Disaster Studies, Policy and Management* 33 (4).

———. 2009b. "The Humanitarian Frontline", Development and Relief, and Religion: What Context, which Threats and which Opportunities? *Third World Quarterly* 30 (4).

Degnbol-Martinussen, John, and Poul Engberg-Pedersen. 1999. *Bistand—udvikling eller afvikling: En analyse af internationalt bistandssamarbejde*. Copenhagen: Mellemfolkeligt Samvirke.

Deneulin, Séverine, and Masooda Bano. 2009. *Religion in Development; Rewriting the Secular Script*. London & New York: Zed Books.

Deneulin, Séverine, and Carole Rakodi. 2011. Revisiting Religion: Development Studies Thirty Years On. *World Development* 39 (1).

DFID. 2005. *Faith in Development*. London: Department for International Development.

Dijk, Teun van. 2006. Ideology and Discourse Analysis. *Journal of Political Ideologies* 11 (2).

Donini, Antonio, and Larry Minear. 2006. *The Humanitarian Agenda 2015: Principles, Power and Perceptions*. Medford: Feinstein International Center.

Eade, John, and David Garbin. 2006. Competing Visions of Identity and Space: Bangladeshi Muslims in Britain. *Contemporary South Asia* 15 (2).

Ebaugh, Helen Rose Fuchs, Janet Saltzman Chafetz, and Paula F. Pipes. 2006. Where's the Faith in Faith-Based Organizations? Measures and Correlates of Religiosity in Faith-Based Social Service Coalitions. *Social Forces* 84 (4).

Edwards, Michael, and David Hulme, eds. 1992. *Making a Difference: NGOs and Development in a Changing World*. London: Earthscan.

Escobar, Arthuro. 1995. *Encountering Development: The Making and Unmaking of the Third World*. Princeton: Princeton University Press.

Esposito, John L. 1998. *Islam and Politics*. 4th ed. Syracuse: Syracuse University Press.

Esposito, John L., and J. Voll. 2001. *Makers of Contemporary Islam*. New York: Oxford University Press.

EU Council. 2012. Council Decision 2012/333/CFSP of 25 June 2012 updating the list of persons, groups and entities subject to Articles 2, 3 and 4 of Common Position 2001/931/CFSP on the application of specific measures to combat terrorism and repealing Decision 2011/872/CFSP. Brussels: *Official Journal of the European Union*. http://eur-lex.europa.eu/LexUriServ/Lex UriServ.do?uri=OJ:L:2012:165:0072:0074:EN:PDF.

Fassin, Didier. 2008. The Humanitarian Politics of Testimony: Subjectification through Trauma in the Israeli-Palestinian Conflict. *Cultural Anthropology* 23 (3).

Ferguson, Barbara. 2006. US Treasury Charges IIROSA Director of Bankrolling Al-Qaeda. *Arab News*, 5. August 2006. http://www.arabnews.com/node/280002 (accessed 25 March 2011).

Ferris, E. 2005. Faith-Based and Secular Humanitarian Organizations. *International Review of the Red Cross* 87 (858).

Flanigan, Shawn T. 2006. Charity as Resistance: Connections between Charity, Contentious Politics, and Terror. *Studies in Conflict & Terrorism* 29(7).

Flyvbjerg, Bent. 2001. *Making Social Science Matter: Why Social Inquiry Fails and How It Can Succeed Again*. Cambridge: Cambridge University Press.

———. 2006. Five Misunderstandings About Case-Study Research. *Qualitative Inquiry* 12 (2).

Foucault, Michel. 1970. *The Order of Things*. New York: Pantheon.

Gasper, Des, and R. Apthorpe. 1996. *Arguing Development Policy: Frames and Discourses*. London: Frank Cass.

Geertz, Clifford. 1973. *The Interpretation of Cultures, Selected Essays*. New York: Basic Books.

Ghafour, P. K. Abdul, and Abdul Aziz Shamsuddin Syed. 2008. International Islamic Relief Organisation-Saudi Arabia (IIROSA) Approves Strategic Plan to Bolster Humanitarian Activities. *Arab News*, 2 May 2008. http://www.arab-news.com/node/311530.

———. 2010. IIROSA Vows to Carry on with Global Humanitarian Programs. *Arab News*, 4 April 2010. http://www.arabnews.com/node/341402?quicktabs_stat2=0.

Ghandour, Abdel Rahman. 2003. Humanitarianism, Islam and the West: Contest or Cooperation? *Humanitarian Exchange Magazine* 25.

———. 2004. The Modern Missionaries of Islam. In *In the Shadow of 'Just Wars': Violence, Politics, and Humanitarian Action*, edited by F. Weissman. Ithaca: Cornell University Press.

Giri, Ananta Kumar, Anton van Harskamp, and Oscar Salemink, eds. 2004. *The Development of Religion, the Religion of Development*. Delft: Eburon.

Gräf, Bettina and Jakob Skovgaard-Petersen, eds. 2009. *Global Mufti. The Phenomenon of Yusuf al-Qaradawi*. London: Hurst Publishers.

Green, Maia, Claire Mercer, and Simeon Mesaki. 2010. Faith in Development.

Building Civil Society in Rural Tanzania. Paper presented at the conference Progressive, Paradoxical, Pragmatic: Exploring Religion and Human Development, Birmingham, 21 July.

Guinane, Kay. 2006. *Muslim Charities and the War on Terror*. Washington DC: OMC Watch.

Haar, Gerrie ter. 2011. *Religion and Development. Ways of Transforming the World* London: Hurst Publishers.

Haar, Gerrie ter, and Stephen Ellis. 2006. The Role of Religion in Development: Towards a New Relationship between the European Union and Africa. *European Journal of Development Research* 18 (3).

Hammack, David C., and Steven Heydemann, eds. 2009. *Globalization, Philanthrophy, and Civil Society: Projecting Institutional Logics Abroad*. Bloomington & Indianapolis: Indiana University Press.

Hamzeh, A. Nizar. 2007. Hizballah. Islamic Charity in Lebanon. In *Understanding Islamic Charities*, edited by J. B. Alterman and Karin von Hippel. Washington DC: Center for Strategic and International Studies.

Harb, Mona. 2008. Faith-Based Organizations as Effective Development Partners? In *Development, Civil Society and Faith-based Organizations: Bridging the Sacred and the Secular*, edited by G. Clarke and M. Jennings. Basingstoke & New York: Palgrave Macmillan.

Harmer, Adele, and Lin Cotterrell. 2005. Diversity in Donorship. The Changing Landscape of Official Humanitarian Aid. *Humanitarian Policy Group Background Paper*. London: Overseas Development Institute.

Harmsen, Egbert. 2008. *Islam, Civil Society and Social Work. Muslim Voluntary Welfare Associations in Jordan between Patronage and Empowerment*. Amsterdam: Amsterdam University Press.

Harper, Malcolm, D. S. K. Rao, and Ashis Kumar Sahu. 2008. *Development, Divinity and Dharma. The Role of Religion in Development and Microfinance Institutions*. Rugby: Practical Action Publishing.

Hatina, Meir. 2006. Restoring a Lost Identity: Models of Education in Modern Islamic Thought. *British Journal of Middle Eastern Studies* 33 (2).

Hattori, Tomohisa. 2003. Giving as a Mechanism of Consent: International Aid Organizations and the Ethical Hegemony of Capitalism. *International Relations* 17 (2).

Haynes, Jeffrey 2007. *Religion and Development. Conflict or Cooperation?* New York: Palgrave Macmillan.

Heberle, Rudolf. 1951. *Social Movements. An Introduction to Political Sociology*. New York: Appleton-Century-Crofts.

Hegghammer, Thomas. 2010. *Jihad in Saudi Arabia. Violence and Pan-Islamism since 1979*. Cambridge: Cambridge University Press.

Held, David. 2009. Restructuring Global Governance: Cosmopolitanism, Democracy and the Global Order. *Millenium Journal of International Studies* 37 (3).

Hernes, Tor 2007. *Understanding Organization as Process. Theory for a Tangled World*. London & New York: Routledge.

Hilhorst, Dorothea. 2003. *The Real World of NGOs: Discourses, Diversity and Development*. London: Zed Books.

Hippel, Karin von. 2007. Aid Effectiveness: Improving Relations with Islamic Charities. In *Understanding Islamic Charities*, edited by J. B. Alterman and K. Von Hippel. Washington DC: Center for Strategic and International Studies.

Høigilt, Jacob. 2013. Islamism and Education: The Nature and Aims of Islamic Schools in the Occupied Palestinian Territories. *Middle East Critique*. Published online.

Holenstein, Anne Marie. 2005. *Role and Significance of Religion and Spirituality in Development Cooperation: A Reflection and Working Paper*. Bern: Swiss Agency for Development and Cooperation.

Howell, Jude, and Jeremy Lind. 2009. *Counter-Terrorism, Aid and Civil Society: Before and After the War on Terror*. Basingstoke: Palgrave Macmillan.

Hulme, D., and M. Edwards, eds. 1997. *NGOs, States and Donors: Too Close for Comfort*. Basingstoke & New York: St. Martin's Press.

Huntington, Samuel P. 1998. *The Clash of Civilizations and the Remaking of World Order*. London: Touchstone.

Hyder, Masood. 2007. Humanitarianism and the Muslim World. *Journal of Humanitarian Assistance*. http://sites.tufts.edu/jha/archives/52.

Ibrahim, Muhammad. 2010a. IIROSA Extending Health Care Services to Half a Million Patients. *Arab News*, 16 July 2010. http://www.arabnews.com/node/350397.

———. 2010b. IIROSA Provides Education for Students in 23 Countries. *Arab News*, 14 August 2010. http://www.arabnews.com/node/352720.

James, Rick. 2009. What is Distinctive about FBOs? How European FBOs Define and Operationalise their Faith. *Praxis Paper*. Oxford: INTRAC.

Jawad, Rana. 2009. *Social Welfare and Religion in the Middle East. A Lebanese Perspective*. Bristol: The Policy Press.

Johnston, Hanks, and Bert Klandermans, eds. 1995. *Social Movements and Culture*. Minneapolis: University of Minnesota Press.

Jones, Ben, and Marie Juul Petersen. 2011. Instrumentalist, Narrow, Normative? Reviewing Recent Work on Religion and Development. *Third World Quarterly* 32 (7).

Jung, Dietrich and Marie Juul Petersen. 2014. Islamic Charity, Social Order and the Construction of Modern Muslim Selfhoods in Jordan. *International Journal of Middle East Studies*.

Juul Petersen, Marie. 2012a. Islamizing Aid: Transnational Muslim NGOs After 9/11. *Voluntas: International Journal of Voluntary and Nonprofit Organizations* 23 (1).

———. 2012b. Trajectories of Transnational Muslim NGOs. *Development in Practice* 22 (5–6).

Kaag, Mayke. 2007. Aid, 'Umma', and Politics: Transnational Islamic NGOs in Chad. In *Islam and Muslim Politics in Africa*, edited by B. F. Soares and R. Otayek. Basingstoke: Palgrave Macmillan.

———. 2008. Transnational Islamic NGOs in Chad: Islamic Solidarity in the Age of Neoliberalism. *Africa Today* 54 (3).

Kadt, Emmanuel de. 2009. Should God Play a Role in Development? *Journal of International Development* 21 (6).

Kanbur, Ravi, and Paul Schaffer. 2007. Epistemology, Normative Theory and Poverty Analysis: Implications for Q-Squared in Practice. *World Development* 35 (2).

Khan, Ahmed Ajaz. 2012. Religious Obligations or Altruistic Giving? Muslims and Charitable Donations. In *Sacred Aid. Faith and Humanitarianism*, edited by M. Barnett and J. Stein. Oxford & New York: Oxford University Press.

Khan, Saad S. 2001. *Reasserting International Islam. A Focus on the Organization of the Islamic Conference and Other Islamic Institutions*. Oxford: Oxford University Press.

Kirmani, Nida, and Ajaz Ahmed Khan. 2008. Does Faith Matter? An Examination of Islamic Relief's Work with Refugees and Internally Displaced Persons. *Refugee Survey Quarterly* 27 (2).

Kochuyt, Thierry. 2009. God, Gifts and Poor People: On Charity in Islam. *Social Compass* 56 (1).

Kohlman, Evan. 2006. The Role of Islamic Charities in International Terrorist Recruitment and Financing. *Working Paper*. Copenhagen: Danish Institute for International Studies.

Kroessin, Mohammed. 2007. Worlds Apart? Muslim Donors and International Humanitarianism. *Forced Migration Review* 29.

———. 2009. Mapping UK Muslim Development NGOs. *Religions and Development Research Programme Working Paper* 30. Birmingham: Birmingham University.

Kumar, Anand. 2009. Terror Financing in Bangladesh. *Stategic Analysis* 33 (6).

Kuran, Timur. 2001. The Provision of Public Goods under Islamic Law: Origins, Impact, and Limitations of the Waqf System. *Law & Society Review* 35 (4).

Kuwait News Agency. 2010. Leading Kuwaiti charity Marks 25th Anniversary, Amir Attends Ceremony. *Kuwait News Agency*. 10 May 2010. http://www.kuna.net.kw/NewsAgenciesPublicsite/ArticleDetails.aspx?id=2082137&Language=en.

Kuzma, Abigal. 2000. Faith-Based Providers Partnering with Government: Opportunity and Temptation. *Journal of Church and State* 42 (37).

Kayaoglu, Turan. Forthcoming. *The Organization of Islamic Cooperation: Politics, Problems, and Potential*. London: Routledge.

Lacey, Robert and Jonathan Benthall, eds. 2014. *Gulf Charities and Islamic Philanthropy in 'The Age of Terror'—and Beyond*. Berlin: Gerlach Press.

Lapidus, I. 2002. *A History of Islamic Societies*. Cambridge: Cambridge University Press.

Levitt, Matthew. 2006. *Hamas: Politics, Charity and Terrorism in the Service of Jihad*. New Haven: Yale University Press.

Lewis, David. 2001. *The Management of Non-Governmental Development Organisations: An Introduction*. London: Routledge.

Lewis, David, Simon Batterbury, A. J. Bebbington, M. Shameem Siddiqi, Sandra Duvall, E. Olsen, and A. Shah. 2003. Practice, Power and Meaning: Frameworks for Studying Organizational Culture in Multi-Agency Rural Development Projects. *Journal of International Development* 15.

Lewis, David, and Nazneen Kanji. 2009. *Non-Governmental Organisations and Development*. London: Routledge.

Lewis, David, and David Mosse, eds. 2006. *Development Brokers and Translators. The Ethnography of Aid and Agencies*. Bloomfield: Kumarian Press.

Lewis, Philip. 2007. *Young, British and Muslim*. London: Continuum International Publishing Group.

Lincoln, Bruce. 2003. *Holy Terrors. Thinking about Religion after September 11*. Chicago: University of Chicago Press.

Long, Norman, ed. 1989. *Encounters at the Interface. A Perspective on Social Discontinuities in Rural Development, Studies in Sociology*. Wageningen: Wageningen Agricultural University.

———. 1992. From Paradigm Lost to Paradigm Regained? The Case for an Actor-Oriented Sociology of Development. In *Battlefields of Knowledge. The Interlocking of Theory and Practice in Social Research and Development*, edited by N. Long and A. Long. London & New York: Routledge.

———. 2001. *Development Sociology—Actor Perspectives*. New York, Routledge.

Long, Norman, and Ann Long, eds. 1992. *Battlefields of Knowledge. The Interlocking of Theory and Practice in Social Research and Development*. London & New York: Routledge.

Lunn, Jenny. 2009. The Role of Religion, Spirituality and Faith in Development: A Critical Theory Approach. *Third World Quarterly* 30 (5).

Ly, Pierre-Emmauel. 2007. The Charitable Activities of Terrorist Organizations. *Public Choice* 13 (1).

Lynch, Cecilia. 2011. Religious Humanitarianism and the Global Politics of Secularism, in *Rethinking Secularism in International Affairs*, edited by Mark Juergensmeyer and Jonathan VanAntwerpen, Oxford: Oxford University Press

Mahmood, Saba. 2005. *Politics of Piety: The Islamic Revival and the Feminist Subject*. Princeton: Princeton University Press.

Malkki, Liisa H. 1996. Speechless Emissaries: Refugees, Humanitarianism, and Dehistorization. *Cultural Anthropology* 11 (3).

Mamdani, Mahmood. 2002. Good Muslim, Bad Muslim: A Political Perspective on Culture and Terrorism, American Anthropologust 104 (3).

Mandaville, Peter. 2001. *Transnational Muslim Politics. Reimagining the Umma*. London: Routledge.

———. 2007. *Global Political Islam*. London and New York: Routledge.

———. 2008. Beyond Islamism? Religious Leaders and Movements in the Contemporary Muslim World. Paper presented at the workshop Religion and Development, Copenhagen, 12. December.

———. 2009. Muslim Transnational Identity and State Responses in Europe and the UK after 9/11: Political Community, Ideology and Authority. *Journal of Ethnic and Migration Studies* 35 (3).

———. 2011. Transnational Muslim Solidarities and Everyday Life. *Nations and Nationalism* 17 (1).

Mandaville, Peter, Farish A. Noor, Alexander Horstmann, Dietrich Reetz, Ali Riaz, Animesh Roul, Hasan Noorhaidi, Ahmad Fauzi Abdul Hamid, Rommel C. Banlaoi, and Joseph Chinyong Liow. 2009. *Transnational Islam in South and Southeast Asia: Movements, Networks, and Conflict Dynamics.* Washington DC: The National Bureau of Asian Research.

Markowitz, L. 2001. Finding the Field: Notes on the Ethnography of NGOs. *Human Organization* 60 (2).

Marranci, Gabriele. 2008. British Muslims and the British State. In *Religious Diversity and Civil Society: A Comparative Analysis*, edited by B. Turner. Oxford: Bardwell Press.

Marshall, Katherine. 2005. Religious Faith and Development: Rethinking Development Debates. Religious NGOs and International Development Conference. Oslo, Norway.

———. 2007. Practitioners, Faith Based Organisations and Global Development Work. A Discussion with Hany El Banna, Islamic Relief. Interview. 3 December 2007. Berkeley Center for Religion, Peace and World Affairs, Georgetown University. http://berkleycenter.georgetown.edu/interviews/a-discussion-with-dr-hany-el-banna-president-and-co-founder-islamic-relief.

———, and Lucy Keough, ed. 2004. *Mind, Heart and Soul in the Fight Against Poverty.* Washington DC: World Bank Publications.

———, and Marisa Bronwyn van Saanen. 2007. *Development and Faith. Where Mind, Heart and Soul Work Together.* Washington DC: World Bank Publications.

Maurer, Bill. 2005. *Mutual Life, Limited: Islamic Banking, Alternative Currencies, Lateral Reason.* Princeton: Princeton University Press.

Mauss, Marcel. 1990 [1923/24]. *The Gift. The Form and Reason for Exchange in Archaic Societies.* London: Routledge.

McAdam, Doug, John McCarthy, and Mayer Zald, eds. 1996. *Comparative Perspectives on Social Movements.* Cambridge: Cambridge University Press.

Meijer, Roel. 2008. Review. Alms for Jihad: Charity and Terrorism in the Islamic World. *International Journal of Middle East Studies* 40 (3).

Melucci, Alberto. 1989. *Nomads of the Present. Social Movements and Individual Needs in Contemporary Society.* London: Hutchinson Radius.

Mercer, Claire. 2002. NGOs, Civil Society and Democratization: A Critical Review of the Literature. *Progress in Development Studies* 2 (1).

Meyer, Katherine, Helen Rizzo, and Yousef Ali. 2007. Changed Political Attitudes in the Middle East. The Case of Kuwait. *International Sociology* 22 (3).

Minear, Larry, ed. 1991. *Humanitarianism under Siege: A Critical Review of Operation Lifeline Sudan.* Trenton: Red Sea Press.

Mitchell, Richard P. 1969. *The Society of the Muslim Brothers.* New York & Oxford: Oxford University Press.

Mosse, David. 2005. *Cultivating Development: An Ethnography of Aid Policy and Practice.* London: Pluto Press.

Munson, Ziad. 2001. Islamic Mobilization. *Sociological Quarterly* 42 (4).

Nadai, Eva, and Christoph Maeder. 2005. Fuzzy Fields. Multi-Sited Ethnography in Sociological Research. *Forum: Qualitative Social Research* 6 (3).

Nagel, Caroline, and Lynn Staeheli. 2009. British Arab Perspectives on Religion, Politics and 'the Public'. In *Muslims in Britain. Race, Place and Identities*, edited by P. Hopkins and R. Gale. Edinburgh: Edinburgh University Press.

Napoleoni, Loretta. 2005. *Terror Incorporated: Tracing the Dollars behind the Terror Networks.* New York: Seven Stories Press.

Nauta, Wiebe. 2006. Ethnographic Research in a Non-Governmental Organization: Revealing Strategic Translations through an Embedded Tale. In *Development Brokers and Translators: The Ethnography of Aid and Agencies*, edited by D. Lewis and D. Mosse. London: Kumarian Press.

Observatoire de l'Action Humanitaire. 2008. *International Islamic Relief Organisation.* http://www.observatoire-humanitaire.org/fr/index.php?page=fiche-ong.php&part=fiche&id=81.

Palmer, Victoria. 2011. Analysing Cultural Proximity: Islamic Relief Worldwide and Rohingya Refugees in Bangladesh. *Development in Practice* 21 (1).

Pfeifer, Karen. 1997. Is There an Islamic Economics? In *Political Islam: Essays from Middle East Report*, edited by J. Beinin and J. Stork. New York: I.B. Tauris.

Pripp, Charles. 2006. *Islam and the Moral Economy: The Challenge of Capitalism.* Cambridge: Cambridge University Press.

Pultz, Karina. 2008. Fra bænkevarmer til dansepartner. Organization of Islamic Conference's nye rolle i international politik. *Research Paper.* Copenhagen: Institut for Strategi.

Purvis, Trevor, and Alan Hunt. 1993. Discourse, Ideology, Discourse, Ideology, Discourse, Ideology. *The British Journal of Sociology* 44 (3).

Quarles van Ufford, Philip, and Matthew Schoeffeleers, eds. 1988. *Religion and Development: Towards an Integrated Approach.* Amsterdam: Free University Press.

Ratcliffe, John. 2007. Islamic Charities after Catastrophes: The Kashmir Earthquake and the Indian Ocean Tsunami. In *Understanding Islamic Charities*, edited by J. B. Alterman and K. Von Hippel. Washington DC: Center for Strategic and International Studies.

Raudvere, Catharina. 2002. *The Book and the Roses.* Istanbul: The Swedish Research Institute in Istanbul.

Reimann, Kim D. 2006. A View from the Top: International Politics, Norms and the Worldwide Growth of NGOs. *International Studies Quarterly* 50.

Renders, Marleen. 2002. An Ambiguous Adventure: Muslim Organisations and the Discourse of 'Development'. *Journal of Religion in Africa* 32 (1).

Rist, Gilbert. 2008. *The History of Development: From Western Origins to Global Faith*. 3rd ed. London: Zed Books.

Roald, Anne Sofie. 1994. *Tarbiya, Education and Politics in Islamic Movements in Jordan and Malaysia*. Lund: Department of Religious History, University of Lund.

Roy, Olivier. 2004. *Globalised Islam. The Search for a New Ummah*. London: Hurst Publishers.

Royal Embassy of Saudi Arabia. 2009. IIRO Contributes $2.39 million for Gaza Relief. 14 January. http://www.saudiembassy.net/latest_news/news01140902.aspx.

Salam, Abdel, and Alex de Waal. 2004. On the Failure and Persistence of Islam. In *Islamism and its Enemies in the Horn of Africa*, edited by Alex de Waal. Bloomington & Indianapolis: Indianapolis University Press.

Salih, Mohamed M.A. 2002. Islamic NGOs in Africa: The Promise and Peril of Islamic Voluntarism. *Occasional Paper*. Copenhagen: Centre of African Studies, University of Copenhagen.

Salvatore, Armando, and Dale F. Eickelman, eds. 2004. *Public Islam and the Common Good*. Leiden & Boston: Brill.

Saudi Press Agency. 2009. Untitled. 26 February. http://www.spa.gov.sa/english/details.php?id=638981.

Schaebler, Birgit, and Leif Stenberg, eds. 2004. *Globalization and the Muslim World: Culture, Religion, and Modernity*. Syracuse: Syracuse University Press.

Schaeublin, Emanuel. 2009. Role and Governance of Islamic Charitable Institutions: The West Bank Zakat Committees (1977–2009) in the Local Context. *CCDP Working Papers*. Geneva: Center on Conflict, Development and Peacebuilding.

Schulze, Reinhard. 2000. *A Modern History of the Islamic world*. New York: New York University Press.

Schwedler, Jilian. 2006. The Third Gender: Western Female Researchers in the Middle East. *PS. Political Science & Politics* 3.

Shaw-Hamilton, James. 2007. Recognizing the Umma in Humanitarianism. In *Understanding Islamic Charities*, edited by J. B. Alterman and K. von Hippel. Washington DC: Center for Strategic and International Studies.

Siddiqui, Ataullah. 1997. Ethics in Islam: Key Concepts and Contemporary Challenges. *Journal of Moral Education* 26 (4).

Silk, John. 2004. Caring at a Distance: Gift Theory, Aid Chains and Social Movements. *Social & Cultural Geography* 5 (2).

Singer, Amy. 2008. *Charity in Islamic Societies*. Cambridge: Cambridge University Press.

Slim, Hugo. 2002. By What Authority? The Legitimacy and Accountability of Non-Governmental Organisations. Paper presented at the International

BIBLIOGRAPHY

Council on Human Rights Policy International Meeting on Global Trends and Human Rights: Before and After September 11, Geneva, 10–12 January.

Smith, S. R., and M. Sosin. 2001. The Varieties of Faith-Related Agencies. *Public Administration Review* 61 (6).

Snow, David A. 2004. Framing Processes, Ideology and Discursive Fields. In *The Blackwell Companion to Social Movements*, edited by D. A. Snow, S. A. Soule and H. Kriesi. Basingstoke: Wiley-Blackwell.

Snow, David A., and Robert D. Benford. 1988. Ideology, Frame Resonance and Participant Mobilization. *International Social Movement Research* 1.

Snow, David A., and Scott C. Byrd. 2007. Ideology, Framing Processes, and Islamic Terrorist Movements. *Mobilization: An International Quarterly Review* 12 (1).

Soage, Ana Belén. 2008. Shaykh Yusuf al-Qaradawi: Portrait of a Leading Islamic Cleric. *Middle East Review of International Affairs* 12 (1).

Soares, Benjamin F., and Rene Otayek. 2007. *Islam and Muslim Politics in Africa*. London: Palgrave Macmillan.

Solberg, Anne Ross. 2007. The Role of Turkish Islamic Networks in the Western Balkans. *Southeast Europe Journal of Politics and Society* 4.

Sparre, Sara Lei, and Marie Juul Petersen. 2007. Islam and Civil Society. Case Studies from Jordan and Egypt. *DIIS Report*. Copenhagen: Danish Institute for International Studies.

Stirrat, R. L., and Heiko Henkel. 1997. The Development Gift: The Problem of Reciprocity in the NGO World. *Annals of the American Academy of Political and Social Science* 554.

Swidler, Ann. 1986. Culture in Action: Symbols and Strategies. *American Sociological Review* 51 (2).

Tammam, Husam and Patrick Haenni. 2003. Egypt's Airconditioned Islam. *Le Monde Diplomatique* September issue.

Tandon, Rajesh. 2000. Riding High or Nosediving: Development NGOs in the New Millennium. *Development in Practice* 10 (3 & 4).

Thaut, Laura. 2009. The Role of Faith in Christian Faith-Based Humanitarian Agencies: Constructing the Taxonomy. *Voluntas: International Journal of Voluntary and Nonprofit Organizations* 20 (4).

Thaut, Laura, Michael Barnett and Janice Gross Stein. 2012. In Defense of Virtue: Credibility, Legitimacy Dilemmas and the Case of Islamic Relief. In *The Credibility of Transnational NGOs. When Virtue is not Enough*, edited by Peter A. Gourewich, David A. Lake and Janice Gross Stein. Cambridge: Cambridge University Press.

Thomas, Scott M. 2004. Faith and Foreign Aid. How the World Bank Got Religion and Why it Matters. *The Brandywine Review of Faith & International Affairs*, Fall edition.

Thompson, John B. 1984. *Studies in the Theory of Ideology*. Berkeley: University of California Press.

————. 1990. *Ideology and Modern Culture: Critical Social Theory in the Era of Mass Communication*. Stanford University Press.

Tomalin, Emma. 2012. Thinking about Faith-Based Organisations in Development: Where Have We Got to and What Next? *Development in Practice* 22 (5–6).

————, and R. Leurs. 2010. Mapping the Work of Faith-Based Organisations in India, Pakistan, Tanzania and Nigeria. Paper presented at the conference Progressive, Paradoxical, Pragmatic: Exploring Religion and Human Development, Birmingham, 21 July.

Tvedt, Terje. 1998. *Angels of Mercy or Development Diplomats? NGOs and Foreign Aid*. Oxford & Trenton: James Currey & Africa World Press.

————. 2002. Development NGOs: Actors in a Global Civil Society or in a New International Social System? *Voluntas: International Journal of Voluntary and Non-Profit Organizations* 13 (4).

Tyndale, Wendy, ed. 2006. *Visions of Development. Faith-Based Initiatives*. Aldershot: Ashgate.

Ukiwo, Ukoha. 2010. The Development Activities of Faith-Based and Secular NGOs in Nigeria. Paper presented at the conference Progressive, Paradoxical, Pragmatic: Exploring Religion and Human Development, Birmingham, 21 July.

UN Security Council Committee pursuant to resolutions 1267 (1999) and 1989 (2011) concerning Al-Qaida and associated individuals and entities. 2015. The list established and maintained by the Al-Qaida Sanctions Committee with respect to individuals, groups, undertakings and other entities associated with Al-Qaida (last updated 19 February 2015). New York: United Nations. http://www.un.org/sc/committees/1267/pdf/AQList.pdf

UNICEF. 2008. UNICEF Signs an Agreement with the International Islamic Relief Organization. *UNICEF*. 9 June 2008. http://www.unicef.org/media/media_44413.html.

US Department of the Treasury. n.d. *Designated Charities and Potential Fundraising Front Organisations for FTOs* http://www.treasury.gov/resource-center/terrorist-illicit-finance/Pages/protecting-fto.aspx.

Vicini, James. 2009. Top Court Lets Stand Saudi Immunity in 9/11 Case. *Reuters*. 29 June 2009. http://www.reuters.com/article/2009/06/29/us-sept11-saudi-lawsuit-idUSTRE55S3PB20090629.

Waal Alex de. ed. 2004. *Islamism and its Enemies in the Horn of Africa*. Bloomington: Indiana University Press.

Wagemakers, Johannes. 2010. *A Quietist Jihadi-Salafi. The Ideology and Influence of Abu Muhammad al-Maqdisi*. Unpublished PhD Thesis. Nijmegen: Radboud University.

Weiss, Holger. 2002. Reorganising Social Welfare Among Muslims: Islamic Voluntarism and Other Forms of Communal Support in Northern Ghana. *Journal of Religion in Africa* 32 (1).

Westby, David L. 2002. Strategic Imperative, Ideology and Frame. *Mobilization: An International Quarterly* 7(3).

Wiktorowicz, Quintan. 2001. *The Management of Islamic Activism. Salafis, the Muslim Brotherhood and the State in Jordan, SUNY Series in Middle Eastern Studies.* Albany, NY: State University of New York Press.

———. 2004. *Islamic Activism. A Social Movement Theory Approach.* Bloomington: Indiana University Press.

Williams, J. 1995. *PC Wars. Politics and Theory in the Academy.* New York: Routledge.

Wilson, John B. 1973. *Introduction to Social Movements.* New York: Basic Books.

Woodhead, Linda, and Paul Heelas. 2000. *Religion in Modern Times.* Sussex: Wiley Blackwell.

Wuthnow, Robert J. 2011. Taking Talk Seriously: Religious Discourse as Social Practice. *Journal for the Scientific Study of Religion* 50 (1).

Yaylaci, Ismail. 2007. Communitarian Humanitarianism. The Politics of Islamic Humanitarian Organizations. Unpublished paper.

———. 2008. Communitarian Humanitarianism? The Politics of Islamic Humanitarian Organizations. Paper presented at the workshop Religion and Humanitarianism, Cairo, 3–5 June.

Yıldız, Ahmet. 2003. Politico-Religious Discourse of Political Islam in Turkey: The Parties of National Outlook. *The Muslim World* 93 (2).

Zaman, Muhammad Qasim. 2004. The 'Ulama of Contemporary Islam and their Conceptions of the Common Good. In *Public Islam and the Common Good*, edited by A. Salvatore and D. F. Eickelman. Leiden: Brill.

Zubaida, Sami. 2004. Islam and Nationalism: Continuities and Contradictions. *Nations and Nationalism* 10 (4).

INDEX

Disasters Emergency Committee:
members of, 126
Direct Aid: 76, 103
donors: 9, 13, 22, 36, 62, 64, 79, 84,
91, 93–4, 102, 105, 115, 118, 123,
131–2, 174–5; agencies, 51, 55–6;
base, 74, 126–7; governmental,
23–4; individual, 51, 54–5, 63, 84,
91–2, 118, 126, 142–3, 147, 149,
164; institutional, 54–5, 63,
117–18; Muslim, 94, 117, 174;
multilateral, 23–4; policies, 21;
relationship with recipients, 95–8;
Western, 58, 94, 118, 127
Dubai Charity Association: 57
Dunant, Henry: role in founding of
International Red Cross (1862),
19
duty: 19, 29, 97, 140; human, 84, 90,
173; Islamic, 146; moral, 20,
146–8; of care, 145–6; religious,
90, 145, 150

education: 19, 22–3, 30, 45, 47, 67,
83, 111, 124, 138, 141, 147, 149,
152–3, 158–9; access to, 86;
development, 121; Islamic, 86,
104–7, 120, 173; lack of, 87;
moral, 90, 110; political/religious
use of, 26–7; Qur'an, 139;
religious, 35, 86; systems, 18, 160;
use in aid strategy, 98–9, 101,
103–8
Effective Partnership in Information
for Better Humanitarian Work:
76
Egypt: 33, 48–9, 100, 119; independence of, 25; migrants from, 31
Egyptian Human Relief Agency:
119
El Ehsan Society: 53

EMDAD: 57
emergency relief: 22, 41, 152–3;
programs, 99–100
empowerment: 63, 98, 166; economic, 17, 151, 153, 157; Islamic
forms of, 175; use in aid strategy,
99, 108–10, 113
Enlightenment: 18
equality: 90, 97, 147; gender, 63,
134–5, 158, 165, 175
Ethiopia: 41, 71
European Council for Fatwa and
Research: establishment of
(1997), 31; members of, 31
European Institute of Human
Sciences: establishment of (1992),
31
European Commission:
Humanitarian Office (ECHO),
51, 78, 118–19, 155, 162, 164, 174
European Union (EU): 52

Facebook: profile pages on, 75
Fahd of Saudi Arabia, King: foreign
aid donations of, 48–9
Faisal of Saudi Arabia, King: 30
faith-based organisations: 3–4, 55,
60, 74, 132–5, 155, 164, 166,
168–9, 177, 179; added value of,
164, 174; moderate, 12, 116, 166;
use in secular development, 56
Faysal Bank: establishment of
(1994), 29
Federation of Islamic Organisations
in Europe: 31, 119; establishment
of (1989), 31
First World War (1914–18): 19, 25
fiqh: 105
Foundation for Human Rights and
Freedoms and Humanitarian
Relief (IHH): establishment of
(1995), 48

Embassy Bombing (1998), 2, 50,
59, 64
Khaled, Amr
Al Khalifa, Sheikh Issa Ben
Mohamed: President of Social
Reform Association, 71
Kinder USA: 57
King Abdul Aziz University: 67
King Faisal International Award for
Serving Islam: 110–11
Kuwait: 5, 30, 34, 62, 64, 66, 69,
72–3, 77, 79, 90, 92, 94, 103, 110,
123; government of, 64, 180;
Kuwait City, 41; Ministry of
Awqaf, 111; Ministry of Social
Development, 111; zakat system
in, 29
Kuwait Joint Relief Committee: 78,
101, 111
Kuwait University: College of
Shariah, 66

La Benevolencija: 50
bin Laden, Osama: NGOs accused
of supporting, 52
Lashkar-e Taiba
League of Nations: establishment of
(1919), 20
Lebanon: 5
legitimacy: 9, 28, 50, 59, 62, 66, 169,
176–7; organisational, 127, 136;
popular, 55; religious, 72–4, 132,
134; strategies for generating,
69–71
Lewis, David: 4
Libya: Muslim Brotherhood branch
in, 25
LIFE for Relief and Development:
57
Logical Framework Analysis: 125,
125, 128

logo: 69, 76, 126–7, 132

Maatouq, Abdullah: background of,
66–7
Makka al Mukarrama Charity
Foundation: 103
Make Poverty History Campaign:
126
Malawi Muslim Agency: 40
Malaysia: zakat system in, 29
Mali: 117
Mandaville, Peter: 6–7
Marshall Plan (1947): 20–1
Martyrs Foundation: 53
Al Masjed al Aqsa Charity
Foundation: 52
Mawdudi, Sayeed Abul A'ala:
founder of Jama'at-e Islami, 27
Médecins sans Frontiers: 44;
perceived as promoting Western
values, 43
Melucci, Alberto: 3
Mercy Relief International: banned
by Kenyan government (1998),
50; offices of, 48
Mercy USA for Relief and
Development: 57
Merhamet: 50
Methodist Church's Fund for Relief
and Development: 50
migration: 7, 30–1; economic waves
of, 31; Muslim, 31
Milli Görüs: role in establishment of
IHH, 48
missionaries/missionary organisations: 58, 87, 112; Christian, 43–4;
perception of Western NGOs as,
43; religiosity, 88, 178; transnational, 33
moderate: 73, 88, 115–16, 134–6,
166, 171; Muslim NGOs, 12, 55,
60, 74, 129; political, 56

130, 140, 142, 163, 173–4, 177;
development, 51, 126, 135, 140,
157, 166; Muslim, 2–14, 17, 36–7,
39–42, 45–6, 48–51, 54, 58, 60–1,
72, 74, 76, 86, 88, 102–3, 108, 113,
133, 164, 166–72, 174–5, 177,
180; networks, 59; relationships
with political organisations, 2;
religious, 3–4, 7, 55, 74, 162; role
of media in, 42; secular, 23, 35, 43,
122, 132, 135, 177; terrorist, 171;
transnational, 2–6, 9–14, 17, 20,
22, 33–4, 36, 39–42, 45, 48, 51, 58,
61, 64, 102, 126, 134, 168–70,
172, 175, 177; Western, 39, 42,
44–6, 51, 58, 76, 78, 88, 126, 136,
179
non-Muslims: 30, 44, 50–1, 88–9,
103, 121–2, 132, 135; conversion
of, 26, 58, 113; recipients, 89; staff,
122, 134; use of zakat donations
for, 143; Western, 102

Office for Services to the
Mujahedeen: 49
Operation Lifeline Sudan: establish-
ment of (1989), 45
Organisation for Economic
Cooperation and Development
(OECD): 34; Development
Assistance Committee, 179–80
oil revenues: 28, 36, 42
ONTRAC: 126
Order of the British Empire (OBE):
recipients of, 117
Organisation of Islamic Call (MDI):
criticisms of Western NGOs, 44;
personnel of, 44
Organisation of the Islamic
Conference (OIC): 28, 33, 71,
117, 179; establishment of (1969),

30; Islamic Development Bank,
30, 34, 67, 109, 117; Islamic
Solidarity Fund, 30
Ottoman Empire: collapse of, 25
Oxfam International: 20, 33, 121,
129, 132, 137–8, 164; organisational structure of, 32

Pakistan: 33, 72, 75, 117, 143–4,
160, 180; borders of, 48;
Earthquake (2005), 127;
Independence of (1947), 27;
Lahore, 27; Peshawar, 47; zakat
system in, 29
Palestine: 55, 144; Muslim
Brotherhood branch in, 25
Palestinian Association in Austria
pan-Islamism: 27–8; pan-Islamic
solidarity, 30
particularism: 50, 143–4; opposition
to, 34; pragmatic, 89, 112;
religious, 34, 87
Persian Gulf War (1990–1):
belligerents of, 49
Philippines: 22, 52, 63
Popular Committee for Fundraising
positioning: 37, 40, 60, 83, 170–1,
174
post-colonialism: 25, 35
poverty: child, 133; conceptions of,
85, 89–90
prayer/prayer rooms: 71, 90, 104,
107, 130, 160
Prince of Wales, Prince Charles:
visit to Islamic Relief, 115–16
Prince's Trust: 127
privatisation: 22–3
productivity: 109; language of,
109–10
professional: 15, 32, 35, 79–80, 96,
113, 119–20, 123–5, 129, 131–2,

134–6, 150, 162; authority, 74, 78, 84, 123, 127–8, 131, 133, 173, 177; knowledge, 77; relations, 66, 74
professionalism: 95, 122, 124; conceptions of, 129–30; financial, 177
Project Cycle Management: 125
project site: 6, 154; visits to, 10
proselytization: 23–4, 58, 141; aggressive, 59, 102
purification: 27; of interest money, 29; ritual, 101

Al-Qaeda: alleged connection to transnational Muslim NGOs, 2, 51–3, 64, 171
al-Qaradawi, Yusuf: 33, 46, 66, 72–3, 90, 102–3, 107, 111; background of, 28–9; *Role of Zakat in the Resolution of Legal Alms, The* (1972), 29; role in establishment of Islamic financial institutions, 29–30, 41–2, 65
Qatar: 57
Qatar Charity: 57
Qatar Islamic International Bank: establishment of (1991), 29
Qatar Islamic Fund for Zakat and Alms: establishment of, 29
Al Quds International Foundation: 53
Qur'an: 7, 90, 98, 140, 142–3, 146, 173; recitation of, 70, 105–6, 161; study of, 101, 105–6, 139, 178; verses of, 70, 107
Qur'an schools: 30, 35, 45, 101, 106, 154; establishment of, 58–9; organisations involved in running of, 101
al-Qurashi, Farid: background of, 65

Qurbani: 98, 157; offerings, 32; sacrifices, 154–7
Qutb, Muhammad: *Program for Islamic Education*, 105
Qutb, Sayyed: 27, 33

Rabita Trust: 52
Rainbow Family: 142
Ramadan packages: meals, 101, 155
Ramadan, Tariq: 72
Al Rashid Trust: 52
rationale: 9, 15, 83, 93, 95–6, 98, 110, 137, 141, 149–50, 167, 173; of aid, 89–91, 145–6; religious, 110; of solidarity, 110, 113
recipients: 34–5, 43, 50, 79, 84–5, 87–8, 90–1, 179; groups, 13, 92; invisibility of, 92; of charity, 153
Red Cross/Red Crescent Societies: Code of Conduct, 126; Kuwaiti, 46, 66; members of, 48; role in establishment of Humanitarian Forum, 76; Saudi, 46–7
Al Rehmat Trust: 53
relief: 30, 46, 76, 78–9, 86–7, 89, 98, 100–2, 117, 139, 148, 153–4, 180; aid as, 47, 99–100; emergency, 22, 41, 100, 151–2; humanitarian, 19–20, 132; international, 123–4; programmes, 70, 100
religion: 4, 6, 22, 25–6, 35, 56, 58, 69, 72, 74, 83, 86–7, 102, 104, 109–10, 128, 130–1, 139–40, 142, 144–7, 151, 153, 155, 158, 160–1, 163, 169, 170, 176, 178–9; added value of, 175; differing conceptions of, 131–2; relationship with aid, 100, 111, 163–4; secular notions of, 35–6, 159; study of, 3, 7
religiosity: 13, 24, 56–7, 60, 71, 78, 106, 130, 132, 155, 157, 165, 170, 175, 177–8; conservative, 136;